# Summary of Contents

# Build Your Own Standards Compliant Website Using Dreamweaver 8

## by Rachel Andrews

# Build Your Own Standards Compliant Website Using Dreamweaver 8

by Rachel Andrews

Copyright © 2005 SitePoint Pty. Ltd.

**Expert Reviewer**: Molly Holzschlag   **Editor**: Georgina Laidlaw
**Managing Editor**: Simon Mackie   **Index Editor**: Bill Johncocks
**Technical Editor**: Craig Anderson   **Cover Design**: Alex Walker
**Technical Director**: Kevin Yank   **Cover Illustration**: Jess Mason
**Printing History**:
    First Edition: September 2005

Published by SitePoint Pty. Ltd.

424 Smith Street Collingwood
VIC Australia 3066.
Web: www.sitepoint.com
Email: business@sitepoint.com

ISBN 0-9752402-3-4
Printed and bound in the United States of America

## About the Author

Rachel Andrew is Managing Director of Web solutions provider edgeofmyseat.com. When not writing code, she writes about writing code, and is the coauthor or author of several books promoting the practical usage of Web standards alongside other everyday tools and technologies. Rachel takes a commonsense, real-world approach to Web standards, with her writing and teaching being based on the experiences she has in her own company every day. Rachel has been using Dreamweaver since the release of version 2, and is a member of the Web Standards Project, working particularly to ensure standards support in authoring tools such as Dreamweaver. Rachel is the author of *The CSS Anthology: 101 Essential Tips, Ticks & Hacks*, also published by SitePoint.

Rachel lives in the UK with her partner Drew and daughter Bethany. When not working, they can often be found wandering around the English countryside hunting for geocaches and nice pubs that serve Sunday lunch and a good beer.

## About the Expert Reviewer

Molly E. Holzschlag is a well-known Web standards advocate, instructor, and author. Among her thirty-plus books is the recent *The Zen of CSS Design*, coauthored with Dave Shea. The book artfully showcases the most progressive csszengarden.com designs. Molly is an expert invited to the GEO working group at the World Wide Web Consortium (W3C) and is a steering committee member of the Web Standards Project (WaSP). She also serves as Advisory Board Member to the World Organization of Webmasters. A popular and colorful individual, Molly maintains a blog at—where else?—http://molly.com/

## About The Technical Director

As Technical Director for SitePoint, Kevin Yank oversees all of its technical publications—books, articles, newsletters and blogs. He has written over 50 articles for SitePoint, but is best known for his book, *Build Your Own Database Driven Website Using PHP & MySQL*. Kevin lives in Melbourne, Australia, and enjoys performing improvised comedy theatre and flying light aircraft.

## About SitePoint

SitePoint specializes in publishing fun, practical, and easy-to-understand content for Web professionals. Visit http://www.sitepoint.com/ to access our books, newsletters, articles and community forums.

# Table of Contents

# Introduction

Traditionally, visual tools like Dreamweaver have received a lot of bad press. Ardent hand-coders point to various examples of terrible markup produced by such tools as evidence for the claim that Visual Tools Are Bad. However, using a visual tool can really help to reduce development time and, if you're someone who works in a visual way, such tools can inspire far more creativity than can a text file full of markup.

For those working in a development team, tools such as Dreamweaver can become invaluable, enabling designers and developers with different skillsets and abilities to work together on a project without destroying each other's work.

I started working with Dreamweaver when it was in version 2, and the product has certainly grown and matured since those early days. Back then, we were at a point at which the nonstandard versions of the markup used by each of the major browsers—Netscape and Internet Explorer—differed so greatly that developers sometimes had to build two sites, and detect the browser version being used before displaying the appropriate site to the visitor. Our layout tool was the table, and Dreamweaver helped us to create nested table layouts populated by spacer images as we tried to achieve the goal of having our design "look the same in both browsers."

Things have changed a lot since those days, and Dreamweaver has moved with the times. The last few releases have steadily shifted from the assumption that everyone creates sites using tables and font tags, towards a product that supports and enhances the workflow of CSS developers, and those who are concerned about Web standards and accessibility.

Whether, like me, you're a longtime Dreamweaver customer who wants to know how to use the latest version of Dreamweaver to build standards-compliant, accessible sites, or you're a relative Dreamweaver novice, I hope you'll find this book useful.

By reading this book from cover to cover, you'll use Dreamweaver 8 to build a Website that validates to XHTML Strict, uses a CSS layout, and addresses the challenges of accessibility every step of the way. While Dreamweaver 8 can assist you in producing standards compliant Websites, any tool is only as good as the person operating it. This book will help you to understand the different decisions that need to be made, and how best to use Dreamweaver to reach your goals.

Through the process of building an example site that uses a realistic workflow for development, Dreamweaver beginners and old hands alike should learn how to create standards compliant Websites using Dreamweaver 8.

# Who Should Read This Book?

This book is great for both Dreamweaver novices and more experienced users.

If you're already a Dreamweaver user, but you want to expand your knowledge and learn how to use Dreamweaver 8 to create sites that are accessible, standards compliant, and use CSS for layout, this book is for you. In the coming pages, we'll look at all of the new tools included in this version of the product—tools that make designing with CSS far easier than ever before.

If you've never used Dreamweaver, but you want or need to, this book will help you to learn Dreamweaver the right way, without compromising accessibility or standards-compliance. In it, we'll work through the process of creating a Website—building a document in XHTML Strict and styling it using CSS, before moving on to building the site itself—and we'll cover lots of Dreamweaver functionality along the way.

# What's In This Book?

**Chapter 1: *What are Web Standards?***
In this first chapter, we take a look at Web standards: what they are, why they're important, and who they're designed to help. This chapter sets the scene for the decisions we'll be making throughout the rest of the book.

**Chapter 2: *Planning the Site and Setting up for Development***
A successful project starts with good planning. In this chapter, we make some major decisions about how we'll develop our site, thinking specifically about the layout and the structure of the site, and setting up our tools so we're ready to get started.

**Chapter 3: *XHTML and Semantics***
This chapter discusses XHTML, clarifying how it differs from HTML, and how we can work with it in Dreamweaver. We also discuss how best to structure a document, using XHTML elements, to ensure that it is accessible to all users.

**Chapter 4: *Constructing the Document***

Armed with a knowledge of XHTML, we put theory into practice in this chapter, as we build a document that will become the homepage of our site. We walk through the process of using Dreamweaver to create a document that validates as XHTML Strict, and find out how to validate our markup using Dreamweaver and other tools.

**Chapter 5: *CSS and Dreamweaver***

In this chapter, we explore Dreamweaver's Cascading Style Sheets (CSS) tools. Dreamweaver 8 comes with some excellent new tools designed to improve your CSS design workflow; the new unified CSS panel, and CSS `div` visualisation are among the tools that are explained in this chapter.

**Chapter 6: *Constructing the Layout with CSS***

Here, we use Dreamweaver's powerful CSS tools to create a style sheet for our document. By employing CSS, we can create a visual layout without compromising the accessibility of the document that we developed in Chapter 4.

**Chapter 7: *Accessibility***

Dreamweaver contains many tools to help us create accessible Websites, and we've been using them throughout the book. This chapter provides some more information on the use of those tools, discusses the process of validating documents for accessibility, and considers the ways in which users' differing needs can be met through good design.

**Chapter 8: *Building the Site***

Now that we have a layout and a stylesheet, we can build the site. We create a page design that we can use as a template for any internal pages that are developed for the project, and utilize server-side includes as a means to reuse common elements of the site.

**Chapter 9: *Forms and Third-party Services***

Forms can present problems for many users, so, in this chapter, we'll create a form using a variety of the accessibility features that Dreamweaver offers. And, as we integrate the Atomz search facility into our site, we learn firsthand that using third-party solutions doesn't always necessitate a compromise on standards compliance.

**Chapter 10: *Alternate Style Sheets***

This final chapter looks as the ways in which we can utilize the power of CSS to provide visitors a variety of alternate style sheets with which to use the site. We create a large-print style sheet, a low-images style sheet, and one that displays only when the document is printed.

# Further Reading

Although this book doesn't assume knowledge of CSS, neither does it provide a complete treatment of the subject. If the following chapters pique your interest in CSS, and you'd like to learn more about it, there are a couple of other SitePoint books that I can recommend.

*HTML Utopia: Designing Without Tables Using CSS*[1] represents a thorough introduction and complete guide to CSS. Like this book, *HTML Utopia: Designing Without Tables Using CSS* walks you through the creation of a site design using CSS, step by step. It also includes a comprehensive CSS reference that has made it an invaluable desk reference for thousands of designers and developers.

*The CSS Anthology: 101 Essential Tips, Tricks & Hacks*[2], my first book for SitePoint, will teach you to achieve practical results quickly. This book was designed to give readers fast, easy-to-follow answers to common questions: readers may jump between the many solutions, picking up tidbits suited to their projects and their needs.

# The Book's Website

Located at http://www.sitepoint.com/books/dreamweaver1, the Website supporting this book will give you access to the following facilities.

## The Code Archive

As you progress through the text, you'll note a number of references to the code archive. This is a downloadable ZIP archive that contains complete code for all the examples presented in this book.

---

[1] http://www.sitepoint.com/books/css1/
[2] http://www.sitepoint.com/books/cssant1/

# Updates and Errata

The Errata page on the book's Website will always have the latest information about known typographical and code errors, and necessary updates for changes to technologies.

# The SitePoint Forums

While I've made every attempt to anticipate any questions you may have, and answer them in this book, there is no way that *any* book could cover everything there is to know about designing, developing, and producing Websites. If you have a question about anything in this book, the best place to go for a quick answer is http://www.sitepoint.com/forums/—SitePoint's vibrant and knowledgeable community.

# The SitePoint Newsletters

In addition to books like this one, SitePoint offers free email newsletters.

*The SitePoint Tech Times* covers the latest news, product releases, trends, tips, and techniques for all technical aspects of Web development. The long-running *SitePoint Tribune* is a biweekly digest of the business and moneymaking aspects of the Web. Whether you're a freelance developer looking for tips to score that dream contract, or a marketing major striving to keep abreast of changes to the major search engines, this is the newsletter for you. *The SitePoint Design View* is a monthly compilation of the best in Web design. From new CSS layout methods to subtle PhotoShop techniques, SitePoint's chief designer shares his years of experience in its pages.

Browse the archives or sign up to any of SitePoint's free newsletters at http://www.sitepoint.com/newsletter/.

# Your Feedback

If you can't find an answer through the forums, or you wish to contact me for any other reason, the best place to write is books@sitepoint.com. We have a well-manned email support system set up to track your inquiries, and if our support staff is unable to answer your question, they send it straight to me.

Suggestions for improvement as well as notices of any mistakes you may find are especially welcome.

# Acknowledgements

I have been very fortunate to have a fantastic team working with me as I've written this book. Thank you to the team at SitePoint—in particular, to Simon Mackie—for making this book a reality. As always, it has been a pleasure working with you.

Thanks also to my expert reviewer, Molly E. Holzschlag, whose insightful comments have ensured that decisions made while writing this book have been thoroughly thought through. Having a reviewer who I respect very much as an author was, I believe, a great benefit to this project, and I thank Molly for her support and encouragement, as well as her excellent eye for technical issues.

To those at Macromedia who have worked with The Web Standards Project, who have listened, and who have worked to ensure that Dreamweaver has become a tool that supports standards, thank you.

Finally, these few words that I add in my acknowledgements cannot possibly convey how grateful I am to my family, to Drew and Bethany. For putting up with my deadline-induced craziness once again, I thank you and love you both very much.

# What are Web Standards?

If you've bought this book, you probably already have an interest in the subject of "Web standards," and are curious about the application of standards in a site that's built with Dreamweaver. Perhaps you already have an understanding of Web standards, but you're not sure how to use Dreamweaver to create compliant code. Or perhaps you're a Dreamweaver user who wants to comply with Web standards, use CSS more extensively, and produce more accessible documents. Either way, this book has the answers you need: it will show you how work to Web standards using Dreamweaver.

As we'll discover in the course of this chapter, there are excellent commercial reasons why sites should be developed to meet Web standards. The decision to adopt Web standards shouldn't be about jumping on a bandwagon, or keeping up with the latest Web development fashion. It's about producing good quality work, and knowing that your development approach will benefit your clients or employers as well as site visitors.

# Web Standards Defined

As we'll be concerned with Web standards throughout this book, let's take a moment to clarify exactly what we're talking about.

Web standards are specifications that direct the use of development languages on the Web, and are set by the World Wide Web Consortium (or W3C)[1]. These specifications cover languages such as HTML, XHTML, and CSS, along with a range of other languages, such as MathML, a markup language designed to represent mathematical equations, that you might come across if you have a specific need. The W3C also publishes the Web Content Accessibility Guidelines (WCAG)—recommendations that address the accessibility of Web pages—via the Web Accessibility Initiative (WAI).

### Get the Spec, Direct!

You can read these specifications and recommendations at the W3C site, though they're a little heavy going at times.

☐ HTML 4.01: http://www.w3.org/TR/html4/

☐ XHTML 1.0: http://www.w3.org/TR/xhtml1/

☐ CSS 1: http://www.w3.org/TR/CSS1/

☐ CSS 2.1: http://www.w3.org/TR/CSS21/

☐ WCAG 1.0: http://www.w3.org/TR/WAI-WEBCONTENT/

In this book, we'll use the XHTML 1.0, CSS 1 and 2.1, and WCAG 1.0 specifications and recommendations, although you'll be glad to know that we won't be doing too much reading of the actual W3C documents themselves!

# Who Needs Web Standards?

You might have a vague notion that Web standards are a good thing, but many sites—including many big name sites—don't comply with Web standards, and *they* certainly seem to manage perfectly well. So why *should* we make the effort to comply with Web standards? Are there any real benefits in doing so? Who needs Web standards, and who needs to take notice of the W3C specifications and recommendations?

---

[1] http://www.w3.org

# Web Designers and Developers

At the top of the list of people who need to worry about Web standards are people like us: the designers and developers who put together Websites. Will the time we spend learning how to develop to Web standards pay off for us?

## Cleaner Markup Makes Bug-fixing Quicker

If you validate your pages using W3C validators, at least you'll know that invalid markup is not the cause of any page display errors you might be experiencing. Sometimes, the process of validating a page, and fixing the errors that are found, can clear up display issues caused by elements not being closed correctly, or misspelled tags.

Even if validating your document doesn't fix the issue, at least you know that the problem exists within a valid document. Once you know that the problem isn't an error, you can start looking at other issues, such as the differing implementations of CSS in various browsers.

## Complying with Accessibility Requirements is Easier

If you create valid XHTML markup, and you ensure that your document is semantically correct, and you separate your document's content from its presentation (all of which we'll discuss in this chapter), you'll already have made considerable progress on many of the accessibility checkpoints outlined in WCAG 1.0. It's also important to recognize that accessibility isn't designed just for those with disabilities. An accessible site is able to be read by many different devices, including search engine indexers and "limited-resource" devices, such as mobile phones and PDAs, which don't have the processing power to cope with messy, nonstandard markup.

## Forward Compatibility

If you consider how your newly developed page looks in only a few current browsers, how can you be sure that it will display well in the next new browser? New browsers may display your pages badly, leaving you scrambling to find and fix problems as complaints come in. If you rely on tags that are specific to certain browsers, or have been removed from the specification entirely, you leave yourself open to this problem.

Complying with Web standards won't eradicate this problem completely; however, standards compliance makes the serious failure of your design less likely, as browser manufacturers now follow the standards, too. While they may occasionally misinterpret some part of the specification, they're unlikely to stop supporting it altogether. If the worst does happen, and a new browser has a strange effect on your standards-based Website, fixing it is likely to be easier than fixing a non-compliant site. If you're experiencing a problem, it will probably have affected other standards-complaint sites. The great minds of the Web community will be figuring out fixes and writing articles to explain their solutions. And, as we've already discussed, bug fixing in a compliant document is far easier than in a non-compliant document.

## Easier Redesigns

Have you ever had to redesign a Website by ripping the text from it and starting from scratch? Have you ever seen markup that was so littered with font tags and tiny table cells that it was easier to just start over? I know I have, and it's a slow process that can chew up a good deal of the time and money dedicated to a site redesign.

Separating the document's content from its presentation won't just give you a warm glow of standards compliance: it means that the next time someone has to redesign the site, they won't need to copy all the text out of the Web documents. All of the site text will have been marked up using semantic (X)HTML, and all of the presentational information—the stuff the site owners want to change—will be stored in a CSS file that can be replaced easily.

Some clients won't even wait for a redesign before they start asking you to make changes: they'll wait until you've almost finished their mammoth site, then ask you to "just switch that column from the left to the right." With a standards compliant site whose page layout is controlled by CSS, you can move page elements around easily, without needing to hack away at complex table structures on many pages. This makes changes to page layouts comparatively simple.

The separation of structure from presentation can also make it easier to provide added features, such as a high-contrast, low-graphics version of the site for visitors who prefer to use the site that way. Why create separate text-only versions of all your pages when you can simply swap out the style sheets?

# Browser Manufacturers

The manufacturers of browsers that access the Websites we build do take notice of Web standards. In the past, browser manufacturers added their own, proprietary tags and attributes to the basic languages. But now, more than ever, they're working to comply with the standards, and, certainly with the newest browsers, attempts are being made to display (X)HTML and CSS as described in the specifications.

Web browsers will, for the foreseeable future, attempt to render even the most poorly marked up, invalid code, because if they didn't, hundreds of thousands of badly written sites would display as a complete mess—and the general public would most probably blame the browser, not the Web designer. However, other devices, which don't have the rendering power of a desktop computer, rely far more heavily on the standards compliance of the markup they encounter.

# Authoring Tool Manufacturers

Authoring tool manufacturers—such as Macromedia, which creates Dreamweaver—have to follow Web standards just as Web designers do, as, increasingly, their customers demand that these authoring environments output valid markup. Traditionally, visual development environments received bad press for creating messy, invalid markup; however, newer versions of the leading visual development environments have cited standards compliance and accessibility features as main selling points. The manufacturers are definitely listening—and responding—to the market's demands.

# Web Users

The users of the Websites we design also benefit from our adoption of Web standards, even if they don't realize it! Perhaps they unwittingly use sites that specifically have been developed to display well in the most popular browser. If those users switch to a different browser, they might find that they no longer enjoy such a great online experience, as the proprietary markup used by those sites won't work in the new browser. A standards compliant site has a far greater chance of working well across all browsers, both those that were in existence when you developed the site, and the new browsers that will launch later in the site's lifetime.

In addition, a Website that's developed in line with accessibility recommendations is likely to be accessible to users who might find browsing the Web a frustrating experience. The Web should offer opportunities for easier shopping, reading, and research to visually impaired or otherwise disabled users. It shouldn't frustrate them with sites that use proprietary markup, or other techniques that effectively lock out of the site anyone who doesn't use a "regular" browser in a "regular" way.

# Using Web Standards

How do we ensure that we're using these Web standards correctly? What does it take to comply with the standards?

First, we need to conform to the specification. This means that we should use only those elements and attributes that are included in the specification, avoiding the proprietary elements introduced by browser manufacturers, such as Internet Explorer's `<marquee>` tag, and Netscape's `<blink>` tag. We should also avoid using elements that appeared in earlier specifications (such as HTML 3.2) and have since been removed when we're working on documents developed to a later specification.

# Creating a Valid XHTML Document

We'll use XHTML throughout this book, so we'll be working to the W3C's XHTML 1.0 Recommendation[2] (in W3C parlance, a "recommendation" is a specification). XHTML is basically the latest version of HTML, and was designed to replace HTML as the markup language for Web pages. Though it's a reformulation of HTML as XML, XHTML is almost identical to HTML, apart from a few small differences that we'll discuss in Chapter 3.

You can create an XHTML document through Dreamweaver's New Document dialog (File > New...). Make sure Basic page is selected in the Category list, then select HTML from the Basic page listing that appears, as shown in Figure 1.1. You can then select one of the XHTML options from the Document Type (DTD) drop-down list.

Clicking Create will create the new document. Switch to Code View, by clicking the Code button at the top of the document window, to see exactly what's included in a simple XHTML document. This is illustrated in Figure 1.2.

---

[2] http://www.w3.org/TR/xhtml1/

## Figure 1.1. Creating a new XHTML document in Dreamweaver.

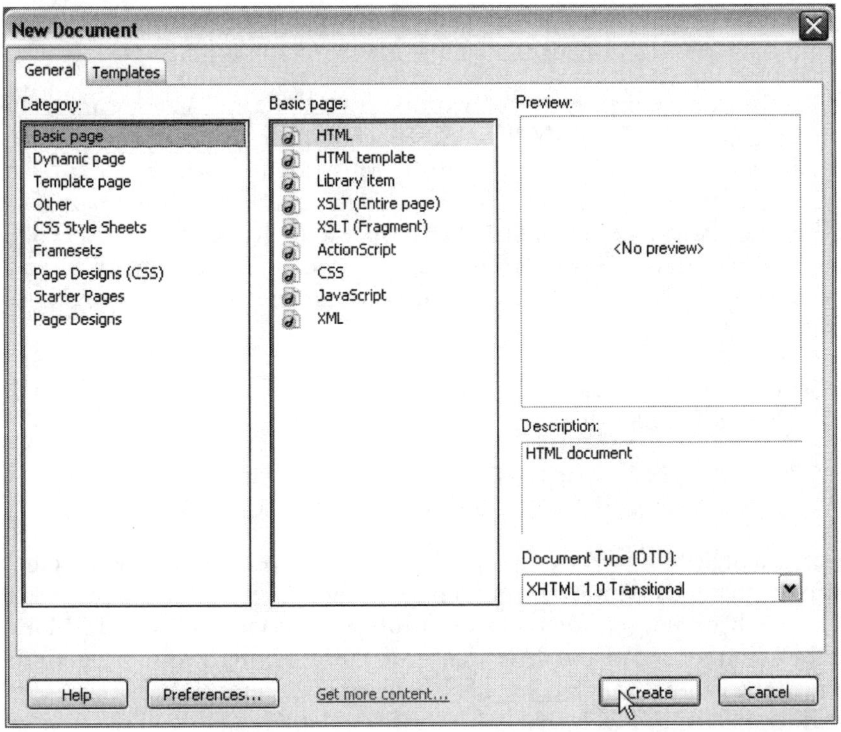

## Figure 1.2. Displaying the new XHTML document in Code View.

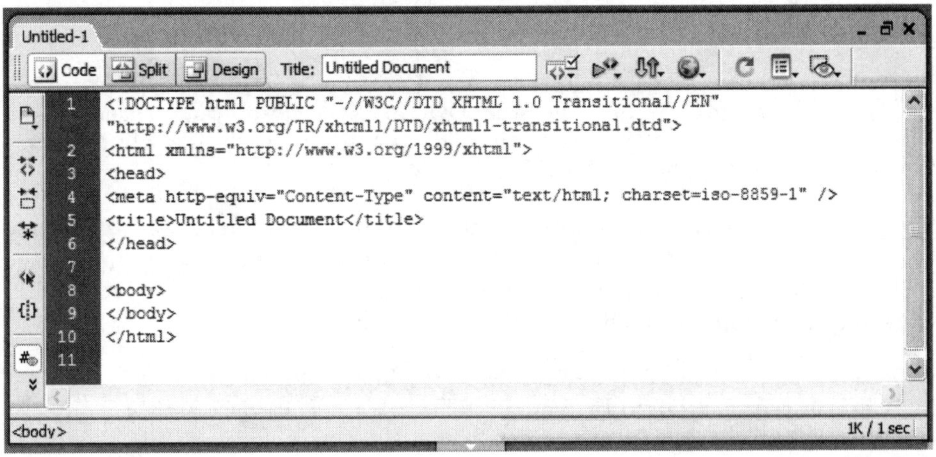

The first line of the document will look something like this:

```
<!DOCTYPE html PUBLIC "-//W3C//DTD XHTML 1.0 Transitional//EN"
    "http://www.w3.org/TR/xhtml1/DTD/xhtml1-transitional.dtd">
```

This is called the **document type declaration**, or DOCTYPE. As you can easily infer from its name, the DOCTYPE declares what your document is—which (X)HTML specification you're working to. In this example, we're working to XHTML 1.0 Transitional, Dreamweaver 8's default. The Transitional part tells us something else about the version of XHTML that we're working with. XHTML 1.0 comes in three "flavors:" Strict, Transitional, and Frameset. Dreamweaver uses the Transitional DOCTYPE by default, and Frameset if you insert frames into the document.

**XHTML Strict** is, as you would expect, the strictest form of XHTML. An XHTML Strict DOCTYPE looks like this:

```
<!DOCTYPE html PUBLIC "-//W3C//DTD XHTML 1.0 Strict//EN"
    "http://www.w3.org/TR/xhtml1/DTD/xhtml1-strict.dtd">
```

If you're using a Strict DOCTYPE, you can't use any **deprecated** elements (tags) or attributes in the document; nor can you use frames. Deprecated elements are those that have been flagged for removal in future versions of XHTML. Many deprecated elements control the appearance of the page, performing the kinds of functions that can be handled by CSS. The main difference between Strict and Transitional DOCTYPEs is that, with the Strict DOCTYPE, you're far more limited in terms of the presentational attributes and elements you can include in the document.

## Using the Strict DOCTYPE in Dreamweaver

Dreamweaver isn't quite as careful as it could be about adhering to the standard. If you use the Strict DOCTYPE, take extra care to validate your documents and replace any invalid attributes. Typically, it will be quite easy to replace them with CSS.

The Frameset DOCTYPE supports the use of frames, and Dreamweaver will use it automatically if you include any frames in your document. The Frameset page will then reference at least two other HTML pages, which can use any DOCTYPE they like. The Frameset DOCTYPE looks like this:

```
<!DOCTYPE html PUBLIC "-//W3C//DTD XHTML 1.0 Frameset//EN"
    "http://www.w3.org/TR/xhtml1/DTD/xhtml1-frameset.dtd">
```

HTML 4.01 offers the same three DOCTYPE flavors—Transitional, Strict and Frameset—which work in exactly the same way as the above XHTML DOCTYPEs. If you used one of these, you would need to mark up your document in HTML, rather than XHTML. We'll explore the differences between HTML and XHTML later in this book, as we start to create our Website.

# Validating your Document

How can you ensure that a document you've created in HTML or XHTML is valid, and conforms to the specification? Run it through the W3C Validator[3] shown in Figure 1.3.

To use the validator, you can enter the URL of the page you'd like validated (if it's live on the Web), or you can upload a file from your computer.

**Figure 1.3. Using the W3C Validator.**

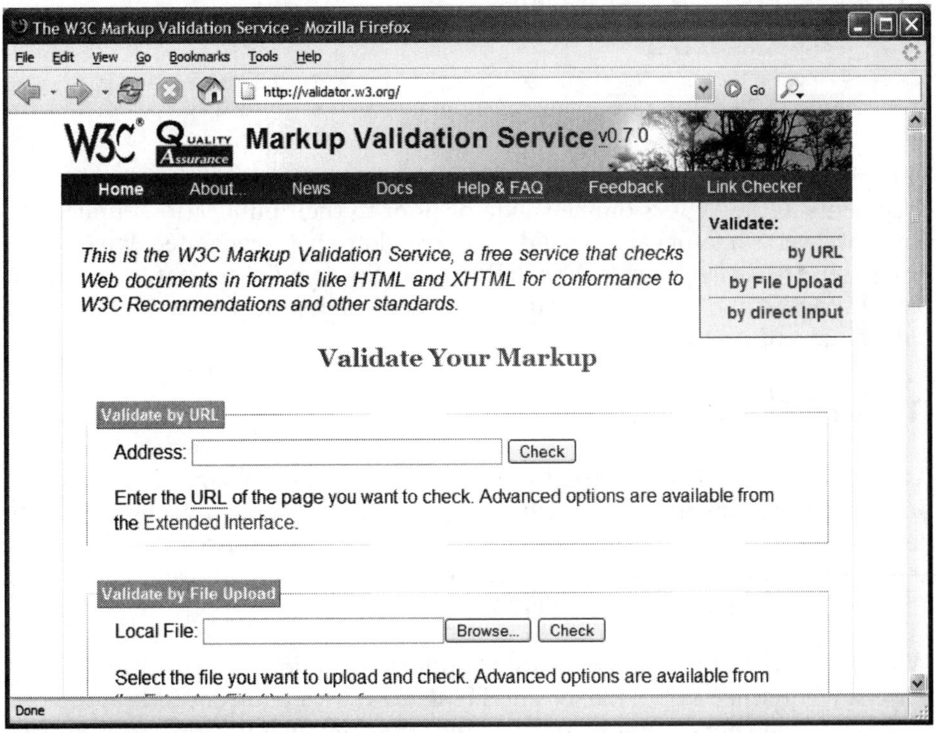

---

[3] http://validator.w3.org/

Once you've told the W3C Validator where to find your (X)HTML, click the Check button. A page will display, announcing the joyful news that your page is valid, or providing a list of errors that you can work through before you re-check the page's validity. If you've been working in Dreamweaver to create an XHTML document, you should have very few errors to fix; however, later in this book, we'll look at some of the more common errors that can occur as we build Websites.

To help you ensure the validity of your pages during development, Dreamweaver provides a built-in validator. To run the validator, select File > Check Page > Validate Markup, or click the Validate Markup button. The validation results appear at the bottom of the window. As shown in Figure 1.4, you can choose to validate the current document, the entire local site, or selected files within the site.

## Figure 1.4. The validator in Dreamweaver.

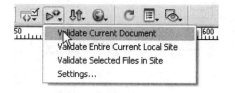

Though this validator provides a useful check as you go along, I always check my documents at the W3C's online validator prior to their publication online. The Dreamweaver validator cannot validate any markup that's generated dynamically using a server-side language such as PHP or ASP. So, if you're generating pages—or parts of pages—in this way, you'll definitely need to use the online validator after uploading your pages.

# Using Valid CSS

As we'll discover when we build our site, CSS replaces all of the deprecated presentational elements in HTML, as well as adding plenty of scope for interesting design ideas that aren't possible using HTML alone. CSS is also a Web standard, and the W3C has developed specifications against which we can validate our CSS code,[4] just as we do for (X)HTML.

When it comes to CSS, you have three options for validation: point to a file on a live server (either a CSS file, or an HTML page with embedded CSS), upload a CSS file from your computer, or paste the CSS directly into a text area. As with

---

[4] http://jigsaw.w3.org/css-validator/

the (X)HTML validator, the result will either be a congratulatory message, or a list of errors for you to fix before revalidating your style sheet. Dreamweaver does not offer a built-in CSS validator.

# Validating for Accessibility

When designing a Website, designers and developers can become consumed by the way the pages display in a Web browser, or range of browsers; we can forget that, for many people, just getting the content is all that matters. Many Web users employ some kind of **assistive technology**—such as a **screen reader**, which reads the text of the page aloud—or have a disability that makes using the Web in the way that most of us do, with a graphical display in a Web browser, very difficult, if not impossible.

Through its Web Accessibility Initiative (WAI), the W3C offers recommendations that we can follow to ensure that our sites are accessible to these users; therefore, we should check that our sites comply with the WCAG 1.0 recommendations. As we'll see in Chapter 7 and Chapter 8, validating the accessibility of Web documents is rather more tricky than checking your documents for valid (X)HTML and CSS. "Yes" and "no" answers are not always provided for the WCAG 1.0 recommendations' different checkpoints.

Dreamweaver contains an accessibility validator, which can be run from the Reports dialog (Site > Reports...), as shown in Figure 1.5. Check the Accessibility checkbox and click Run.

**Figure 1.5. Running an accessibility report from the Reports dialog.**

The report that displays in the Results Panel will include notes such as, "Color is not essential," (which appears in Figure 1.6); this relates to a checkpoint that advises that the use of color in the document should not be essential to users' understanding of the page. You would fail this checkpoint if, for example, the only way you communicated the status of an article on your site was through color-coded icons. In this case, your pages wouldn't be accessible to users who could not differentiate between the colors. You would pass the checkpoint if you used both color-coding and a textual status note. Of course, there's no way for an automatic validator to know which approach you've taken, so you need to make your own, manual check and decide whether you pass or fail a checkpoint. And, to do so in an informed way, you need to have an understanding of what each point means.

That said, Dreamweaver *can* help: in the Reference tab of the Results Panel, you'll find the UsableNet Accessibility Reference depicted in Figure 1.6, which explains the checkpoints and provides methods by which you can check whether your site passes or fails each one. Right-click on any checkpoint and select More Info... to display an explanation of that checkpoint.

## Figure 1.6. The UsableNet Accessibility Reference displaying in the Results tab of the Reference Panel.

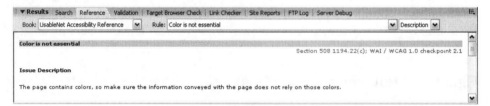

There are also online accessibility validators, the most popular of which is WebXACT[5] (previously known as Bobby), and Cynthia Says[6]. These are accompanied by the same provisos as the Dreamweaver validator in that the results these systems provide require interpretation: they cannot give you a "yes" or "no" answer.

---

[5] http://webxact.watchfire.com/
[6] http://www.cynthiasays.com/

# Applying a Semantic Document Structure

Implied in our adherence to Web and accessibility standards is the adoption of semantic document structure. A semantic document uses HTML tags for their meanings, not their appearance. For example, a semantic document would use the <h1>, <h2>, and similar tags to mark up a page's headings. If we didn't want to display the default appearance of these headings, we could easily change it using CSS. Similarly, the use of an unordered list (<ul>) tag to mark up a list of links would be preferable to separating those links with line breaks. If we want the list of links to appear without bullets, we can achieve the effect using CSS.

We will look at this issue in more depth in Chapter 3; however, here's a simple example. If I were to mark up a section of this chapter as an XHTML document, I might end up with something that looks like Figure 1.7.

## Figure 1.7. Marking up the chapter as XHTML.

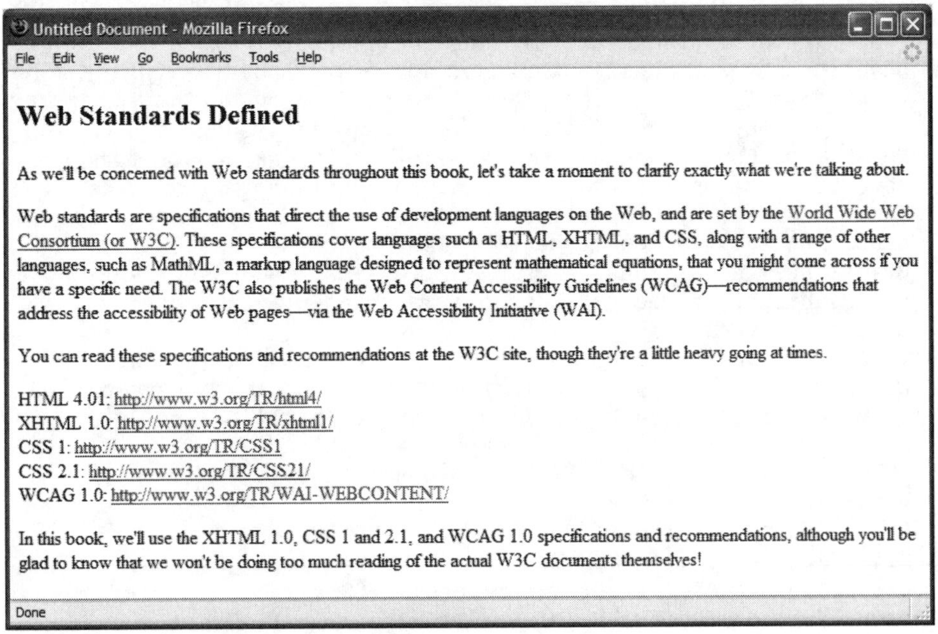

The markup for the page could be something like this:

```
<!DOCTYPE html PUBLIC "-//W3C//DTD XHTML 1.0 Transitional//EN"
    "http://www.w3.org/TR/xhtml1/DTD/xhtml1-transitional.dtd">
```

```
<html xmlns="http://www.w3.org/1999/xhtml">
<head>
<title>Untitled Document</title>
<meta http-equiv="Content-Type" content="text/html;
    charset=iso-8859-1" />
<style type="text/css">
<!--
.heading {
  font-size: 24px;
  font-weight: bold;
}
-->
</style>
</head>

<body>
<p class="heading">Web Standards Defined</p>
<p>As we'll be concerned with Web standards throughout this book,
   let's take a moment to clarify exactly what we're talking
   about.</p>
<p>Web standards are specifications that direct the use of
   development languages on the Web, and are set by the
   <a href="http://www.w3.org/">World Wide Web Consortium (or
   W3C)</a>. These specifications cover languages such as HTML,
   XHTML, and CSS, along with a range of other languages, such as
   MathML, a markup language designed to represent mathematical
   equations, that you might come across if you have a specific
   need. The W3C also publishes the Web Content Accessibility
   Guidelines (WCAG)&mdash;recommendations that address the
   accessibility of Web pages&mdash;via the Web Accessibility
   Initiative (WAI).</p>
<p>You can read these specifications and recommendations at the
   W3C site, though they're a little heavy going at times.</p>
<p>HTML 4.01: <a href="http://www.w3.org/TR/html4/">
   http://www.w3.org/TR/html4/</a><br />
   XHTML 1.0: <a href="http://www.w3.org/TR/xhtml1/">
   http://www.w3.org/TR/xhtml1/</a><br />
   CSS 1: <a href="http://www.w3.org/TR/CSS1">
   http://www.w3.org/TR/CSS1</a><br />
   CSS 2.1: <a href="http://www.w3.org/TR/CSS21/">
   http://www.w3.org/TR/CSS21/</a><br />
   WCAG 1.0: <a href="http://www.w3.org/TR/WAI-WEBCONTENT/">
   http://www.w3.org/TR/WAI-WEBCONTENT/</a></p>
<p>In this book, we'll use the XHTML 1.0, CSS 1 and 2.1, and WCAG
   1.0 specifications and recommendations, although you'll be glad
   to know that we won't be doing too much reading of the actual
```

```
  W3C documents themselves!</p>
</body>
</html>
```

As so many designers are now comfortable with the use of CSS for styling text, we often see text that's marked up as a paragraph (i.e. it appears between <p> and </p> tags), but is styled as a heading using CSS. To be semantically correct, I should have used a h1 element (as that denotes a heading), then used CSS to make it display as required.

Take a look at the list of URLs for the different W3C specifications: they've been split onto separate lines using the <br/> tag. The correct way to structure these links would have been as an unordered list. We could even indicate that this content constitutes a note using a <div> tag:

```
<div class="note">
<p>You can read these specifications and recommendations at the
  W3C site, though they're a little heavy going at times.</p>
<ul>
  <li>HTML 4.01 <a href="http://www.w3.org/TR/html4/">
    http://www.w3.org/TR/html4/</a></li>
  <li>XHTML 1.0 <a href="http://www.w3.org/TR/xhtml1/">
    http://www.w3.org/TR/xhtml1/</a></li>
  <li>CSS 1 <a href="http://www.w3.org/TR/CSS1">
    http://www.w3.org/TR/CSS1</a></li>
  <li>CSS 2.1 <a href="http://www.w3.org/TR/CSS21/">
    http://www.w3.org/TR/CSS21/</a></li>
  <li>WCAG 1.0 <a href="http://www.w3.org/TR/WAI-WEBCONTENT/">
    http://www.w3.org/TR/WAI-WEBCONTENT/</a></li>
</ul>
</div>
```

A document can be perfectly valid against its specification while structured in a non-semantic manner. We need to use common sense and judgment to look at our documents and decide whether we're using the correct tags to mark up each element on the page.

Thanks to CSS, the look and feel of the document need not be compromised by our use of correct elements and adherence to semantic document structure. However, marking up documents correctly is extremely beneficial when we start to consider site visitors who don't use traditional Web browsers to read content. We'll discuss this issue more throughout this book.

# Separating Presentation from Document Structure

Another issue that's implied by working to Web standards is that of separating presentation from content. The content comprises the semantic document that we discussed in the last section; the presentation is what makes it appear as it does on a computer, projector, or printed page.

If you're using a Transitional DOCTYPE, you can include in your document many tags and attributes that do not describe what the different elements in the document are, but instead, state how they should look. Presentational tags include `<font>` and `<center>`, and can be replaced using CSS. Other attributes are used for presentational elements such as borders: for example, `<img border="0" />`.

Using such presentational elements can make it difficult to change the way elements look. Best practice Web development entails the separation of the structure of a document from its presentational aspects. This separation is achieved by the use of CSS, wherever possible, to dictate how the document should look. If you want to validate against a Strict DOCTYPE, for the most part you'll be required to apply this separation, as the tags and attributes that are absent from the Strict DOCTYPEs are largely presentational.

This separation of structure from presentation also underlies the recommendation that tables not be used for page layout purposes. The `<table>` tag was initially designed to describe tabular data, such as that found in a spreadsheet, not to force page elements into certain locations on the page. If your page uses a table to lay out page elements, you've mixed your structure and presentation—even though the page may well validate to a Strict DOCTYPE.

# Summary

In this chapter, we've learned what Web standards are, and explored the core issues that we must consider if we want to develop Web pages to Web standards. We've also looked at some of the reasons why Web standards are helpful to those designing for the Web, and why investing time to understand this approach will pay off in future.

As is the case with all visual development environments, Dreamweaver has not achieved a reputation for creating clean markup. For many, however, developing in a visual environment is a better way to work than hand-coding HTML and CSS in a text editor. This book will discuss how you can use Dreamweaver to ensure that your work is standards compliant, and addresses all of the issues we mentioned in this chapter: valid markup and CSS, semantic document structure, the separation of structure from presentation, and meeting accessibility recommendations. Any tool—be it Notepad or Dreamweaver—is only as good as its operator, so let's move on and create a standards compliant Website using Dreamweaver 8.

# Site Planning and Setting up for Development

Before we dive in and start developing our site, we need to make some decisions about how the site will look, how it will be hosted, and how it will be structured. The Website we'll build through the course of this book will be called Code Spark; it will be a Web design resource site much like sitepoint.com. I have chosen this as the subject matter for the site not because I assume that every reader wants to build a Web design resource site, but because the concepts that we'll explore while creating this site are common to many other types of Website. The decisions we'll need to make during this project will parallel the kinds of options you'll have to consider around most of the sites you'll build. Whether you follow this book, creating the Code Spark resource site using the example graphics provided, or using the techniques described here to develop your own project, is entirely up to you.

# The Code Spark Site Design

## Features of the Code Spark Website

Before we can begin to design the layout of the site, we need to consider the site's features, so that we know exactly what we need to include in the layout. Code Spark is a Web design and development tutorial site, so we'll have to handle tutorials that explore design and development techniques, and articles that discuss interesting developments in the area of Web design.

## Tutorial Pages

The tutorials will comprise the majority of the site's content, so we obviously need a design that facilitates the formatting of this type of content. Tutorials tend to include a number of screenshots—which might be quite wide—and code samples, which need to be formatted so that the tutorial author's line breaks are preserved. We want to ensure that our article page allows for the display of such page elements.

We'll also want to make sure that, if readers like the tutorial they're reading, they'll be able to find similar tutorials on the Code Spark site. Perhaps the easiest way to do this is to add to the tutorial page a list of other articles written by that author.

## The Homepage

We'll want to make the focus of Code Spark—Web design and development tutorials—obvious from the get-go, so we'll present a number of regularly updated feature tutorials on the homepage of the Website. This way, new visitors can quickly and easily ascertain what the site's about, and returning visitors can see what's new at a glance.

## Site Navigation

Once we've prepared and published our tutorial content, we're going to need to give visitors various ways to find it. The subject of "Web design and development" is fairly broad, so our content will need to be sensibly categorized. This way, visitors can quickly access all the articles that discuss Dreamweaver, CSS, or PHP development, for example. A tutorials index page, which displays the categories list, along with a couple of sample tutorials, will give the user an immediate understanding of the information contained in the categories. Making a list of these categories available on every page of the site helps to reinforce the content categories in the minds of users, and gives them quick, easy access to the latest tutorials on the topics in which they're most interested.

A list of the most popular and highly rated tutorials is a good way to allow the cream of your Website to rise to the top. By making it easy for users to find your site's best content from the homepage, your visitors will be more likely to read those tutorials and come away with a good impression of Code Spark—perhaps even telling their friends about it. A sitemap is also very useful to visitors: it's a well-known tool that allows users to quickly get a feel for the way the Code Spark content is organized, and gives them a direct pathway to the tutorials that interest them.

Now, navigating the site by browsing its carefully thought-out categories might be good for users who are looking to improve their CSS skills, for example. But if a user needs a tutorial on a specific topic—such as building a CSS-based three-column page layout—that person's going to want a faster way to locate it. By providing a search field, you make it very easy for users to quickly find specific tutorials, a task that—as you'd know if you've ever had to visit a huge site like Microsoft's Developer Network (MSDN)—can otherwise be very difficult indeed.

As we're concerned with accessibility, we want to add features that will help visitors use the site, such as a style sheet switcher that allows users to increase and decrease the font size, and a list of keyboard shortcuts that they can use to navigate the site. We'll also need to provide a page that explains what the Website's all about, and a way for visitors to get in touch with the people who run the site.

Bearing all of the above in mind, we can make a list of the important features that our site requires. It needs:

- ❑ Navigation to the main parts of the site: the tutorial index, information about the site and the people who run it, the contact page, and the sitemap

- ❑ A list of the tutorial categories

- ❑ A search facility

- ❑ A featured tutorials display on the homepage

- ❑ A large area for the presentation of article content on individual tutorial pages

# Designing the Site

Once you've created a list of key elements, you can come up with a page layout either on paper or in a graphics application. To begin the Code Spark project site, let's take a look at a design created in Fireworks by SitePoint's Alex Walker, and pictured in Figure 2.1, so we can discuss the implementation of a layout that makes use of graphics, while still adhering to Web standards.

# Figure 2.1. Alex's homepage design, incorporating our requirements.

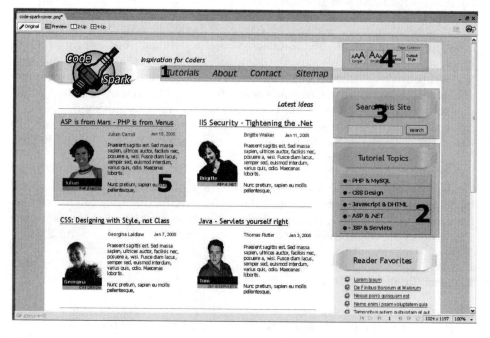

This design incorporates each of the elements we identified as being required on the homepage:

- **1** Our main navigation displays along the top.
- **2** Category links and a "reader favorites" section appear down the right-hand side.
- **3** The search field is also on the right.
- **4** Our accessibility controls appear in the top-right corner.
- **5** The featured tutorials make up the main content area.

This process of thinking through the elements that you want to include before you come up with a layout will save you struggling find space later for extra elements that you hadn't expected to use.

The site's tutorial page layout shown in Figure 2.2 includes a large content area, allowing us to easily publish articles that contain images and blocks of example code.

## Figure 2.2. The tutorial page layout, showing the content area.

Whether you're at the homepage, an article page, or any other location on the site, a number of consistent page elements are present: the header, which includes the Code Spark logo, the top navigation, and accessibility features that we'll discuss later; and the bar to the right of the page, which contains the search box, along with elements that change depending on where you are located within the site. This sidebar provides quick, easy access to tutorial topics.

The content area on the homepage will contain two columns in which we'll highlight the latest articles and tutorials posted on the site. When users click through from this display to an article page, the article content fills the complete width of this main content area. Ours will be a liquid layout: one that stretches to fill the users' browser windows, regardless of their screen resolutions.

### Liquid or Fixed Width?

A **fixed width layout** (one that doesn't grow and shrink with the size of the browser window) needs to be narrow enough to ensure that users with low screen resolutions don't have to scroll sideways to read the site's content. In practice, this fact means that we really need to design for users operating at a resolution of 800 x 600 pixels, unless we know that the majority of our target users will have a resolution of at least 1024 x 768 pixels. Designers often use fixed width layouts because they find it easier to position graphically intense designs within a known page width.

For a content rich site, however, using a **liquid layout** (one that expands and shrinks with the browser window's size) can be a good design choice. Of course, you should always check your work at a resolution of 800 x 600 pixels to ensure that a horizontal scrollbar doesn't appear at this resolution, and that the columns are not ridiculously narrow, but users with higher screen resolutions will have greater flexibility in the ways they view the site.

# Structuring the Site

Now that we have a site design, we can begin to think about how we'll put the site together, and the technologies we'll use to do so. Once again, some time spent planning will help to make the site's development more streamlined once we begin.

# Dealing with Common Elements

We've already identified some common page elements in our design; some of these elements are present on every page, while other elements are present on some—but not all—pages. We can use the fact that we have these common elements in the site design to make development easier.

## The "Copy, Paste, Copy, Paste" Technique

In developing a site, you might work by creating a new document, writing the XHTML code, applying your CSS, and then, when you're ready to create a new page, simply copying and pasting into the new document all of the common elements that appeared in the last document. In this way, all of your site's files contain potentially large amounts of markup—and possibly images—that are duplicated on each page.

This isn't too much of a problem, until you decide to change a graphic in the header, and have to open up every page of the site to copy and paste in the new logo markup. The use of CSS does reduce the need to copy and paste common elements between files—much of this information can be found in the CSS file that controls the site's pages—however, there are still many elements that need to appear in the individual page document. As such, when you create pages in this way, some copying and pasting is inevitable. Finally, you must upload all of the altered pages to the Website in order to have the revised logo display.

# Dreamweaver Templates

If you have any experience in Dreamweaver, you may be aware of **Dreamweaver Templates**. A template is basically a normal HTML page that Dreamweaver can use as a basis from which to create new pages. You mark one or more regions of the template as being editable, optional, or repeating. These will be the only areas that Dreamweaver will allow you to update in pages based on that template; the rest are locked by Dreamweaver, as shown in Figure 2.3.

### Figure 2.3. A page based on a Dreamweaver template with a single editable region.

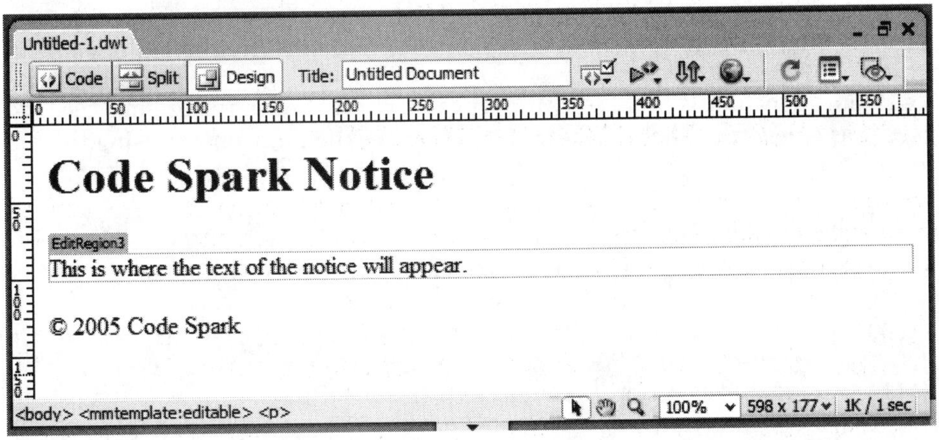

Dreamweaver locks parts of the page by placing special HTML comments in your markup. These comments indicate which areas are locked, and which are editable, as shown below.

```
<h1>Code Spark Notice</h1>
<!-- TemplateBeginEditable name="EditRegion3" -->
<p>This is where the text of the notice will appear. </p>
<!-- TemplateEndEditable -->
<p>&copy; 2005 Code Spark</p>
```

The really useful aspect of using Dreamweaver Templates is that if you change any part of the main template, Dreamweaver will ask whether or not you want

25

it to update all other pages based on this template, saving you the time and hassle of copying and pasting the changes across your site.

Templates help us avoid copying and pasting common elements, which is great. However, it can't help us overcome the task of having to re-upload all the changed Website files, which we have to do whether we use Dreamweaver Templates or some other design approach. And of course, Dreamweaver Templates don't benefit designers who don't use Dreamweaver: it's the only program that knows how to handle these templates.

# Server Side Includes (SSI)

Our third option for the management of repeated sections of markup is to make use of use **Server Side Includes (SSI)**. SSI allows you to merge two or more files before your page is presented to the browser. The **include file**, or **include**, is simply a file into which the repeated section of code has been copied. It isn't a complete XHTML document in itself: it's just a part of your complete document.

To create an include, simply copy the repeated content from the original file, and save it as a new file. Then, include that file in the main document using the following line:

```
<!--#include file="newfile.html" -->
```

As an example, you might have an XHTML document that looks like this:

```
<!DOCTYPE html PUBLIC "-//W3C//DTD XHTML 1.0 Strict//EN"
    "http://www.w3.org/TR/xhtml1/DTD/xhtml1-strict.dtd">
<html xmlns="http://www.w3.org/1999/xhtml">
<head>
<meta http-equiv="Content-Type" content="text/html;
    charset=iso-8859-1" />
<title>Code Spark Notice</title>
</head>
<body>
<h1>Code Spark Notice</h1>
<p>This is where the text of the notice will appear.</p>
<p>&copy; 2005 Code Spark</p>
</body>
</html>
```

The content from the top of this document all the way down to the <h1> heading is common to all pages of the Website, as is the content from the copyright notice onwards. We could divide this page into three parts: the top, the bottom and the middle—the middle being the only part that will change.

By copying the top and bottom parts of the document into `top.html` and `bottom.html`, respectively, we can replace them in the original document with the include information.

```
<!--#include file="top.html" -->
<p>This is where the text of the notice will appear.</p>
<!--#include file="bottom.html" -->
```

Once this file has been uploaded to a Web server (we'll set one up later in this chapter), anyone who views the page with a Web browser will see the file exactly as it was before you employed SSI. The Web server intercepts the `#include` file code in our HTML, and replaces it with the specified file, as shown in Figure 2.4.

## Figure 2.4. Creating a complete document from three files using Server Side Includes.

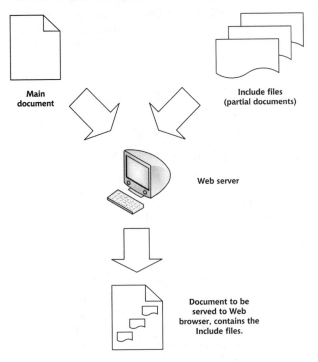

Main
document

Include files
(partial documents)

Web server

Document to be
served to Web
browser, contains the
Include files.

To create new files that contain the same top section, we simply add the appropriate include line to each page on which we want the top section to display. Then, if we want to change the logo, we simply edit it within the `top.html` file, and re-upload that file. All of the pages that include `top.html` will automatically show the new logo.

Server Side Includes are an incredibly useful way to create documents that are easy to maintain, and, given that our tutorial site is likely to become quite large as we add new tutorials, SSI represents a good choice for us. After all, we don't want to have to copy and paste our changes, then re-upload all our files every time we make a change to a section; nor do we want to lock anyone who works on the site into using Dreamweaver. If the site was a brochure site that had only a few pages and wasn't expected to develop any further than that, you might decide against using SSI. However, having maintained a number of large sites over the years, I know that—in the case of Code Spark, at least—SSI will save us a lot of time and energy later on.

Dreamweaver understands includes: when you load a page that contains an include directive, it will display the part of the document that's contained in the SSI. However, you need to open the include file directly in order to make any changes to it. We'll look at how we can work with Dreamweaver and SSI when we move on to build our site.

### Using Built-In Functions to Include Files

If you're building a site using PHP, ASP.NET, or some other server-side language, you may be able to use that language's built-in functions to include files. These methods tend to offer better error handling features, but you're unlikely to need these features if your content is static.

In PHP, you can make use of `include`, `require`, `include_once` or `require_once`.[1] In ASP, `Server.Execute` is similar, but not quite the same.

# Setting up a Web Server

Since we're building what could potentially become a large static content site, we'll employ SSI to reuse the code for the common parts of each page. If we want to test and view the site complete with all the included portions of each page, we'll need to run a local Web server. In this instance, "Web server" refers to the software that responds to browser requests by sending back Web pages. This

---

[1] See http://www.php.net/manual/en/language.control-structures.php for more information.

software is responsible for the heavy lifting involved in SSI: intercepting `#include` commands in HTML files, and replacing them with the specified files. The term "Web Server" can also be used to refer to the computer that hosts a Website.

You may already have Apache or IIS installed if you perform any server-side Web development in languages such as PHP, Perl, or ASP. If you're unsure whether or not you have a Web server installed, try typing **`http://localhost/`** into your Web browser: this will request the default page from your local Web server, if one is running. Both Apache and IIS install a test page; if you see such a page, it will be pretty obvious which Web server you're running. If you see only an error message complaining that localhost could not be found, you may need to install a Web server.

If you're running Apache, you may want to skip to the section called "Testing SSI " below; if you're using IIS, skip straight to the section called "Using IIS as your Local Web Server". If you're not already running a local Web server, we can set up the Apache Web server in order to process our includes. Apache is available for all major platforms, and is free to download and use.

# Installing Apache

Apache is used on almost 70% of the Web servers that run sites on the Internet.[2] If you've ever used shared hosting on a Linux server, it's likely that your site was running on Apache. The Apache Web server is an Open Source project that's free to download and install, with installers provided for most operating systems.

---

[2]Statistics according to http://news.netcraft.com/

# Windows

## Figure 2.5. Downloading the Apache installer.

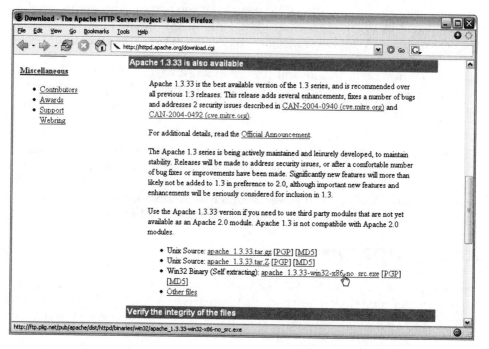

To install Apache on Windows, go to http://httpd.apache.org/, click on Download, and grab the "Win32 Binary (Self Extracting)" version, as shown in Figure 2.5. I'll be using Apache 1.3 throughout this discussion, but the instructions are more or less the same for Apache 2, if you wish to use that instead.

Locate and run the downloaded executable file, and progress through the setup questions by clicking Next. Don't worry if you don't understand the options presented; they're not important in the case of our simple testing server.

## Installing Apache Alongside IIS

You can use IIS to serve Web pages with server-side includes—a job it does perfectly well—but if you want to install Apache on a computer that already has IIS, use these instructions[3] to do so.

---

[3] http://www.evolt.org/article/Recap_IIS_and_Apache_together/18/1700/

If you type **http://localhost/** into your Web browser following a successful installation, Apache's test page will display (localhost, as mentioned before, refers to your computer). By default, Apache will look in the directory C:\Program Files\Apache Group\Apache\htdocs\ to find files to serve. To change this setting, we need to edit httpd.conf, the main Apache configuration file. From the Start menu, select All Programs > Apache HTTP Server > Configure Apache Server > Edit the Apache httpd.conf Configuration File to open this file in Notepad. Find the line that starts with DocumentRoot, as shown in Figure 2.6.

## Figure 2.6. Editing `httpd.conf` in Notepad

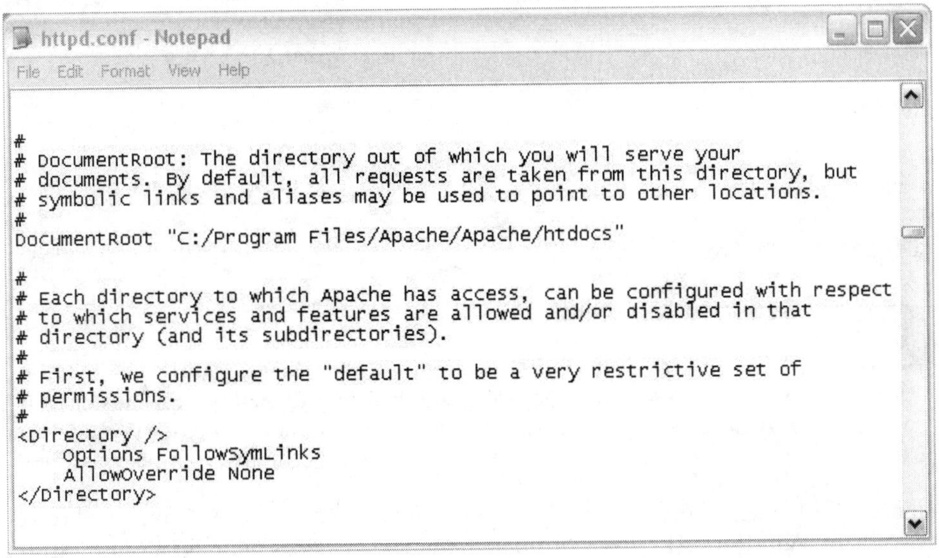

```
#
# DocumentRoot: The directory out of which you will serve your
# documents. By default, all requests are taken from this directory, but
# symbolic links and aliases may be used to point to other locations.
#
DocumentRoot "C:/Program Files/Apache/Apache/htdocs"

#
# Each directory to which Apache has access, can be configured with respect
# to which services and features are allowed and/or disabled in that
# directory (and its subdirectories).
#
# First, we configure the "default" to be a very restrictive set of
# permissions.
#
<Directory />
    Options FollowSymLinks
    AllowOverride None
</Directory>
```

This snippet tells the server where your Website files are stored. Let's change this location to one that's more easily accessed. Create a folder on your C: drive called Apache Sites, then change the line in httpd.conf as follows:

```
#
# DocumentRoot: The directory out of which you will serve your
# documents. By default, all requests are taken from this
# directory, but symbolic links and aliases may be used to point
# to other locations.
#
DocumentRoot "C:/Apache Sites"
```

### Back up Before you Edit!

Before you edit `httpd.conf`, make a backup copy of the file so that if it all goes wrong, and Apache fails to start, you have a copy of the original file with which you can replace the edited file. `httpd.conf` can be found in `C:\Program Files\Apache Group\Apache\conf`.

The original directory will also be referenced later in the file, in a section that looks like this:

```
#
# This should be changed to whatever you set DocumentRoot to.
#
<Directory "C:/Program Files/Apache Group/Apache/htdocs">
```

Change this to:

```
#
# This should be changed to whatever you set DocumentRoot to.
#
<Directory "C:/Apache Sites">
```

### Security Matters!

Resist the temptation to reuse an existing folder to host your Website, or—even worse—to set `DocumentRoot` to `C:/`. Remember: the outside world may be able to gain access to the directory you set up for your Website; you don't want strangers to be able to download or modify your personal files!

In order for Apache to take notice of any changes to `httpd.conf`, we need to restart it. In Windows XP, you can do so from the Services Management console, which can be opened by selecting Services from the Administrative Tools menu, or by selecting Run... from the Start menu and typing **services.msc** into the dialog that appears. To restart Apache, locate Apache in the list of services, right-click on it, and select Restart.

# Mac OS X

If you're running Mac OS X, you're in luck! Apache is already installed: you simply need to start it up. To do so, access System Preferences, select Sharing, and start up Personal Web Sharing. You should then be able to enter **http://localhost/** in your browser to view the Apache test page. On the Mac, this page is served from /Library/WebServer/Documents/—a location to which you may or may not have access, depending on the way your user profile is set up. Fortunately,

Apache on the Mac is also configured to give each user his or her own Web space at `http://localhost/~username/`. The files for this directory are located in the `Sites` folder of your home directory.

# Testing SSI

Before we complete this part of the setup procedure, we need to check that SSI works properly on our system. To do this, we'll create a very simple Web page that contains an include. Create the following two files in your text editor:

File: **hello.html**

```
<p>Hello, World!</p>
```

File: **ssi_test.shtml**

```
<!DOCTYPE html PUBLIC "-//W3C//DTD XHTML 1.0 Transitional//EN"
    "http://www.w3.org/TR/xhtml1/DTD/xhtml1-transitional.dtd">
<html xmlns="http://www.w3.org/1999/xhtml">
<head>
<title>Testing SSI</title>
<meta http-equiv="Content-Type" content="text/html;
    charset=iso-8859-1" />
</head>
<body>
<!--#include file="hello.html" -->
</body>
</html>
```

You should now be able to open a browser, type

**`http://localhost/ssi_test.shtml`**

into the address bar, and see "Hello, World!" display on the Web page as in Figure 2.7.

# Enabling SSI

If you see a blank page, or the code from `ssi_test.shtml`, you need to tweak your Apache configuration to enable SSI. Open your `httpd.conf` file, and look to see if the following lines are present and uncommented.

```
AddType text/html .shtml
AddHandler server-parsed .shtml
```

## Figure 2.7. Confirming that SSI works correctly.

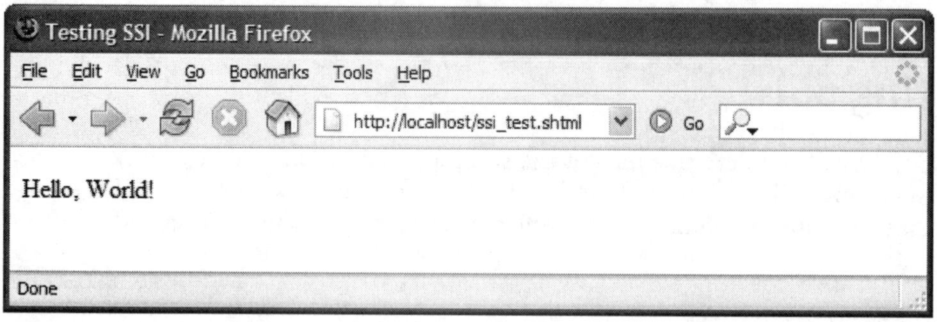

Testing SSI - Mozilla Firefox

File   Edit   View   Go   Bookmarks   Tools   Help

http://localhost/ssi_test.shtml   Go

Hello, World!

Done

## Got a Comment?

In `httpd.conf`, lines beginning with # are ignored by Apache. These are comments. These lines provide you with the ability to add notes to the file, or disable certain options without deleting them. For example, the following options are disabled in `httpd.conf`. To re-enable them, we'd remove the # from the start of each line.

```
# AddType text/html .shtml
# AddHandler server-parsed .shtml
```

If these lines are not present in the file, add them: they ensure that files with the extension `.shtml` are parsed by the server. Next, locate the following section:

```
#
# This should be changed to whatever you set DocumentRoot to.
#
<Directory "C:/Apache Sites">

#
# This may also be "None", "All", or any combination of "Indexes",
# "Includes", "FollowSymLinks", "ExecCGI", or "MultiViews".
#
# Note that "MultiViews" must be named *explicitly* ---
# "Options All" doesn't give it to you.
#
    Options Indexes FollowSymLinks MultiViews
```

In the `Options` line, add `Includes` to the list to enable SSI for that directory:

```
    Options Indexes FollowSymLinks MultiViews Includes
```

You should also check that the following line is not commented out:

```
AddModule mod_include.c
```

You'll need to restart Apache in order for the server to take notice of your changes. Once you've done so, re-test your page in the browser.

### SSI Default on Mac OS X

The default installation of Apache on Mac OS X should have SSI enabled. If it doesn't, or you need to edit httpd.conf for some other reason, you may need to log in as an administrative user.

# Using IIS as your Local Web Server

If you already have IIS installed and set up as your local Web server, you should be able to use the .shtml extension to parse files that contain SSI directives. To test SSI, create the hello.html and ssi_test.shtml files as described in the previous section, and save them to the directory C:\Inetpub\wwwroot. Run the test by loading **http://localhost/ssi_test.shtml** in your browser.

If your test include page doesn't work, you'll need to check that pages with the .shtml extension are being parsed. To do this, open the IIS Management Console (Control Panel > Administrative Tools > Internet Information Services). Right-click on your Website and select Properties. Select the Home Directory tab in the Default Web Site Properties dialog, then click the Configuration button.

Check that .shtml is listed under Extension and that its executable path ends in ssinc.dll, as shown in Figure 2.8.

# Hosting your Site

The site that we'll create should be able to be hosted on any standard hosting account that allows the use of Server Side Includes. This requirement should be covered by even the most basic packages of most shared hosting accounts. However, if you already have a hosting account and want to check that SSI is available, simply upload the test pages we created earlier to test our own servers. If those pages work, SSI is available to you.

**Figure 2.8. Checking that `.shtml` is being parsed to enable includes on IIS.**

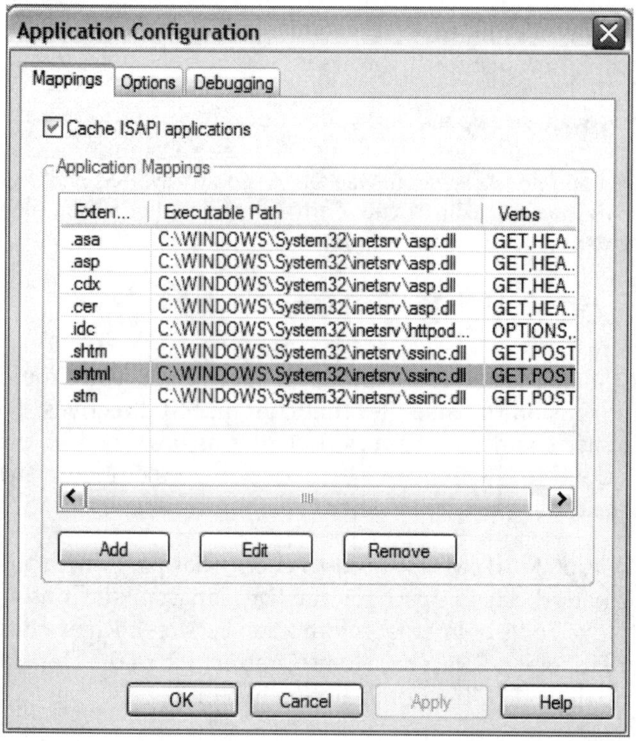

# Setting up Dreamweaver

Now that your server is set up and ready, let's create a directory for the Code Spark Website. Go to the Web server's root folder (`C:\Apache Files` for Apache; `C:\Inetpub\wwwroot` for IIS) and create a folder called `codespark`. This folder will be accessible as `http://localhost/codespark/`.

Now, we're ready to set up Dreamweaver and begin development on the site. Open Dreamweaver, and select Site > New Site.... This should open the Site Definition wizard. In the first screen, name your site **codespark** and enter its URL: **http://localhost/codespark**.

After clicking Next, you'll be asked if you want to work with a server-side language. You do not need to use server-side technology to create the site in this book, as we're using Server Side Includes, but the server technologies Dreamweaver is asking about here are those it uses to work with database-driven Websites in ASP, PHP, ASP.NET, JSP, and ColdFusion. Select No in this dialog, and move on.

In the next screen, select the radio button labeled Edit directly on server using local network, then browse for the site directory that you have created.

## Figure 2.9. The wizard displaying a summary.

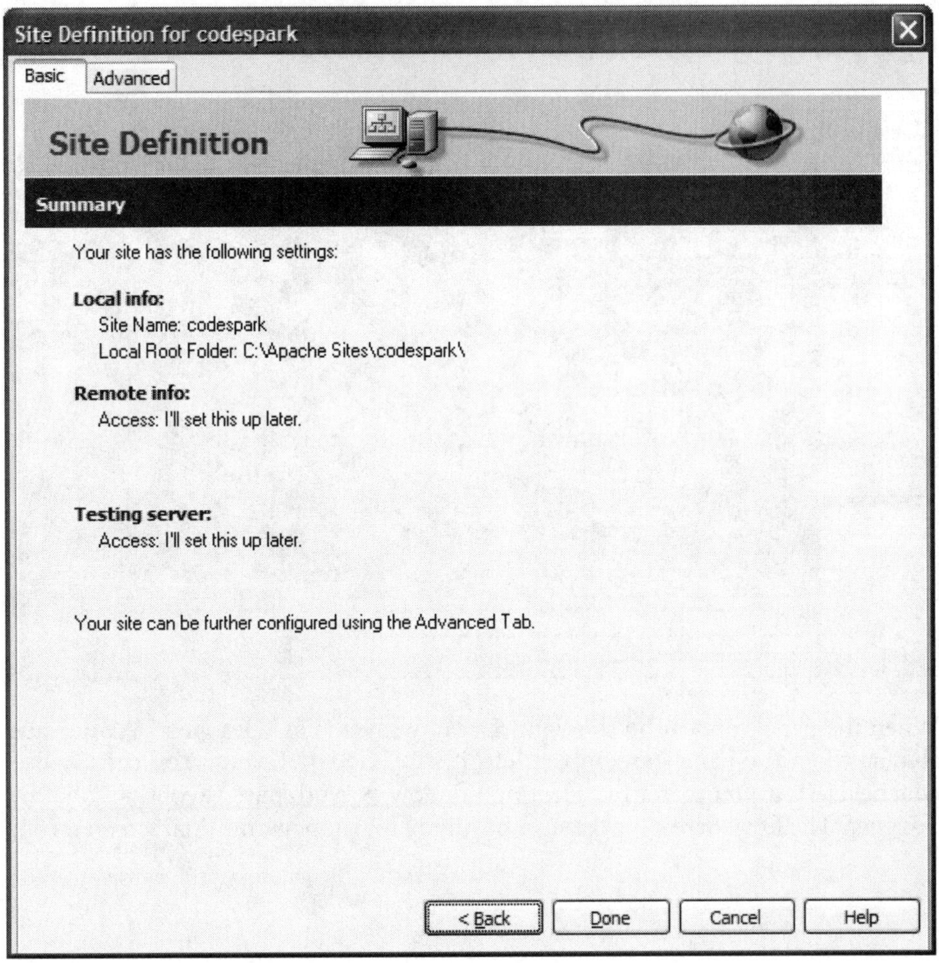

Following this step, the wizard completes, providing a summary of the details of your site's creation similar to that shown in Figure 2.9. If it all seems fine, click Done to create the site and open it in Dreamweaver.

# Your Workspace

Depending on the selection that you made when you installed Dreamweaver, you should now be presented with a large gray screen with panels positioned either on its left (as shown in Figure 2.10) or its right.

## Figure 2.10. The Dreamweaver 8 Workspace.

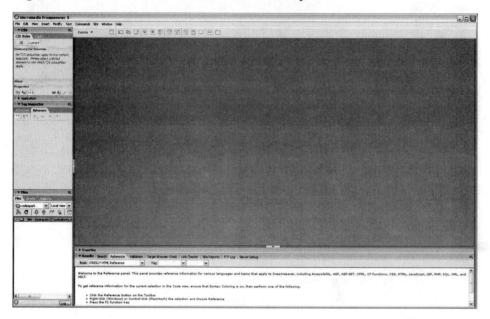

When the panels appear on the right, Dreamweaver is in "Designer" Workspace layout; when the panels are on the left, it's in "Coder" layout. You can choose whichever view you prefer by selecting Window > Workspace Layout > Coder or Designer. The Dual Screen option can be handy for those with a dual screen setup.

## Figure 2.11. Changing the Workspace.

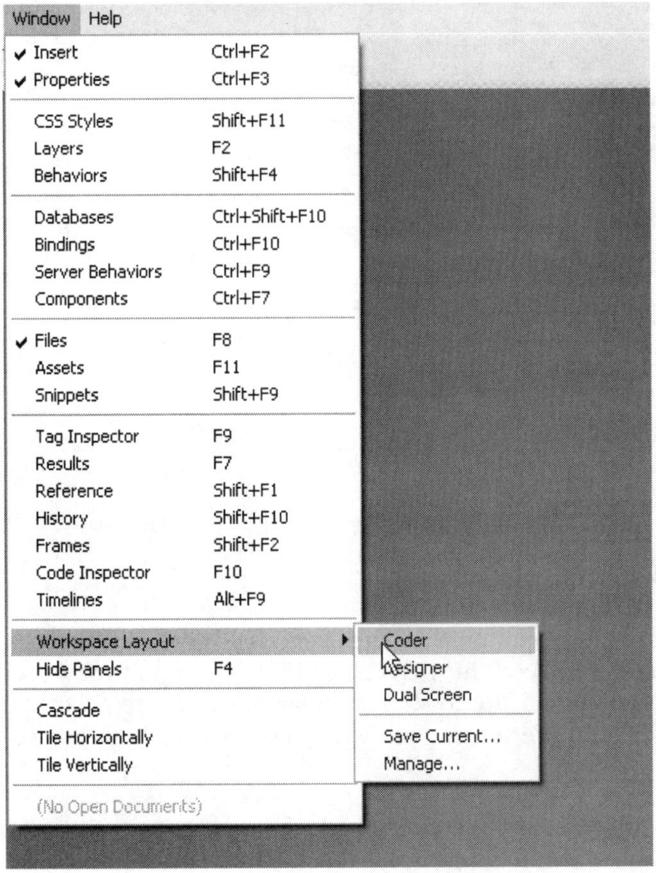

| Window | Help | |
|---|---|---|
| ✔ Insert | Ctrl+F2 | |
| ✔ Properties | Ctrl+F3 | |
| CSS Styles | Shift+F11 | |
| Layers | F2 | |
| Behaviors | Shift+F4 | |
| Databases | Ctrl+Shift+F10 | |
| Bindings | Ctrl+F10 | |
| Server Behaviors | Ctrl+F9 | |
| Components | Ctrl+F7 | |
| ✔ Files | F8 | |
| Assets | F11 | |
| Snippets | Shift+F9 | |
| Tag Inspector | F9 | |
| Results | F7 | |
| Reference | Shift+F1 | |
| History | Shift+F10 | |
| Frames | Shift+F2 | |
| Code Inspector | F10 | |
| Timelines | Alt+F9 | |
| Workspace Layout | ▶ | Coder |
| Hide Panels | F4 | Designer |
| | | Dual Screen |
| Cascade | | Save Current... |
| Tile Horizontally | | Manage... |
| Tile Vertically | | |
| (No Open Documents) | | |

I tend to work with the panels on the left, so the screenshots in this book will show that configuration; however, the way you like to arrange your Workspace is a personal choice: it won't make any difference to the project.

### Dreamweaver Panels Explained

If you're new to Dreamweaver, you'll find that you soon pick up the different panel and toolbar purposes as we use them. Each time we use a new panel or tool I'll explain how to locate it and use its basic functionality. All panels can be opened and closed from the Window menu. Each panel is grouped with other panels that do similar things. You can switch between them using the tabs at the top of the panel group, as shown in Figure 2.12 below.

### Figure 2.12. The Assets Panel is part of the Files Panel group.

# Setting Preferences

You can make many changes to the way that Dreamweaver operates by setting your own preferences. There are certain preferences that it's important to set correctly when you're developing a site to Web standards, so, before we create our first page, let's make sure we're starting out with these essential preferences in place.

Open the Preferences dialog (Edit > Preferences) and select the General category to display the information shown in Figure 2.13. Make sure that:

1. Allow Multiple Consecutive Spaces is unchecked. If this option is checked, it will allow you to insert a series of non-breaking spaces ( ) each time you press **space** more than once. If you need to add more space to your layout, it's best to do so with CSS, to ensure that Dreamweaver isn't working against you!

2. Use <strong> and <em> instead of <b> and <i> is checked. <b> and <i> are prime examples of presentational markup: they don't convey the reason *why* an element is bold or italicized, just the fact that it is styled as such. <em> and <strong> tell the browser (or Web indexer, screen reader, or any other program that wants to parse the site) that the text is emphasized or strongly emphasized. This is another example of the semantic document

structure we discussed in Chapter 1. We will discuss screen readers, and the way they read out text, in more detail in Chapter 7 and Chapter 8.

3. Use CSS instead of HTML tags is checked. This one's fairly self-explanatory: we don't want Dreamweaver inserting any <font> tags for us!

## Figure 2.13. Setting General preferences.

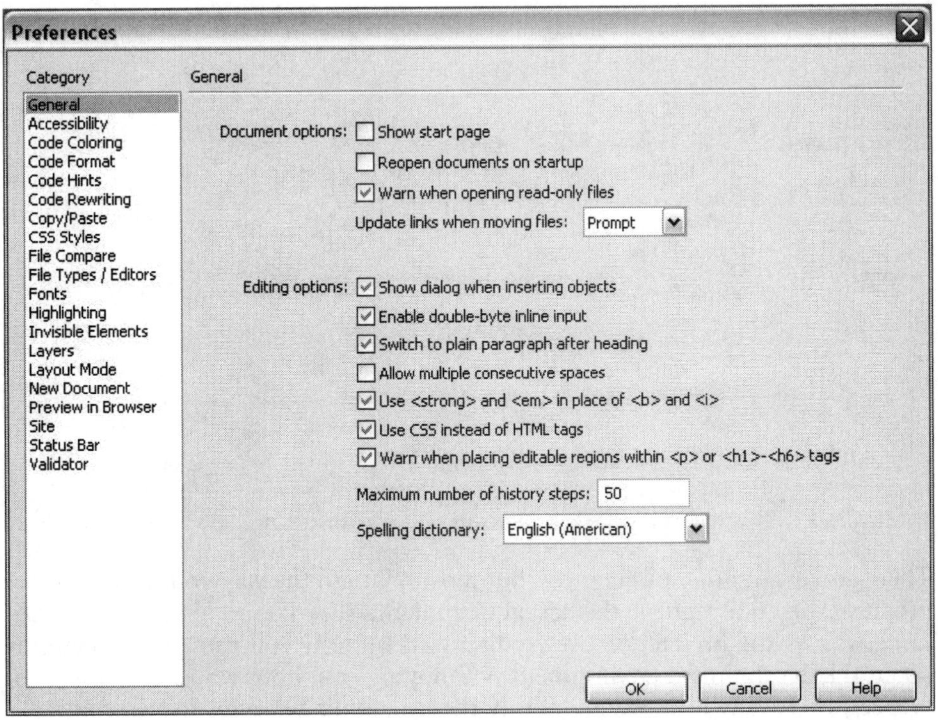

Select the Accessibility category, under Show Attributes when Inserting, and check all four checkboxes, as shown in Figure 2.14. This means that, when you enter any of these elements, Dreamweaver will display additional dialogs that prompt you to enter the accessibility attributes for those elements. This makes it less likely that you will forget to enter these important attributes as you create a document.

## Figure 2.14. Setting Accessibility preferences.

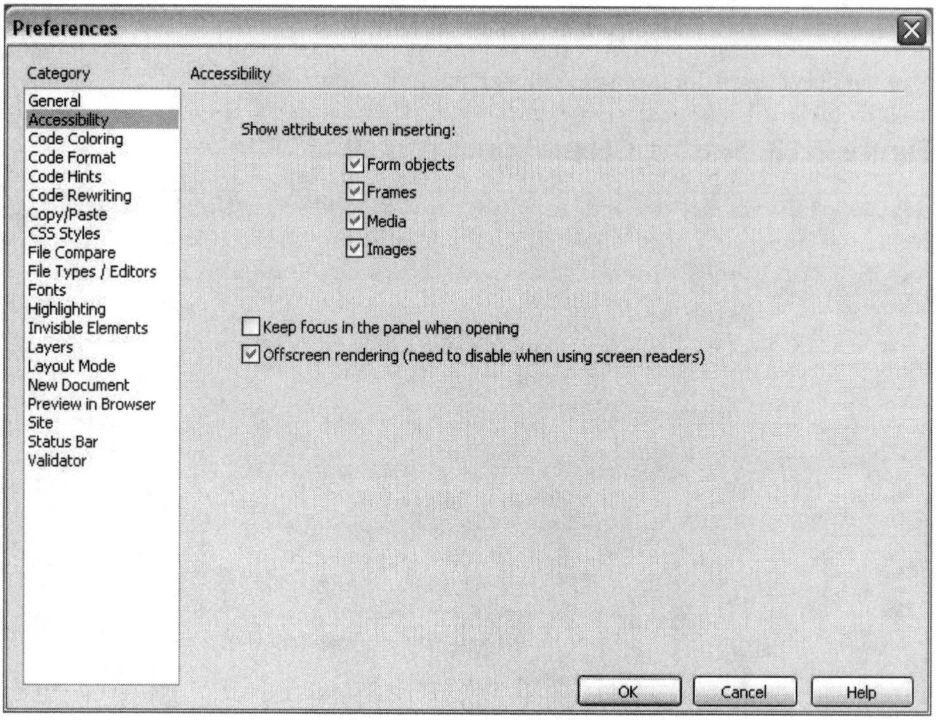

There are lots of other preferences, but most relate to the way you work with the product: they don't affect the actual documents that you're working on in the same way as the preferences we've discussed here. If you find that something about the development environment is annoying you, however, check your preferences: there may be a way to modify the program's behavior to suit you.

# Summary

In the course of this chapter we've made some key decisions about how we'll proceed with the development of this site. We've decided on the elements that we want to include in our site, and we've come up with a layout that contains all those elements. We have considered the best way to build our site in order to manage the common elements that will display on every page of the site, and, because the site could become very large as we add articles and tutorials, we've decided to use Server Side Includes (SSI) to manage these common elements. In order to do so—and be able to test the site locally—we installed a Web server and checked that SSI works. Finally, we created the site in Dreamweaver, and set up the preferences we need in order to get a head start on the path to developing a standards compliant Website.

Making these kinds of decisions at the start, and setting our systems up on the basis of these decisions, means that you can begin the development process with a clear understanding of where you're heading, and what you hope to achieve. It's important to consider how the site will grow and develop. You can't preempt everything that might possibly happen, but, when planning the development, if you consider how the site might be likely to evolve over the next year, these expectations can support your decision-making process. For example, we might not have made the decision to use SSI if the site was never going to be any more than a three-page brochure site, as the issues of copying and pasting and re-uploading content would not have existed for that type of project.

In the next chapter, we'll look at XHTML. We'll discover how it's different than the HTML you may already have used, and how Dreamweaver can help you to use XHTML in a site's development.

# XHTML and Semantics

Dreamweaver MX was the first version of Macromedia Dreamweaver to provide support for those working in XHTML—a development that reflected the fact that many developers have moved from HTML to XHTML. In this chapter, we'll explore XHTML in some depth. We'll understand why it's different from HTML, why we might want to use it in preference to HTML, and how we could go about doing so.

In this chapter, we'll see not only how valid XHTML is written, but also, how to structure an XHTML document correctly in order that our content is accessible to all users.

## What is XHTML?

XHTML is basically the union of two languages: HTML and XML. You're probably already familiar with HTML, but XML may need a brief introduction.

## XML

Extensible Markup Language (XML) is a general-purpose language for structuring data in a way that's easy for both humans and computers to read, as shown here:

```
<?xml version="1.0" encoding="iso-8859-1"?>
<orders date="March 31 2006" xmlns="http://myshop.com/orders.dtd">
  <order productID="52478">
    <description>Dreamweaver 8 (OS X)</description>
    <recipient>
      <name>Sally Smith</name>
      <address>
        <street>474 Smith St.</street>
        <city>Collingwood</city>
        <state>Victoria</state>
        <zipCode>3068</zipCode>
        <country>Australia</country>
      </address>
    </recipient>
  </order>
  <order productID="52477">
    <description>Dreamweaver 8 (Windows)</description>
    <recipient>
      <name>John Jameson</name>
      <address>
        <street>Level 5, 142 Park Avenue</street>
        <city>New York</city>
        <state>New York</state>
        <zipCode>10167</zipCode>
        <country>United States</country>
      </address>
    </recipient>
  </order>
</orders>
```

We can see that this code comprises a list of two orders made on March 31, 2006: one for Dreamweaver 8 for Mac OS X (to be delivered to Sally Smith in Australia), and the other for Dreamweaver 8 for Windows (to be delivered to John Jameson in New York).

The actual tags that are used here aren't part of XML; XML defines only how the tags are written. It's up to the entities that create and consume these files to agree on the actual tags that are used. In this way, we can define lots of useful languages within XML; XHTML is one of these.

# XHTML

XHTML came into being as a recommendation that was released by the W3C on January 26, 2000. XHTML represented a reformulation of HTML—the original language of Websites—into an XML application designed to meet the future needs of the Web. Indeed, XHTML can be regarded as the latest version of HTML, as no further HTML specifications will be developed or released.

As XHTML is a reformulation of HTML, rather than a completely new markup language, it will seem very familiar to anyone who has already used HTML. There are very few differences between XHTML and HTML, which makes life easy for the Web developer who wishes to work in XHTML. We will discuss these differences in this chapter, and see why we might want to use XHTML over HTML.

# What Makes a Valid XHTML Document?

In order to create a valid XHTML document right from the start, we need to include certain elements in that document before we begin marking up content. We're fortunate in that Dreamweaver will give us a valid XHTML document as a starting point, if we use File > New... to open the New Document dialog, then select Basic Page, HTML, and then select one of the XHTML 1.0 document types from the Document Type (DTD) drop-down list. The default selection is XHTML 1.0 Transitional, which will create a page containing the following markup.

```
<!DOCTYPE html PUBLIC "-//W3C//DTD XHTML 1.0 Transitional//EN"
    "http://www.w3.org/TR/xhtml1/DTD/xhtml1-transitional.dtd">
<html xmlns="http://www.w3.org/1999/xhtml">
<head>
<title>Untitled Document</title>
<meta http-equiv="Content-Type" content="text/html;
    charset=iso-8859-1" />
</head>

<body>
</body>
</html>
```

## The DOCTYPE

A valid XHTML document must use an XHTML DOCTYPE. We discussed DOCTYPEs in Chapter 1; you'll remember that this line identifies the specification to which the document is written. The XHTML Transitional DOCTYPE is:

```
<!DOCTYPE html PUBLIC "-//W3C//DTD XHTML 1.0 Transitional//EN"
    "http://www.w3.org/TR/xhtml1/DTD/xhtml1-transitional.dtd">
```

## Using the XML Declaration

Sometimes, you'll see an **XML Declaration**, like the one shown below, as the first line of an XHTML document.

```
<?xml version="1.0" encoding="UTF-8"?>
```

This XML Declaration, which declares that the document is XML, is recommended but not required. This line was inserted by Dreamweaver MX. However, Dreamweaver 8 doesn't insert the XML Declaration, as it has the unfortunate effect of switching Internet Explorer 6 into "Quirks Mode"—a special mode that disregards Web standards in favor of Internet Explorer 5's nonstandard rules.

# The `html` Element

```
<html xmlns="http://www.w3.org/1999/xhtml">
```

The `html` element is known as the root element of the document. To be a valid XHTML document, this element needs to include the `xmlns="http://www.w3.org/1999/xhtml"` part; this attribute, part of XML, states that the elements in the document comply with the XHTML standard, by default.

## XML Namespaces

The actual tags used in an XML document can be defined by one or more document type definitions, or DTDs (these are different from the DOC-TYPEs, document type *declarations*, that we discussed earlier). DTDs can be linked into an XML document using the `xmlns` attribute.[1] Each DTD is given a "namespace," which forms a prefix for the tags that are part of that DTD. One DTD may be given the "default namespace" (which has no prefix), but other DTDs used in the document require unique prefixes.

For example, if we wanted to add some XML from our order list to an XHTML document, we could add a namespace to our document like so:

```
<html xmlns="http://www.w3.org/1999/xhtml"
    xmlns:ord="http://myshop.com/orders.dtd">
```

---

[1] Strictly speaking, `xmlns` attributes do not need to point to a DTD, as evidenced by the URL used to identify the XHTML namespace (`http://www.w3.org/1999/xhtml`). XML actually allows any text string to identify an XML namespace. Using the public URL of the relevant DTD is simply a useful convention to use for custom XML document types. None of this really matters for our purposes, however.

Within the XHTML document, we could then use the `ord:` prefix to indicate that the element is from the order list DTD:

```
<h2>Orders Placed</h2>
<ord:orders>
  <ord:order productID="52478">
    <ord:description>Dreamweaver 8 (OS X)</description>
    <ord:recipient>
      <ord:name>Sally Smith</ord:name>
      <ord:address>
        <ord:street>474 Smith St.</ord:street>
        <ord:city>Collingwood</ord:city>
        <ord:state>Victoria</ord:state>
        <ord:zipCode>3068</ord:zipCode>
        <ord:country>Australia</ord:country>
      </ord:address>
    </ord:recipient>
  </ord:order>
</ord:orders>
```

# The head Element

```
<head>
<title>Untitled Document</title>
<meta http-equiv="Content-Type" content="text/html;
    charset=iso-8859-1" />
</head>
```

The `head` element contains the `title` element, which gives the page a title. In the snippet above, you can see that Dreamweaver has inserted "Untitled Document" by default: there are many thousands of documents on the Web titled "Untitled Document" because their authors forgot to change the documents' titles!

In the head of the document we can also see a `<meta>` tag. This `<meta>` tag declares the `Content-Type` of the document, as well as the character encoding used.

# The body Element

```
<body>
</body>
```

Here's the body element, into which you'll place all of the content that you wish to make available to your site's visitors.

# XHTML and HTML: the Differences

There are only a few rules to keep in mind when using XHTML instead of HTML. Although we'll use Dreamweaver to write our XHTML—and can rely on the program to do a pretty good job of it—it's worth understanding the differences between the two languages. It's inevitable that, sometimes, you'll need to hand-code markup, or edit markup you've copied from other sources in order to make it XHTML compliant.

## Quoting Attribute Values

In HTML, it's perfectly valid not to quote attribute values. For example, the following image markup is valid HTML:

```
<img src="/img/me.jpg" alt="A picture of me" height=400 width=200>
```

To make this valid XHTML, you need to insert quotes around the attribute values, `height="400" width="200"`. Dreamweaver writes both HTML and XHTML with quoted attribute values; however, you might find that markup you've copied from other sources contains these unquoted HTML values.

## Closing all Empty and Non-empty Elements

As you'd probably expect, a **non-empty element** is any element that contains something—for example, text, scripts or other data content—between a start and end tag. p and li are examples of non-empty elements. In HTML, we aren't required to close these elements, so the following list is valid HTML.

```
<ul>
  <li>List item one
  <li>List item two
  <li>List item three
</ul>
```

However, this would constitute invalid XHTML, as the li element has not been closed. This issue has been rectified in the valid XHTML markup below:

```
<ul>
  <li>List item one</li>
```

```
  <li>List item two</li>
  <li>List item three</li>
</ul>
```

What about elements such as hr, img, and br? These **empty elements** must also be closed. In XML, you can do this with <hr></hr>, or by using XML's shorthand notation, <hr/>. Unfortunately, older browsers would likely balk at such odd markup. As you might have guessed, the clever folks who put together XHTML came up with a solution to this problem: use the shorthand notation, but insert a space between the element's name and the closing slash (<hr />). This still represents valid XML, so XHTML-aware browsers won't have a problem with it, and older browsers see the closing slash as an unrecognized attribute.

# Avoiding Minimizing Attributes

HTML supported minimizing attributes, or leaving out an attribute's value when it's not required. Consider this example of attribute minimization:

```
<input type="checkbox" checked>
```

Above, the attribute checked indicates that the checkbox should be checked when it displays on the page. XML doesn't support minimizing attributes in the same way HTML does, so to achieve this using valid XHTML, we need to give these attributes a value:

```
<input type="checkbox" checked="checked" />
```

Here, the value of the attribute becomes the same as its name. This is the case for several attributes that are minimized in HTML:

☐ selected="selected"

☐ disabled="disabled"

☐ readonly="readonly"

# Writing Elements and Attributes in Lowercase

XHTML requires that all tags and attributes be written in lowercase. HTML is not case-sensitive: we could even use a mixture of upper- and lowercase with that language. Yet XML is case sensitive, so XHTML requires the use of lowercase tags, as illustrated in the below example.

```
<p>This line is <em class="formal">valid</em> XHTML</p>
<p>This line is <STRONG STYLE="text-transform: uppercase;">
  not</STRONG> valid XHTML</p>
```

# Nesting Elements Properly

Web browsers are generally very tolerant of errors in HTML, but less tolerant of errors in XHTML. The following example constitutes invalid HTML and XHTML, but would generally display as the author (probably) intended:

```
<p><em>This text is emphasized</p></em>
```

In HTML, tags must be nested correctly; that is, the last tag that was opened must be the first tag that's closed. This requirement becomes even more important when we start to use XML, and to mark up our document for meaning. Thus, we need to edit the above to nest our tags correctly:

```
<p><em>This text is emphasized</em></p>
```

# Using `id` Instead of `name` to Identify Elements

HTML allows us to use the `name` attribute to identify particular elements on the page. `name` could be used for a number of purposes: to reference an element using JavaScript, to name a form element so that it could be collected once the form had been submitted, and more. Here's `name` in action:

```
<form method="post" action="/cgi-bin/search.cgi">
  <img src="search.gif" name="Image1" alt="Search ">
  <input type="text" name="searchField">
  <input type="submit" value="Search">
</form>
```

In XHTML, we must use the `id` attribute instead:

```
<form method="post" action="/cgi-bin/search.cgi">
  <img src="search.gif" id="Image1" alt="Search " />
  <input type="text" id="searchField" name="searchField" />
  <input type="submit" value="Search" />
</form>
```

Have a close look at that, and note that I've left the `name` attribute on the `<input>` tag. Form fields are the one place where the `name` attribute is still kosher; however, it isn't used to identify these elements in the document: it's used to supply the variable name under which the field's value will be submitted. In XHTML Strict, that's the only purpose for which the name attribute may be legally used.

Dreamweaver will add both name and id attributes to a given element (giving both attributes the same values) in an XHTML Transitional document.

### The id Must be Unique

Unlike names, elements' id attributes must be unique: there cannot be more than one element with a particular id in any given document.

# Why use XHTML?

We've explored the differences between XHTML and HTML, and we now have a clearer understanding of each language. But the fact remains that we can create a standards compliant, accessible and semantic Website that validates to HTML 4.01 if we want to. Why should we consider moving to XHTML?

## Creating Clean Markup

HTML allows developers to write markup in a very flexible manner. It isn't very strict with the application of rules such as closing tags like <p>. For example, consider the following:

```
<p>This is a paragraph.
<p>This is another.
```

HTML allows this markup, rather than demanding that the closing </p> tag be used to mark up the end of the paragraph, like so:

```
<p>This is a paragraph.</p>
<p>This is another.</p>
```

HTML allows the creation of simpler, but more ambiguous markup, whereas in XHTML every opening tag must be matched by its closing tag. While it might seem like quite a good idea to take a flexible approach to markup, which enables people with little technical expertise to easily create documents for the Web, this approach can also cause a number of problems, particularly where these untidily marked-up documents are to be read by devices that don't have the processing power of a desktop computer.

# Making Code Easier for Machines to Process

XHTML is easier than HTML for a computer to process because XHTML does not permit the flexibility allowed by HTML. This means that documents marked up using XHTML are more easily read or displayed by devices other than a conventional Web browser—devices such as screen readers, Web-enabled phones, Braille readers, and search engines.

# Boosting the Portability of Content

The content that you've marked up within your Web page is valuable in its own right; in the future, you might want to reuse it in a different format. If that content was marked up using HTML—even valid HTML—it would be more difficult to reuse the content in another application than if it was marked up in XHTML. XHTML's rigorous conformance to XML rules means that it's far easier to transform an XHTML document into some other format. This would be very useful if you had decided to rebuild your site with a database-driven back-end, for example, and needed to get all that marked-up content into the new database.

# Allowing Integration with other XML Applications

XHTML allows the incorporation of tags from other XML applications such as MathML, SMIL (Synchronized Multimedia Integration Language), and SVG (Scalable Vector Graphics). This might not seem particularly useful right now, unless you have a very specialized requirement, but XHTML's integration capabilities are likely to become more important in the future.

# XHTML in Dreamweaver

Having read through all the do's and don'ts in the previous sections, you'll be glad to know that we'll be letting Dreamweaver write most of the XHTML markup for us. Now, let's take a look at the tools Dreamweaver provides to help us write valid XHTML documents.

# Creating New Pages

We have already seen that Dreamweaver can create new pages either in HTML or XHTML. Once Dreamweaver recognizes that your page has an XHTML DOCTYPE, it will insert elements using the correct XHTML syntax, rather than

HTML. You can confirm whether or not Dreamweaver is working in XHTML by looking to see if (XHTML) displays in the title bar, as shown in Figure 3.1.

## Figure 3.1. Dreamweaver displaying XHTML in the title bar.

In Design View, type **Shift-Enter** to insert a line break. Switch into Code View to have a look at the markup that was entered. Dreamweaver will have inserted the correct `<br />` tag instead of HTML's `<br>`. Try adding an image: you'll note that Dreamweaver closes the image tag correctly. There is little difference between the way we work with Dreamweaver in HTML, and in XHTML. As long as Dreamweaver knows which type of document we're working on, it will write the correct markup for us.

# Creating a Frameset

If you need to create a frameset, Dreamweaver will help you to use the correct DOCTYPE.

In your new XHTML document, create a frameset with a top frame using the Insert Frames button—as shown in Figure 3.2, you'll find it in the Layout panel of the Insert toolbar.

## Figure 3.2. Creating a frameset in Dreamweaver.

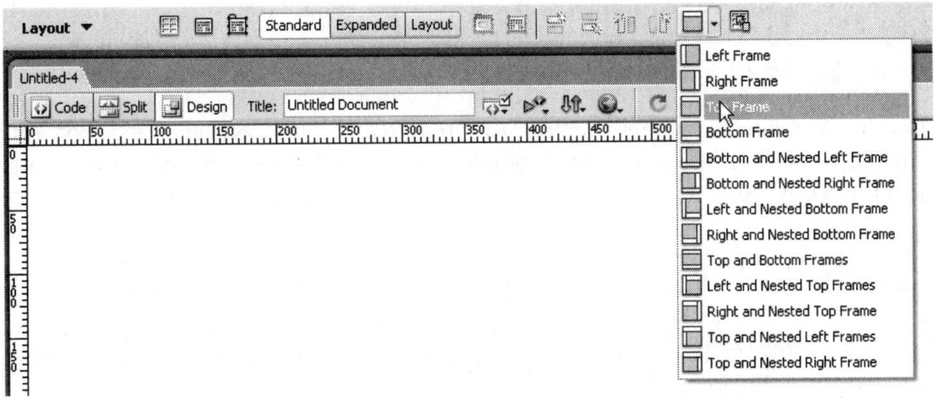

Your existing page will become the bottom frame, while a new top frame is created within a frameset. If you look at the source of the individual frames, they should use an XHTML Transitional DOCTYPE.

```
<!DOCTYPE html PUBLIC "-//W3C//DTD XHTML 1.0 Transitional//EN"
    "http://www.w3.org/TR/xhtml1/DTD/xhtml1-transitional.dtd">
```

Now, take a look at the containing frame. This frame should have a XHTML Frameset DOCTYPE, as illustrated in the code below, and in Figure 3.3.

```
<!DOCTYPE html PUBLIC "-//W3C//DTD XHTML 1.0 Frameset//EN"
    "http://www.w3.org/TR/xhtml1/DTD/xhtml1-frameset.dtd">
```

## Figure 3.3. Creating a frameset document in Dreamweaver.

# Converting Existing Pages

Once you start working in XHTML, you might like to convert some of your older sites to XHTML. Perhaps you'll need to convert some content marked up with HTML into XHTML format, in order to integrate it with your site. Dreamweaver has a "Convert to XHTML" capability that can make this process very easy.

To convert a document, first open it in Dreamweaver, then select File > Convert. Finally, select the specification to which you'd like to convert your document. You'll need to convert framesets and each framed page individually.

Dreamweaver will do its best to apply the rules of XHTML we discussed previously, but there are likely to be some problems if the original markup wasn't Web standards compliant. You'll need to step through the document and fix these issues yourself. If this seems like a tedious thing to have to do, remember that avoiding such issues is one of the reasons we're using Web standards compliant XHTML:

we're very unlikely to have to go through this rigmarole again. You can, of course, have Dreamweaver find these problems using its built-in markup validator.

## The Dreamweaver Validator

As we discussed in Chapter 1, the document validation process allows you to confirm that your markup complies with the particular specification you've chosen to work to.

Validate your document by selecting File > Check Page > Validate Markup. If the document is constructed using valid XHTML, a message to that effect will display in the Results Panel. If the document is invalid, you'll see a list of errors and the numbers of the lines on which those errors appear, like the one shown in Figure 3.4. These errors are likely to arise from some of the points we discussed above; for example, "Expected end of tag 'img'" means that an image tag in the document requires a closing /> to make it valid XHTML.

**Figure 3.4. Displaying errors in the Results Panel after the XHTML document is validated.**

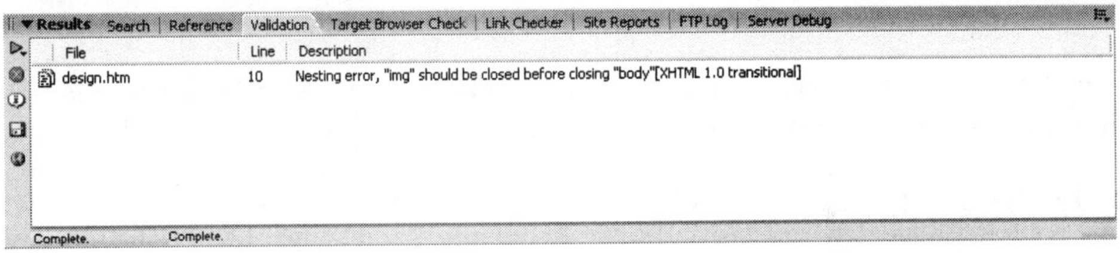

| Results | Search | Reference | Validation | Target Browser Check | Link Checker | Site Reports | FTP Log | Server Debug |
|---|---|---|---|---|---|---|---|---|
| | File | | Line | Description | | | | |
| | design.htm | | 10 | Nesting error, "img" should be closed before closing "body"[XHTML 1.0 transitional] | | | | |

Complete.    Complete.

### Viewing Line Numbers

When working in Code View, you can turn on line numbering in order to make tracking down any problematic lines of code easier. Line numbering can be turned on and off via the View > Code View Options > Line Numbers menu item. You can also double-click the line in the Results Panel to jump to that line in your document, which will be highlighted.

# Semantic Markup

As we've already agreed, we're not concerned simply with writing valid XHTML: we want also to create semantic documents. Semantics is the study of meaning, so a document with semantic markup is a document that contains tags that attempt to convey the meaning of the text. For example, an <h1> tag is used to indicate a top-level heading, while the `<ul>` and `<li>` tags are used to mark lists of items in no particular order. If we use semantic markup, the browser can not only read and display (or, in the case of a screen reader, read aloud) the contents of the page, but knows to display or speak the elements in the appropriate format. As we've seen, when it comes to writing valid XHTML, Dreamweaver will do most of the hard work for us, but when it comes to creating properly structured documents, we need to take a proactive approach ourselves.

One of the biggest issues I experience when working in a visual environment such as Dreamweaver is that it's very easy to become engrossed in how things look, and completely forget about the markup that Dreamweaver generates. For example, it's very easy for me to decide I want to indent some text a few inches from the left-hand side of the screen. The problem is that I can end up with the following markup:

```
<blockquote>
  <blockquote>
    <blockquote>
      <p>My indented text</p>
    </blockquote>
  </blockquote>
</blockquote>
```

This obviously isn't great from a semantic perspective: my indented text is not a quote, and it's certainly not a quote of a quote of a quote!

Making sure our Website looks great in a Web browser is, of course, very important, but it isn't the whole story. Some of our users might not be able to see any part of our design because they're using screen readers or text-only devices. Yet, by taking some care as we create our Web documents, we can give these users an excellent experience without compromising the site's look and feel for other users.

 *Tip*

## Removing CSS Style Rendering

Dreamweaver 8 makes it easy to see what your document will look like without styling when you're working in Design View. The Style Rendering toolbar can be opened by selecting View > Toolbars > Style Rendering. The Toggle Displaying of CSS Styles button switches the CSS in your document on and off, as shown in Figure 3.5.

## Figure 3.5. Toggling CSS style rendering.

# Using Elements Semantically

In this section, we'll take a look at some of the most common elements in XHTML, and see how to use them in Dreamweaver. This is not an exhaustive list, but aims to provide some examples of the more common mistakes that can be made, particularly when we're using a tool such as Dreamweaver.

Throughout this chapter, I use the terms "should" and "shouldn't" in the manner in which they're used in the W3C specifications[2], in order to show that these issues affect the Web standards that we're trying to meet. Each XHTML element should be used in a particular way. Of course, in practice, decisions have to be made as to the types of elements we'll use and the best way to use them; we'll be looking closely at these decisions as we build our site. This chapter explains specifically what the standards tell us; using the type of terminology that's employed by the specifications themselves helps to reinforce the fact that the information provided here isn't personal opinion—it's the standard!

## Headings

XHTML provides six heading levels. These headings can be thought of as being similar to the headings that might be presented in a book:

```
<h1>Introduction</h1>
<h1>Starters</h1>
  <h2>Soups</h2>
    <h3>Vegetable Soup</h3>
    <h3>Pea and Ham Soup</h3>
    <h3>Minestrone</h3>
  <h2>Other Starters</h2>
<h1>Mains</h1>
  <h2>Beef</h2>
```

---

[2] http://www.ietf.org/rfc/rfc2119.txt

```
  <h2>Chicken</h2>
  <h2>Vegetarian</h2>
<h1>Deserts</h1>
  <h2>Cakes</h2>
  <h2>Biscuits</h2>
```

Using Dreamweaver, we can create a heading by selecting the text we wish to style as a heading, then selecting the desired heading level in the Property Inspector, as shown in Figure 3.6.

## Figure 3.6. Creating a level one heading in Dreamweaver.

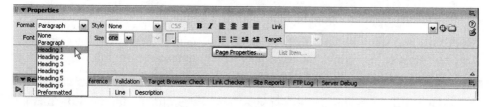

We should use a heading style whenever the text in question logically comprises a heading. We shouldn't use a heading when we simply want large text: use CSS to create that effect.

We should not "fake" headings by styling a paragraph or other element with CSS so that it looks like a heading, but is semantically a paragraph. Pages on which a heading is not distinguished as such can be rendered—or spoken—by the browser in ways that we did not intend, which in turn can cause confusion among users. We'll discuss this in more detail a little later.

Where possible, we should also avoid using an image at a point at which a heading would logically belong in a document. If we used an image, users with screen readers or other text-only devices would not perceive that heading as intended.

# Lists

XHTML places three different types of list at your disposal; lists should be used whenever your content logically comprises a list of items.

The unordered list style usually displays in browsers as a bulleted list; however, you can use CSS to change the bullets' appearance, or even to change the list to run horizontally across the screen, rather than vertically. You create an unordered list in Dreamweaver using the Property Inspector's Unordered List icon, shown in Figure 3.7.

## Figure 3.7. Creating an unordered list.

An unordered list is marked up as follows:

```
<ul>
  <li>250 grams (9 ounces) Plain Flour</li>
  <li>1 teaspoon Baking Powder</li>
  <li>50 grams (2 ounces) Butter</li>
  <li>1 egg</li>
  <li>Half a Cup of Milk</li>
</ul>
```

The ordered list format should be used whenever the order of the items in the list is important. You can create an ordered list in Dreamweaver using the Property Inspector's Ordered List icon, as shown in Figure 3.8.

## Figure 3.8. Creating an ordered list.

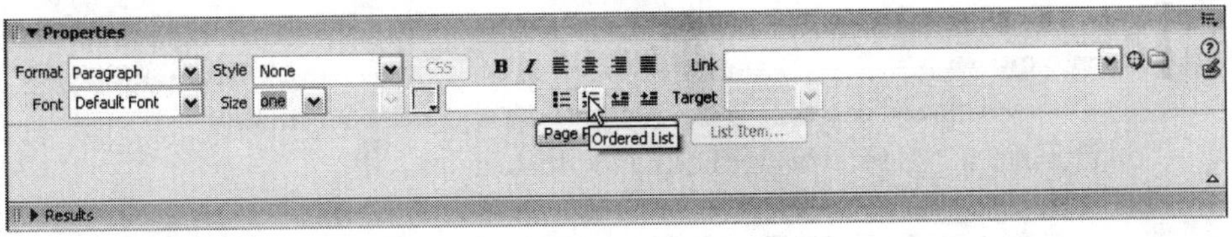

If, after you create an ordered list, you switch into Code View, you'll see the following markup.

```
<ol>
  <li>Preheat the oven to 200 degrees Celsius (400 degrees
    Fahrenheit)</li>
  <li>Put the flour, baking powder and sugar in a mixing bowl,
    then rub in the margarine until the mixture resembles
    breadcrumbs.</li>
  <li>Beat the egg and add it, with the milk, to the rest of the
```

```
    ingredients. Beat into a dough.</li>
  <li>Turn the dough out onto a floured surface and knead it
     briefly.</li>
  <li>But into a greased tray and bake for 45 minutes.</li>
</ol>
```

The `<ol>` element indicates that this is an ordered list. By default, a browser will display these lists as shown in Figure 3.9, but you can use CSS to change the display of any list.

## Figure 3.9. Displaying an unordered list and an ordered list.

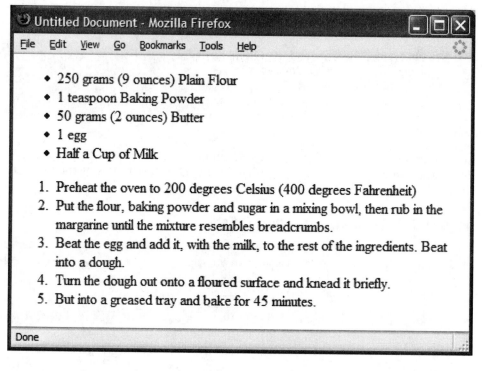

## Correct Structure for Nested Lists

In both ordered and unordered lists, there is the potential to create *nested* lists—lists within lists. In such instances, the sublist must be nested *inside* a list item element of the parent list, as shown in the following example:

```
<ul>
  <li>List item one</li>
```

```
<li>List item two
  <ul>
    <li>Sub item one</li>
    <li>Sub item two</li>
  </ul>
</li>
<li>List item three</li>
</ul>
```

The last type of list is useful if you have list of terms and definitions to mark up; it's called a definition list. You can create a definition list in Dreamweaver using the Insert toolbar's Text panel. To create the list, click the dl button, as shown in Figure 3.10.

## Figure 3.10. Creating a definition list using the Insert toolbar.

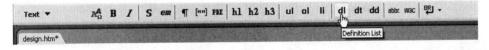

The first item that you type into your definition list will become the first term; hitting **Enter** will move you forward a line to create the definition for that term. Hitting **Enter** once more will create the second definition, and so on.

You'll end up with markup that looks something like this:

```
<dl>
  <dt>Cardamom</dt>
  <dd>An Indian spice from the ginger family.</dd>
  <dt>Caster Sugar</dt>
  <dd>Super fine sugar.</dd>
</dl>
```

## Figure 3.11. Displaying a definition list.

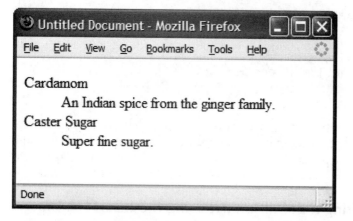

By default, this markup will display in the browser, and in Dreamweaver, as shown in Figure 3.11. Again, you can change this display using CSS.

# Creating Paragraphs and Line Breaks

The difference between a line break and a paragraph is a common source of confusion. A tried and true way of discerning the difference involves marking up a couple of verses of lyrics from a favorite song:

```
<p>
It's time to play the music,<br />
It's time to light the lights,<br />
It's time to meet the Muppets on the Muppet Show tonight!
</p>
<p>
It's time to put on make up,<br />
It's time to dress up right,<br />
It's time to raise the curtain on the Muppet Show tonight!
</p>
```

The paragraph tags tie the verse together. The line break tags are used to mark the end of each line of the verse.

To create a paragraph in Dreamweaver, hit **Enter**; to create a <br /> tag, hit **Shift-Enter**. Whenever you use <br />, consider whether it's the most appropriate element. Would you perhaps be better to create additional space using CSS, or using a paragraph? Maybe the content should really be marked up as a list, as in the example above.

Make sure you don't use line breaks within a paragraph to simulate a list! While this markup might display like an ordered list of items in a Web browser, a screen reader would not be able to present the content as intended:

```
<p>
  1. Preheat the oven to 200 degrees Celsius (400 degrees
  Fahrenheit)<br />
  2. Put the flour, baking powder and sugar in a mixing bowl,
  then rub in the margarine until the mixture resembles
  breadcrumbs.<br />
  3. Beat the egg and add it, with the milk, to the rest of the
  ingredients. Beat into a dough.<br />
  4. Turn the dough out onto a floured surface and knead it
  briefly.<br />
  5. But into a greased tray and bake for 45 minutes.
</p>
```

# Showing Emphasis

We often show emphasis in printed text by making specific words bold or italic. This approach lets the reader understand the emphasis we've placed on particular words: we're not just making them bold or italic for the sake of it. For example, the first time we've used a new or important term in this book, we've bolded that term. We use bold formatting to emphasize these new words to the reader: to flag them as words you'll need to remember.

When we set our preferences back in Chapter 2, we set the checkbox Use <strong> and <em> in place of <b> and <i> in the preferences dialog. Doing this means that the B (for bold) button in the Property Inspector will insert the strong element, and the I (for italics) button will insert the em element, like so:

```
<strong>Make sure that you preheat the oven.</strong> Cooking at
the correct temperature is <em>really</em> important.
```

By default, most Web browsers will display <strong> as bold text and <em> as italicized text. This is why many Web designers incorrectly consider these tags equivalent to <b> and <i>, which are purely presentational and don't provide much meaning. Like almost all tags, the appearance of <strong> and <em> can be changed using CSS.

### What's the Difference Between <em> and <strong>?

The W3C and most of the HTML documentation describes these elements only as "emphasis" and "strong emphasis," which isn't much use. Think of <strong> as a loud, slow voice, and <em> as a raised tone of voice.

## Indenting and the blockquote Element

Dreamweaver's Property Inspector is home to the Text Indent icon shown in Figure 3.12. The only time you should use this icon is to indent text that's a quote.

### Figure 3.12. Using the Text Indent icon.

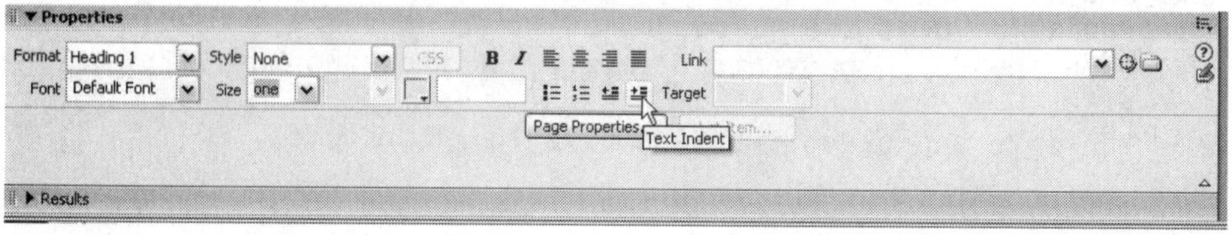

This icon inserts a blockquote element, which is why it's used to mark up quote text. We saw this button's effects in a previous example. In most browsers, this will indent the text slightly to more clearly differentiate the quote from surrounding text.

If you simply want to create an indentation effect on a section of text, the correct way to do so is to use CSS to create padding to the left and right of the element: don't use a structural tag such as <blockquote>.

# Semantic Markup and Text-Only Devices

In Chapter 1, I marked up a part of this book to demonstrate semantic markup. First, I marked it up in a non-semantic manner, my only concern being how it looked. Then, I took the same document and marked it up semantically so that the content structure made sense without the CSS. To get firsthand experience at how difficult it is to understand a document that's written in a non-semantic manner, have a look at such a document in a text-only browser. One easily obtainable, text-only browser is Lynx. You can download versions for Mac, Unix/Linux, and Windows at no cost.

# Windows Install

To install Lynx on Windows, you need to download a copy of the Lynx installer for Windows[3]. Install Lynx onto your system using the product's installer, then run it from the Start menu, or from the Lynx icon on the desktop (if you allowed the installer to create one). On launch, a window that looks something like Figure 3.13 displays.

**Figure 3.13. Launching Lynx for Windows.**

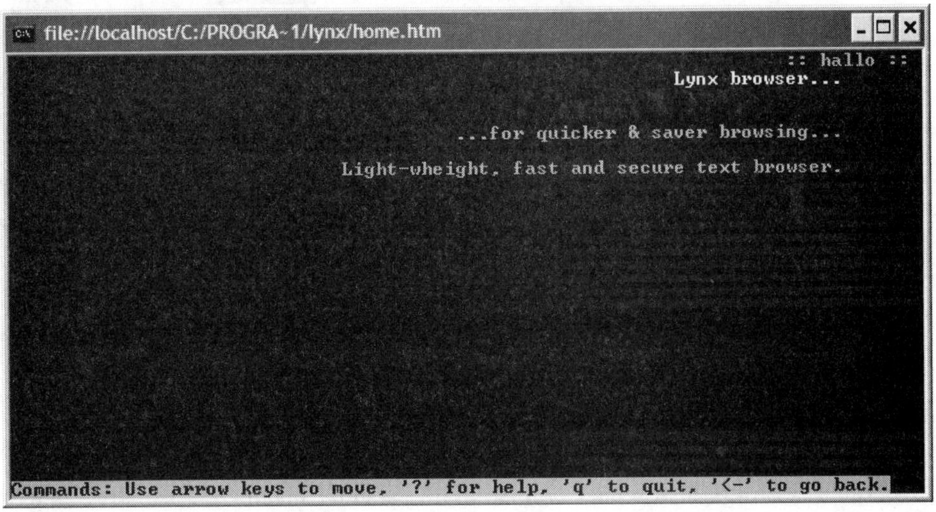

---

[3] http://www.csant.info/lynx.htm

# Mac Install

## Figure 3.14. Running Lynx on Mac OS X.

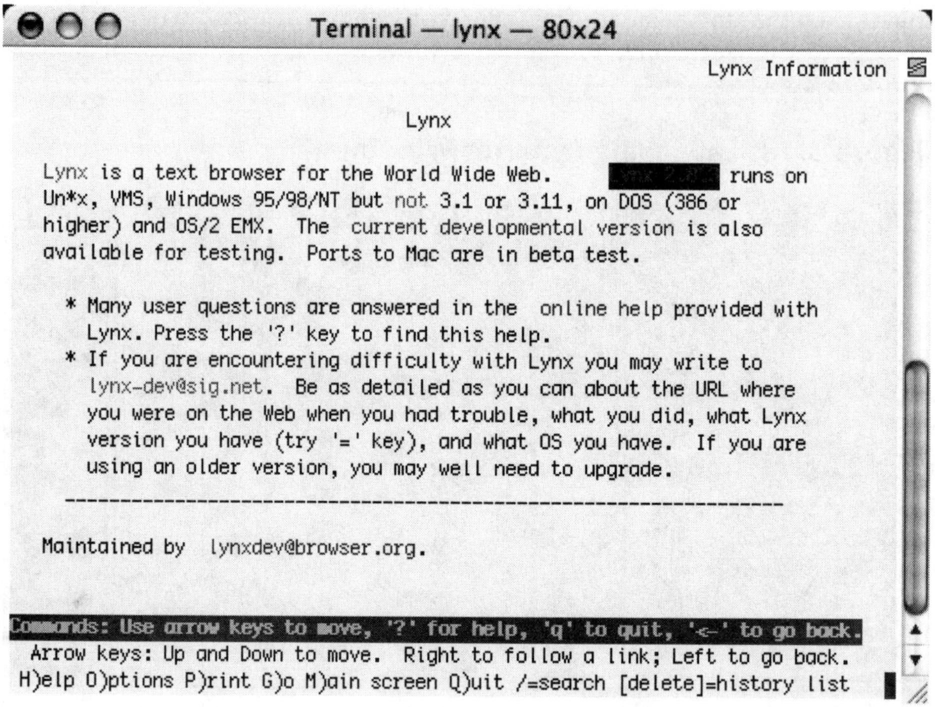

Mac OS X users can also download Lynx:[4] just double-click the downloaded file and follow the instructions. To run Lynx, you may need to open the Terminal application to get access to the command line. Terminal is in the `Utilities` folder located in your `Applications` folder. Figure 3.14 shows the browser in action on the Mac platform.

# Linux

Most Linux or other UNIX users will probably find that Lynx is already installed on their system. If not, a quick Web search should uncover packages developed for your system.

---

[4] http://osxgnu.org/

# Using Lynx

Lynx works identically on Windows, Mac, and Linux machines. To use Lynx, you need to learn some simple commands. First of all, to visit a Website, type **g**.

Lynx will then present a field into which you can type the URL of the site you want to visit, like that shown in Figure 3.15.

### Figure 3.15. Opening a Web page using Lynx.

```
URL to open: http://edgeofmyseat.com/
   Arrow keys: Up and Down to move.  Right to follow a link; Left to go back.
 H)elp O)ptions P)rint G)o M)ain screen Q)uit /=search [delete]=history list
```

Hit **Enter** to have Lynx access this URL. If the site you're trying to visit uses cookies, Lynx will ask if you wish to allow the cookie; type **Y** for yes, or **N** for no, **A** to always accept cookies from the site, or **V** to never accept cookies from this site. If you press **H** while in Lynx, the Lynx help system appears. You can navigate this in the same way you'd navigate a Website.

Once you've loaded a page in Lynx, you can use the arrow keys to navigate it. The up and down arrow keys will let you jump from link to link, from the left to the right—and from top to bottom—of the page. Hit the right arrow key to follow the link you're currently on; the left arrow key will take you back to the previous page.

The up and down arrow keys will select any form fields in the page, too. Select a text field by typing into it. Toggle check boxes and radio buttons by hitting **Enter** when the desired option is selected. To view the options in a drop-down list, select it, hit **Enter**, then use the up and down arrows to scroll through the listed items. Hit **Enter** again to use the selected option. Buttons are "clicked" when you hit the **Enter** key.

You can use Lynx to view local files, which is useful in development. If you're running a local Web server, such as Apache or IIS, you can point Lynx to internal localhost URLs; however, Lynx will also read an HTML file if you pass it the location, for example, `c:\web\myfile.html`.

### Lynx Spacing Snafu

Lynx has trouble with pathnames that contain spaces. Replace any spaces in a file path with **%20** to load the file.

If I view my non-semantic document in Lynx, the display for which is shown in Figure 3.16, I see that every element looks just like a paragraph: it's readable, but no emphasis is placed on any of the sections, so it's not obvious that the heading, "What are Web standards?" is in fact a heading. Imagine reading this entire chapter without any structural clues as to which section is which—this is the effect that text browser users have to endure when reading documents that have not been marked up correctly.

## Figure 3.16. Displaying non-semantic markup in Lynx.

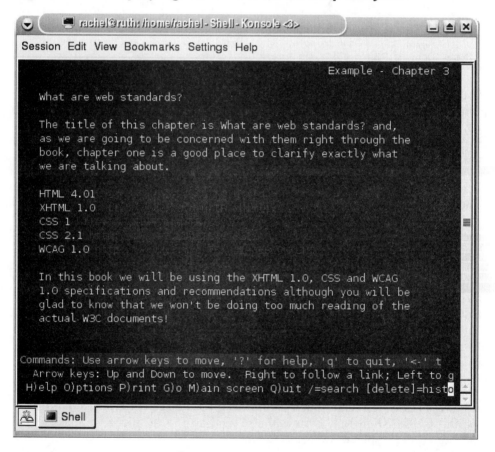

This problem is accentuated for screen reader users. The markup of page headings, lists, and other elements lets the screen reader know to read each section of content in a voice that's appropriate to those particular elements, just as you would if you were to read a page aloud. You'd normally emphasize a heading, leave appropriate pauses between list items, and so on. A screen reader can do this too, provided it knows what the elements are; the only way it can know is if the page elements have been marked up correctly.

Figure 3.17 depicts this same document marked up using a level one heading (<h1>) for the document's heading, and a list to display the Web links. As you can see, Lynx now understands that the heading is a heading, and deals with it as such; Lynx demonstrates that the list is a list by applying an asterisk to each bullet point.

## Figure 3.17. Displaying semantic markup in Lynx.

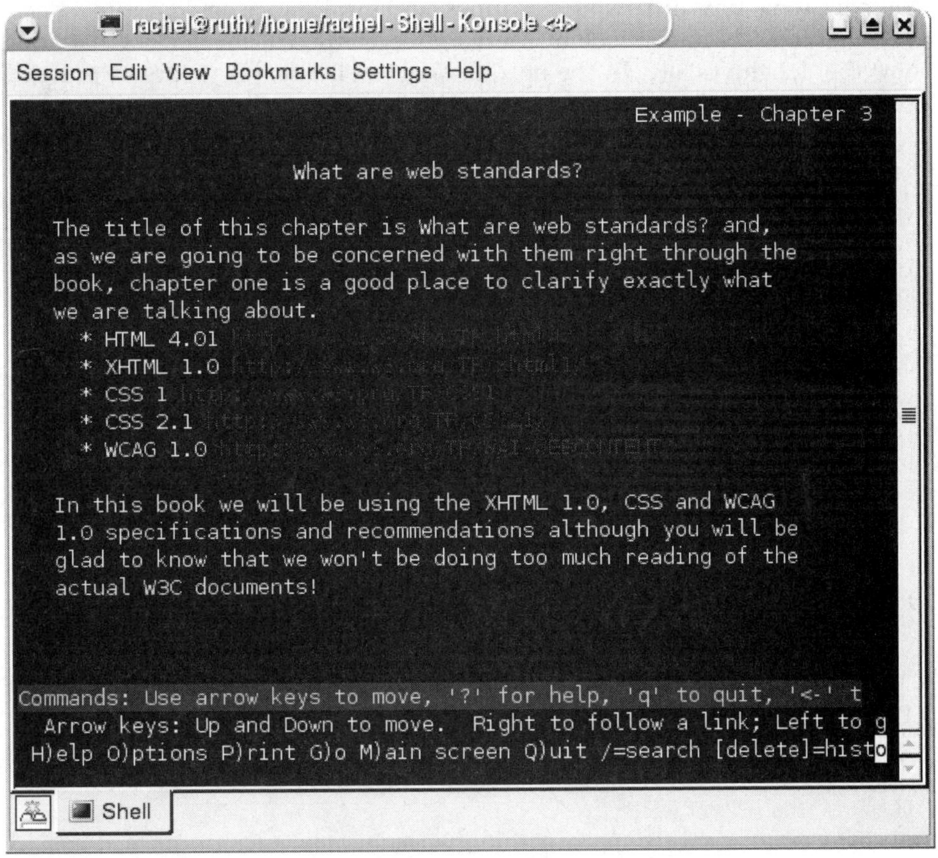

*Tip*

**Lynx Preview**

If you don't have Lynx installed, and you just want a quick preview of a site in a text-only device, use the online Lynx Viewer.[5]

# Summary

In this chapter, we discussed XHTML, including what it is, and why we might want to use it. We also explored the basics of working in XHTML using Dreamweaver.

We spent some time discussing semantics, and saw how we could create a document that could be understood by everyone—even those using devices that don't show the design visually. In the next chapter, we'll put this theory to practical use as we build a layout for our project Website.

---

[5] http://www.delorie.com/web/lynxview.html

# 4

## Constructing the Document

If you're like most people, you probably design a Website by considering how it should look, then moving graphic elements around—either by hand-coding the HTML and CSS, or using Dreamweaver—until the page "looks" the way you want it to.

In this chapter, we're going to take a completely different approach to page design. First, we'll consider how the document should be structured in order to make it valid, accessible, and semantic. Then, in Chapter 6, we'll make the document display as we want it to using CSS.

In this chapter, we'll structure the content of our homepage using XHTML; this will give us a framework for our site.

# The New XHTML Document

In this chapter we are going to develop our document using the XHTML Strict DOCTYPE. XHTML Transitional allows you to use deprecated elements and attributes; most of these are presentational in nature. Using XHTML Strict helps us to remember that presentation belongs in CSS, not in the document: it's a good way to ensure that our site is compliant with Web standards.

There are, however, a few reasons why you might want to use XHTML Transitional:

❑ The site is going to be maintained by someone who's using Dreamweaver, but won't know to remove the presentational attributes inserted by Dreamweaver, which are not valid in XHTML Strict.

❑ You're using a Content Management System—or other third-party code—that will validate to the Transitional DOCTYPE, but contains attributes that aren't permitted in Strict.

❑ You have a specific need to get the layout working in very old browsers, such as Netscape 4. To do so, you're going to use certain presentational attributes (such as border="0" on images), as those browsers provide limited CSS support.

That said, the choice to work to XHTML Strict doesn't have to be your final decision. If you aim for Strict, then realize that some third-party feature is going to require the Transitional DOCTYPE be used, you can always change the DOCTYPE declaration to suit. Developing to the Strict DOCTYPE wherever possible will ensure that you remember to keep presentation in the CSS, where it belongs!

Create a new XHTML document in Dreamweaver by selecting File > New.... In the New Document dialog, select Basic Page and HTML, then choose XHTML 1.0 Strict from the Document Type drop-down, as shown in Figure 4.1. Click Create to create the new XHTML page, and then save this page to the Code Spark site, as homepage-layout.html.

This should give you a blank page in Design View. If you switch into Code View using the buttons above the document window, you'll see your basic XHTML document, as illustrated in Figure 4.2.

This page will become our homepage document. But for now, we're going to concentrate on creating a semantic and standards compliant document that will form a sound basis for the design and structure of the site.

## Figure 4.1. Creating a new XHTML page in Dreamweaver.

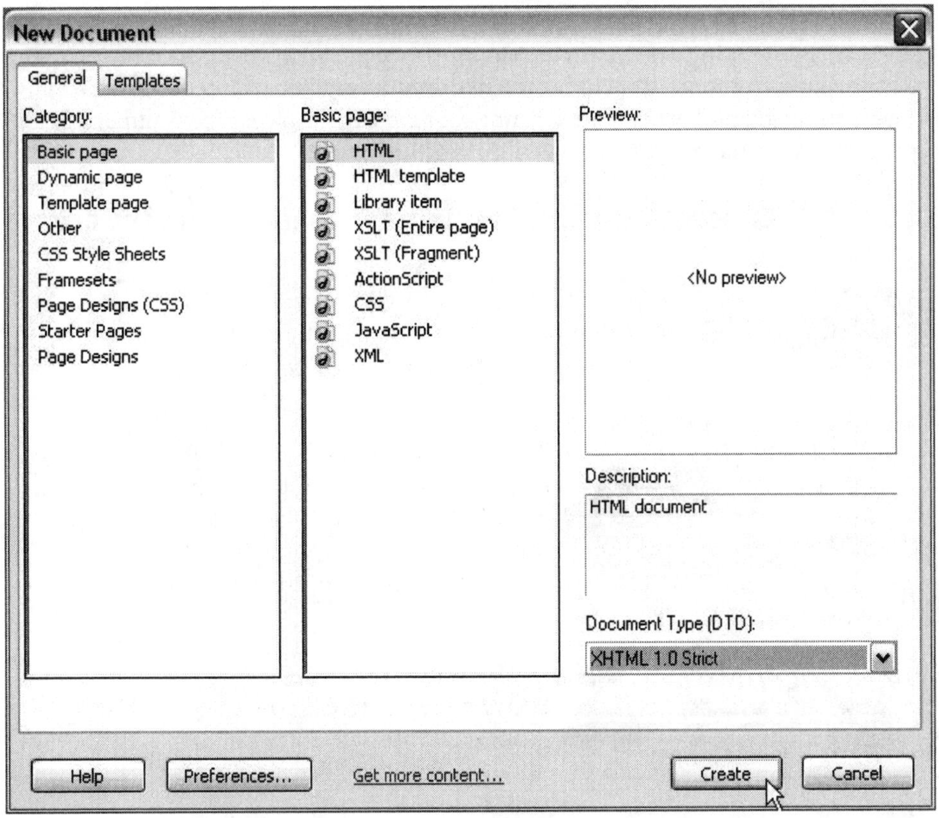

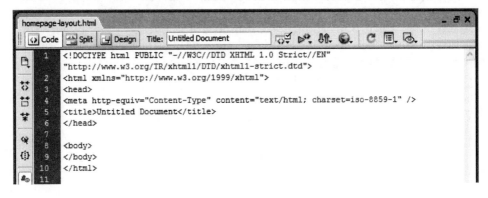

## Figure 4.2. Viewing the code of our basic XHTML document.

# The Main Content Area

Let's start by working on the main part of this document: the page content. On the homepage, the content includes the featured tutorial abstracts, recent tutorials, browser statistics, and other content shown in Figure 4.3. We'll focus our attention on the area that has not been grayed out in this image.

**Figure 4.3. Concentrating on the homepage main content area.**

Using Design View in Dreamweaver, type **Latest ideas** into homepage-layout.html. This will be the main heading on the homepage itself, so it should be marked up as a level one heading. We can do this in Dreamweaver by selecting the heading text, then choosing Heading 1 from the Property Inspector, as illustrated in Figure 4.4.

## Figure 4.4. Creating a level one heading using the Property Inspector.

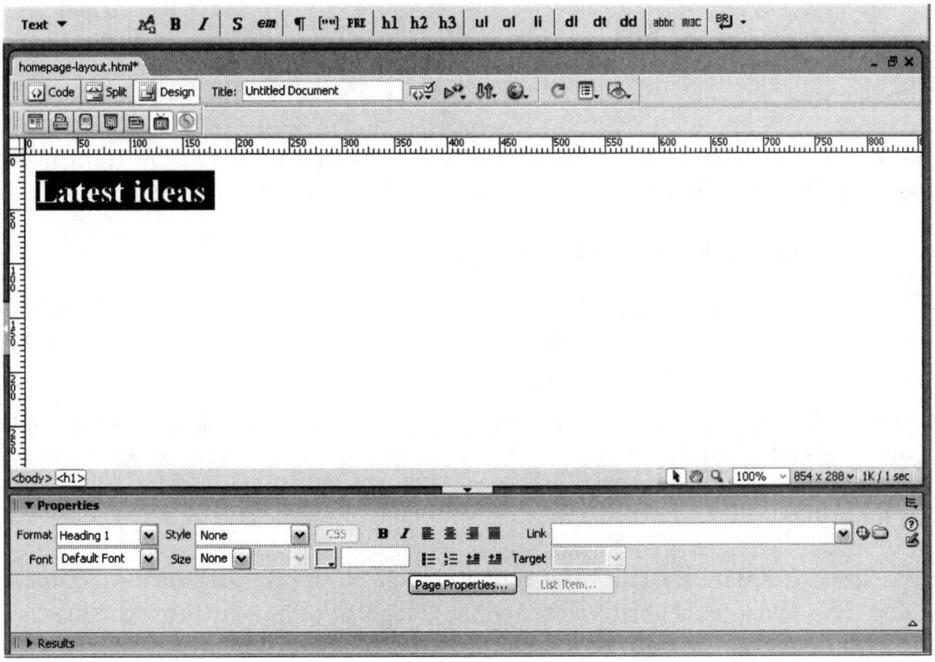

We have six blocks of content on the homepage. The top four contain details of the latest tutorials on the site, and all have the same structure: a heading (which is linked to the tutorial), the author's name and the tutorial's date of publication, a picture of the author, and some text about the tutorial itself. We can create these elements now.

In Design View, hit **Enter** and add the following text:

```
ASP is from Mars – PHP is from Venus
```

Select this text, and make it a level two heading by selecting Heading 2 in the Property Inspector. While the text is still selected, type **#** into the Property Inspector's Link field. This will turn the text into a link, which you can amend to point to the actual tutorial later. Hit **Enter** to create a new paragraph and type: **Julian Carroll Jan 15, 2005**

The image of the author can now be added. To insert an image using Dreamweaver, click the Images button from the toolbar, as shown in Figure 4.5.

## Figure 4.5. Selecting the Images button on the Common panel of the Insert toolbar.

When you click the Images button, a dialog will open to allow you to browse your computer for the author image. Once you've found it, click OK.

 ### All Images are Provided!

All the images we used to build this site are available as part of this book's code archive. If you haven't done so already, go and grab it from site-point.com.

At this point, the Accessibility Attributes dialog, shown in Figure 4.6, should open. This dialog appears if you told Dreamweaver to display accessibility attributes for images within your Preferences. We did this when we set up Dreamweaver in Chapter 2.

Type some alternate text into the box provided by the Accessibility Attributes dialog. This text should clearly describe the image for users who are browsing the site with images turned off, or with a device that cannot display images. As our image includes some text ("Julian—PHP & MySQL") we should to add this information to the alternate text attribute, as you can see in Figure 4.6. I've added the following text:

```
Photo of Julian — PHP and MySQL
```

## Figure 4.6. Adding the image tag's accessibility attributes.

**Image Tag Accessibility Attributes**

Alternate text: Julian - PHP &a

Long description: http://

OK

Cancel

Help

If you don't want to enter this information when inserting objects, change the Accessibility preferences.

Finally, let's add a couple of short paragraphs of text to explain the tutorial. At this point, I've added some dummy placeholder text to fill the space. Our page now displays in Dreamweaver as shown in Figure 4.7.

## Figure 4.7. Displaying the document in Dreamweaver.

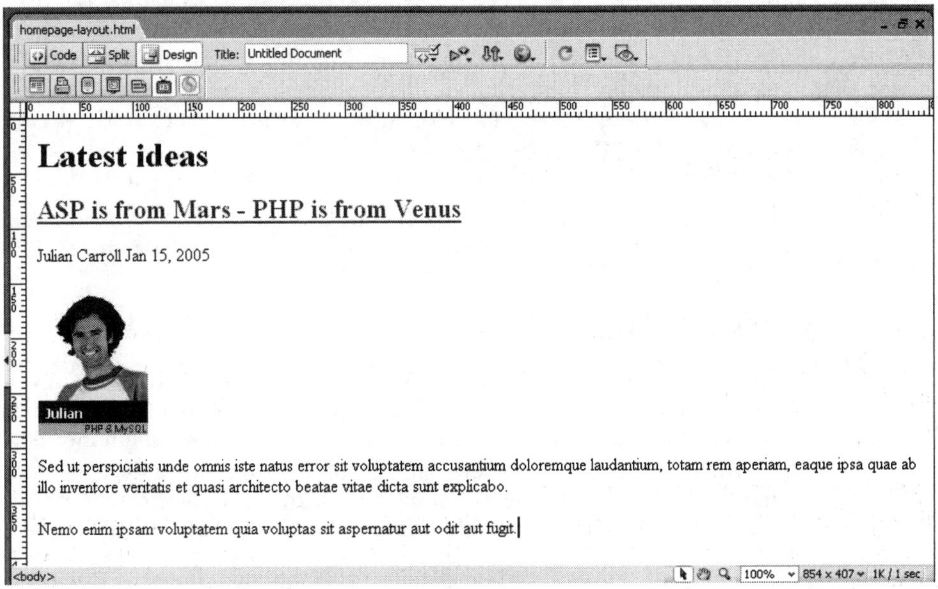

### Download Mock Latin Now!

*Tip*

The dummy text we are using is the standard 'mock Latin' used by designers to fill out mockups. You can download some mock Latin of your very own.[1]

Switch into Code View to see how our XHTML is shaping up. At this point, the document should contain the following markup and content:

File: **homepage-layout.html**

```
<!DOCTYPE html PUBLIC "-//W3C//DTD XHTML 1.0 Transitional//EN"
    "http://www.w3.org/TR/xhtml1/DTD/xhtml1-transitional.dtd">
<html xmlns="http://www.w3.org/1999/xhtml">
<head>
<title>Code Spark layout</title>
<meta http-equiv="Content-Type" content="text/html;
    charset=iso-8859-1" />
```

---

[1] http://www.lipsum.com/

```
</head>

<body>
<h1>Latest ideas </h1>
<h2><a href="#">ASP is from Mars - PHP is from Venus</a></h2>
<p>Julian Carroll Jan 15, 2005</p>
<p><img src="img/julian.jpg" alt="Photo of Julian - PHP and MySQL"
    width="104" height="135" /> </p>
<p>Sed ut perspiciatis unde omnis iste natus error sit voluptatem
  accusantium doloremque laudantium, totam rem aperiam, eaque
  ipsa quae ab illo inventore veritatis et quasi architecto beatae
  vitae dicta sunt explicabo.</p>
<p>Nemo enim ipsam voluptatem quia voluptas sit aspernatur aut
  odit aut fugit.</p>
</body>
</html>
```

*Tip*

## Split that Screen!

If you have enough screen real estate, it can be helpful to work in Dreamweaver's Split Screen View as you create the XHTML document. The Split Screen feature allows you to see the Design and Code Views simultaneously. To switch into Split Screen View, click the Split button above the document window. As shown in Figure 4.8, you'll be able to watch the creation of your markup in Code View as you add elements to the page in Design View.

## Figure 4.8. Working in Split Screen View.

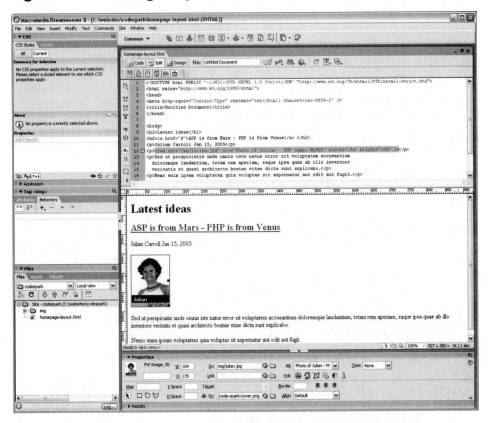

We need to add three sections just like this one for the other featured tutorials. Follow the steps above to add these sections, working from left to right, and top to bottom. Once you've done so, your document should contain the following markup:

File: **homepage-layout.html (excerpt)**

```
<!DOCTYPE html PUBLIC "-//W3C//DTD XHTML 1.0 Transitional//EN"
    "http://www.w3.org/TR/xhtml1/DTD/xhtml1-transitional.dtd">
<html xmlns="http://www.w3.org/1999/xhtml">
<head>
<title>Code Spark layout</title>
<meta http-equiv="Content-Type" content="text/html;
    charset=iso-8859-1" />
</head>
```

```
<body>
<h1>Latest ideas </h1>
<h2><a href="#">ASP is from Mars - PHP is from Venus</a></h2>
<p>Julian Carroll Jan 15, 2005</p>
<p><img src="img/julian.jpg" alt="Photo of Julian - PHP and MySQL"
    width="104" height="135" /> </p>
<p>Sed ut perspiciatis unde omnis iste natus error sit voluptatem
  accusantium doloremque laudantium, totam rem aperiam, eaque
  ipsa quae ab illo inventore veritatis et quasi architecto beatae
  vitae dicta sunt explicabo.</p>
<p>Nemo enim ipsam voluptatem quia voluptas sit aspernatur aut
  odit aut fugit.</p>
<h2><a href="#">IIS Security - Tightening the .NET</a></h2>
<p>Brigitte Walker Jan 11,2005</p>
<p><img src="img/brigitte.jpg" alt="Photo of Brigitte - ASP and
    .NET" width="104" height="135" />   </p>
<p>Sed ut perspiciatis unde omnis iste natus error sit voluptatem
  accusantium doloremque laudantium, totam rem aperiam, eaque ipsa
  quae ab illo inventore veritatis et quasi architecto beatae
  vitae dicta sunt explicabo.</p>
<p>Nemo enim ipsam voluptatem quia voluptas sit aspernatur aut
  odit aut fugit.</p>
<h2><a href="#">CSS: Designing with Style, not class</a></h2>
<p>Georgina Laidlaw Jan 7, 2005</p>
<p><img src="img/georgina.jpg" alt="Photo of Georgina -
    CSS Design" width="104" height="135" /> </p>
<p>Sed ut perspiciatis unde omnis iste natus error sit voluptatem
  accusantium doloremque laudantium, totam rem aperiam, eaque ipsa
  quae ab illo inventore veritatis et quasi architecto beatae
  vitae dicta sunt explicabo.</p>
<p>Nemo enim ipsam voluptatem quia voluptas sit aspernatur aut
  odit aut fugit.</p>
<h2><a href="#">Java - Servlets yourself right</a></h2>
<p>Thomas Rutter Jan 3, 2005</p>
<p><img src="img/tom.jpg" alt="Photo of Tom - JSP and Servlets"
    width="104" height="135" /> </p>
<p>Sed ut perspiciatis unde omnis iste natus error sit voluptatem
  accusantium doloremque laudantium, totam rem aperiam, eaque ipsa
  quae ab illo inventore veritatis et quasi architecto beatae
  vitae dicta sunt explicabo.</p>
<p>Nemo enim ipsam voluptatem quia voluptas sit aspernatur aut
  odit aut fugit.</p>
</body>
</html>
```

# Linking to Other Tutorials

The bottom two sections of the homepage contain slightly different content. They too have headings, but one contains links to other tutorials on the site, while the other displays the latest information about the Web browsers that visitors are using to view the site. First, let's consider the section that contains links to tutorials. The layout for this section is shown in Figure 4.9.

### Figure 4.9. Viewing the layout for the links section.

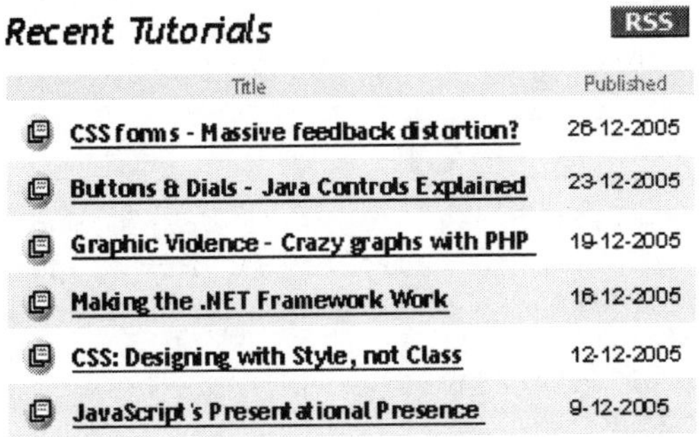
Recent Tutorials
RSS
Title
Published
CSS forms - Massive feedback distortion?
26-12-2005
Buttons & Dials - Java Controls Explained
23-12-2005
Graphic Violence - Crazy graphs with PHP
19-12-2005
Making the .NET Framework Work
16-12-2005
CSS: Designing with Style, not Class
12-12-2005
JavaScript's Presentational Presence
9-12-2005

The "Recent Tutorials" section is laid out in a tabular format, with headings at the top of each column, and the data arranged in the cells that follow. As this is tabular data, it's appropriate to use a table to structure this information in a semantic manner.

First, in Design View, add the RSS button image with the alternative text, **RSS**. Hit **Enter**, and type `Recent Tutorials`; make this into a level two heading using the Property Inspector, and hit **Enter** once again.

Now, let's insert a table. To do this in Dreamweaver, open the Layout Panel of the Insert toolbar, and click the Table button, as shown in Figure 4.10.

### Figure 4.10. Clicking the Table button on the Insert toolbar.

Layout
Standard
Expanded
Layout
Table

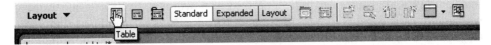

### Dreamweaver's Insert Toolbar

You probably already noticed the drop-down list on the Insert toolbar: this lets you switch between different sets of tools. Dreamweaver calls these sets of tools "panels." You can instead display the different panels as tabs by selecting Show as tabs from this drop-down list.

The Table dialog, shown in Figure 4.11, will open. This enables you to set the features of the table that you are about to insert. Give your table seven rows and two columns. Under the Header section, select Top to convert the cells in the top row of the table into th elements: table headings.

## Figure 4.11. The Table dialog.

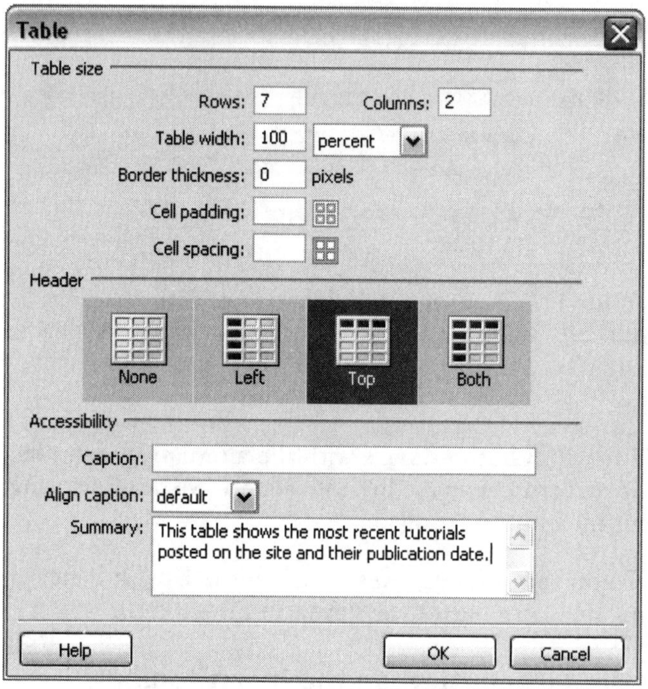

We can also add a summary here. The summary will not display on-screen in a regular graphical browser, but provides screen reader users with additional information about the table, to help them put it into context. This and the caption fields are particularly important if the context of the table is vague because of the way the page has been laid out. In our document, however, it should be easy to understand the content of the table.

Click the OK button in this dialog to insert a table into your document. Now, enter the tabular data into the cells: start with the headings "Title" and "Published" in the top row, then fill in the rest of the tutorials and their publication dates, as shown in Figure 4.12.

## Figure 4.12. Viewing the table in Design View.

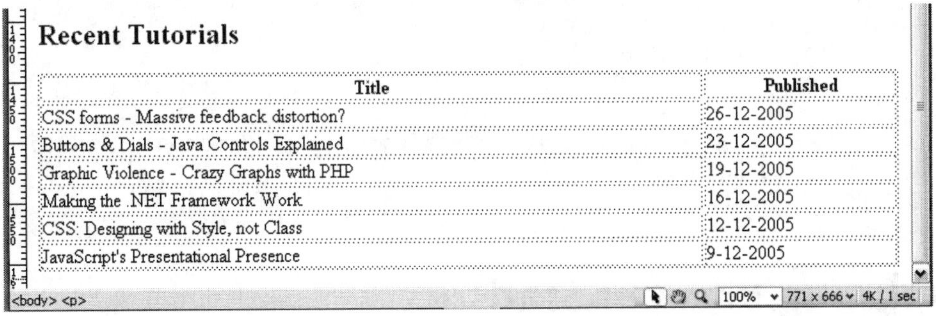

Make each of the tutorial titles into a link by selecting the title and entering a **#** into the Link field of the Property Inspector, just as you did for the tutorial headings. Once you've done this, switch into Code View to review the markup for this section. It should look like this:

```
<h2>Recent Tutorials</h2>
<table width="100%" border="0" summary="This table shows the most
    recent tutorials posted on the site and their publication
    date.">
  <tr>
    <th scope="col">Title</th>
    <th scope="col">Published</th>
  </tr>
  <tr>
    <td><a href="#">CSS forms - Massive feedback distortion?
      </a></td>
    <td>26-12-2005</td>
  </tr>
  <tr>
    <td><a href="#">Buttons &amp; Dials - Java Controls Explained
      </a></td>
    <td>23-12-2005</td>
  </tr>
  <tr>
    <td><a href="#">Graphic Violence - Crazy Graphs with PHP
      </a></td>
```

```
      <td>19-12-2005</td>
    </tr>
    <tr>
      <td><a href="#">Making the .NET Framework Work</a></td>
      <td>16-12-2005</td>
    </tr>
    <tr>
      <td><a href="#">CSS: Designing with Style, not Class
        </a></td>
      <td>12-12-2005</td>
    </tr>
    <tr>
      <td><a href="#">JavaScript's Presentational Presence</a></td>
      <td>9-12-2005</td>
    </tr>
</table>
```

# Displaying Browser Statistics

The final section of this main content area displays browser statistics. This content is shown in the Fireworks design in Figure 4.13.

Figure 4.13 comprises a heading and a pie chart, and illustrates market share for different types of browsers. A text description is provided, along with a legend for the diagram.

To start, add the heading. Then, insert the image; don't forget to add an `alt` attribute that clearly explains what the image is. There's no need to describe the data in the chart: the text below the chart helps with that.

*Tip*

### Making Table Data Accessible

A chart is a great way to display a lot of data succinctly, but it isn't very accessible. To rectify this, you can present the chart's data on a separate page, and use the `img` element's `longdesc` attribute to link to it. We'll take a look at `longdesc` in more detail in Chapter 7.

## Figure 4.13. Designing the browser statistics display for the homepage.

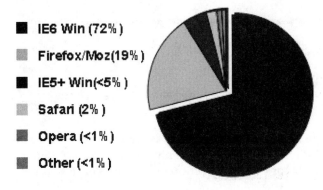

*Browser Stats - December - 04*

- ■ IE6 Win (72%)
- ▨ Firefox/Moz(19%)
- ■ IE5+ Win(<5%)
- ▨ Safari (2%)
- ■ Opera (<1%)
- ■ Other (<1%)

December saw Firefox's market share jump 1% across all
major site categories, presumably on the back of it's 1.0
launch push. Increases of as much as 3% were observed in
some technically-oriented categories.

Overall, though IE6 continued the gradual decrease in
market share it has endured since it held 92% in
November 2003, it since enjoys 4 times greater usage than
any other browser.

We can now add the list. We create lists using the Unordered List button in
Dreamweaver's Property Inspector, shown in Figure 4.14. Type the first list item
into the document as if you were entering a new paragraph, then click the Unordered List button on the Property Inspector. When you hit **Enter**, a new list
item will be created.

## Figure 4.14. Creating an unordered list.

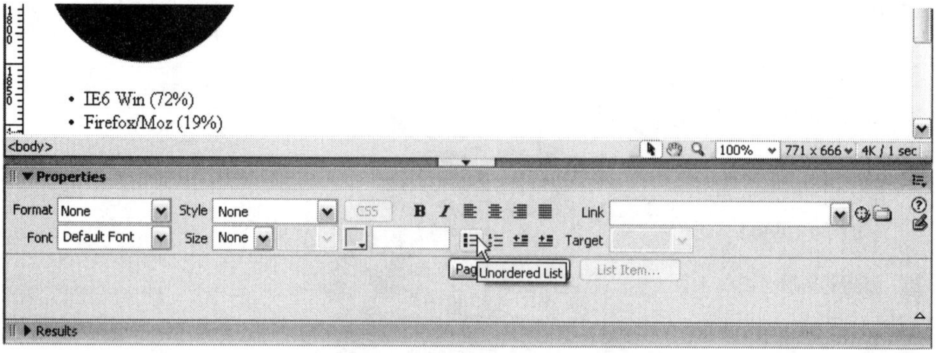

Once you've created all the items in the list, hit **Enter** twice to close the list and create a new paragraph. Now, enter the two paragraphs of text that accompany this section. That's it! The code for this final section of the homepage's content area is now complete:

```
<h2>Browser Stats - December - 04</h2>
<p><img src="img/browser_chart.gif" alt="Pie chart showing
    browser statistics for Dec 2004" width="180" height="180" />
</p>
<ul>
  <li>IE6 Win (72%)</li>
  <li>Firefox/Moz (19%)</li>
  <li>IE5+ Win (&lt;5%)</li>
  <li>Safari (2%)</li>
  <li>Opera (&lt;1%)</li>
  <li>Other (&lt;1%)</li>
</ul>
<p>December saw Firefox's market share jump 1% across all major
    site categories presumably on the back of it's 1.0 launch push.
    Increases of as much as 3% were observed in some
    technically-oriented categories.</p>
<p>Overall, though IE6 continued the gradual decrease in market
    share it has endured since it held 92% in November 2003, it
    still enjoys 4 times greater usage than any other browser.</p>
```

If you view the page in a browser, you'll see all of the content displayed as in Figure 4.15 below: our logical headings, paragraphs, tables, and lists are presented in the browser's default display style.

## Figure 4.15. Displaying the document in Firefox 1.0.

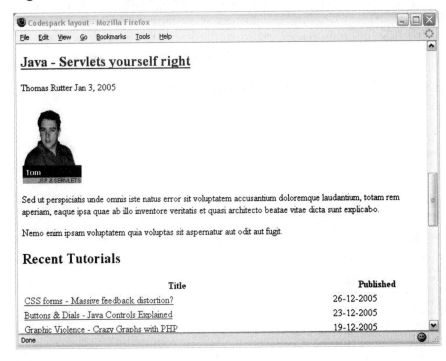

# Other Page Elements

Now that we've completed the structure of the main content area of the homepage, it's time to move on to consider the rest of the page. We have the heading area, which contains the logo and tagline, site controls that help users to change the text size, and the main navigation. We must also consider the content that displays in our layout's sidebar: a search form, as well as quick links to the various topics and other items of interest on the site.

Before we decide where to place these elements within our document, let's take a moment to think about how site visitors are going to use these pages. Users who have a regular Web browser will see the full layout and, using CSS, we will be able to position all the page elements to make the site as usable as possible. It doesn't really matter to these users just where in the document the page elements are located, as they will see the full page design. However, for users of text-only devices, the locations of the various content elements within the actual XHTML document is very important.

Our homepage will be displayed or read aloud by a text-only browser or screen reader in the order in which the content appears in the actual XHTML document, starting with the title. Currently, our document contains only the page content, so, after the title, a screen reader would start to read the first element on the page: our "Latest ideas" heading, as depicted in Figure 4.16.

## Figure 4.16. Displaying the document in the text-only Lynx browser.

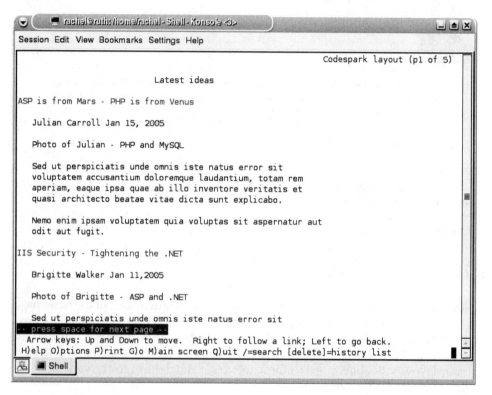

The page's heading section helps orient users by providing information about the site itself—the logo and tagline—as well as quick access to the site's main navigation, including the sitemap, as shown in Figure 4.17.

## Figure 4.17. The heading area, including main navigation.

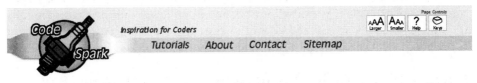

### Easing Text-only Navigation

**Tip**

A sitemap is very useful to visitors who use text-only browsers: it gives them a quick way to jump from page to page without having to follow the complicated navigational structures that, while easy to use in a graphical browser, can be much slower to use via other methods. Remember: to users of screen readers, or those who must tab through Web documents using their keyboard, Web pages are linear documents. A visitor using a screen reader, for example, has to wait for the Web page to be read aloud in order to get to the link they want. A sitemap can save time and frustration for these visitors—as well as those using regular browsers.

As the heading area contains information that will help users to understand the site—and to get around it—it seems logical that we should place this element at the top of the document, before the homepage's main content.

The information that appears in the sidebar, depicted in Figure 4.18, is less important in terms of its ability to help users immediately understand and access the site. As a list of tutorials and information, it could also become quite lengthy.

If we placed this element before the homepage's main content, users of screen readers would need to listen to all this information before they reached the main content; this would start to get rather dull after the first page! For this reason, let's add this section after the page's main content, at the bottom of the current document. We can then position it alongside our main content using CSS.

**Figure 4.18. The sidebar.**

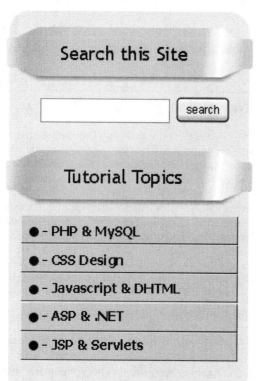

# The Heading and Main Navigation

Now that we've decided where in the document we're going to place the rest of the page elements, we can start to add our heading area.

Return to your document and, in Dreamweaver's Design View, place your cursor just before the "Latest ideas" heading. Switch to Code View to make sure the cursor is outside the h1 element. Switch back to Design View and insert the Code Spark logo (logo.gif), remembering to add appropriate alternate text. Beside the image, type the tagline **Inspiration for Coders**; this should sit beside the bottom of the Code Spark logo.

Next, we'll add our accessibility controls. Hit **Enter** and type **Page Controls**. Our page controls are no more than a list of links, so we'll add them to the page as an unordered list. Click the Unordered list button to insert the first list item, then insert the first accessibility control image, control_larger.gif. Next, make the image into a link: select the image and type **#** into the Link field in the Property Inspector. Hit **Enter** to insert the next item, and repeat the process for the other controls (control_smaller.gif, control_low_graphics.gif and control_default_style.gif).

## Figure 4.19. Creating the heading area of the page.

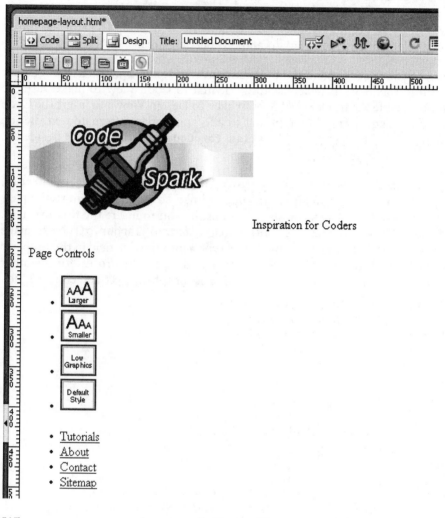

When you peruse your document in Design View, it should look like the display shown in Figure 4.19. Don't worry that it looks a bit untidy right now; we'll use CSS to transform this content later on.

Our final task is to add to this heading area the main navigation, which will link to the Tutorials, About, Contact and Sitemap pages. Once again, the navigation comprises an unordered list of links, so go ahead and add them to the document.

Switching into Code View, we can see the markup that constitutes the heading section:

File: **homepage-layout.html (excerpt)**

```html
<p><img src="img/logo.gif" alt="Code Spark" width="290"
    height="160" />Inspiration for Coders </p>
<p>Page Controls</p>
<ul>
  <li> <a href="#"><img src="img/control_larger.gif"
      alt="Increase Text Size" width="43" height="35"
      border="0" /></a></li>
  <li><a href="#"><img src="img/control_smaller.gif"
      alt="Decrease Text Size" width="43" height="35"
      border="0" /></a></li>
  <li><a href="#"><img src="img/control_low_graphics.gif"
      alt="Low Graphics" width="43" height="35"
      border="0" /></a></li>
  <li><a href="#"><img src="img/control_default_style.gif"
      alt="Default Style" width="43" height="35"
      border="0" /></a></li>
</ul>
<ul>
  <li><a href="">Tutorials</a></li>
  <li><a href="">About</a></li>
  <li><a href="">Contact</a></li>
  <li><a href="">Sitemap</a></li>
</ul>
```

# The Sidebar

The final section that we'll add to the document is the sidebar, which, as we've already decided, will be placed beneath the main content in the structure of our document.

In Design View, place your cursor at the bottom of your main content text, beneath the section about browser statistics. The first part of the sidebar is a search box, so add a level three heading that reads "Search this Site."

To create the search box, add a form element using the Forms Panel of the Insert toolbar, as shown in Figure 4.20. The form will appear as a dotted red outline.

## Figure 4.20. Adding a form.

Insert a text field into your form. When you do so, the Input Tag Accessibility Attributes dialog shown in Figure 4.21 will open, to help you add the correct attributes to the element.

## Figure 4.21. The Input Tag Accessibility Attributes dialog.

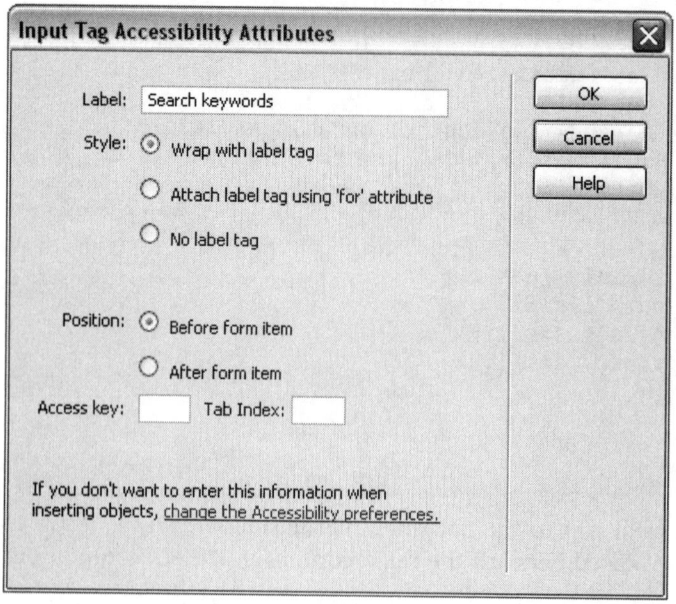

Our original design didn't include a label for the search field, but I'm going to throw one in: it'll help when we come to validate our site for accessibility purposes. In Figure 4.21 above, I added the label **Search keywords** and selected the Wrap with label tag option.

Click OK to insert your text input and label. In the Property Inspector, change the name of the input field to **keywords**. I also added a <br /> after the label Search Keywords, and before the search box. **Shift-Enter** creates a <br /> in Dreamweaver.

Now, insert a button using the Insert toolbar. This button doesn't need a label, so select the No label tag option before you click OK. Select the button, then use the Property Inspector to change the value to **Search**, as shown in Figure 4.22.

### Figure 4.22. Changing the value of the button to "Search."

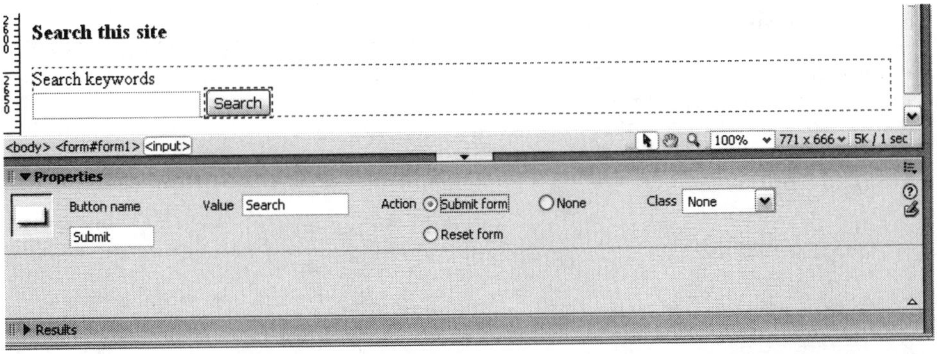

If you check Code View, the markup for the form we just added should look something like this:

File: **homepage-layout.html** (excerpt)

```html
<h3>Search this Site</h3>
<form name="form1" id="form1" method="post" action="">
  <label>Search keywords<br />
  <input name="keywords" type="text" id="keywords" />
  </label>
  <input type="submit" name="Submit" value="Search" />
</form>
```

Add another heading—"Tutorial Topics"—as a level three heading, and mark up the main sections of the site using an unordered list. Make the text in the list items into dummy links, as these will eventually link to the actual sections of the site:

❑ PHP & MySQL

❑ CSS Design

❑ JavaScript & DHTML

❑ ASP & .NET

❑ JSP & Servlets

## Figure 4.23. Viewing the sidebar section after the search feature and three lists are added.

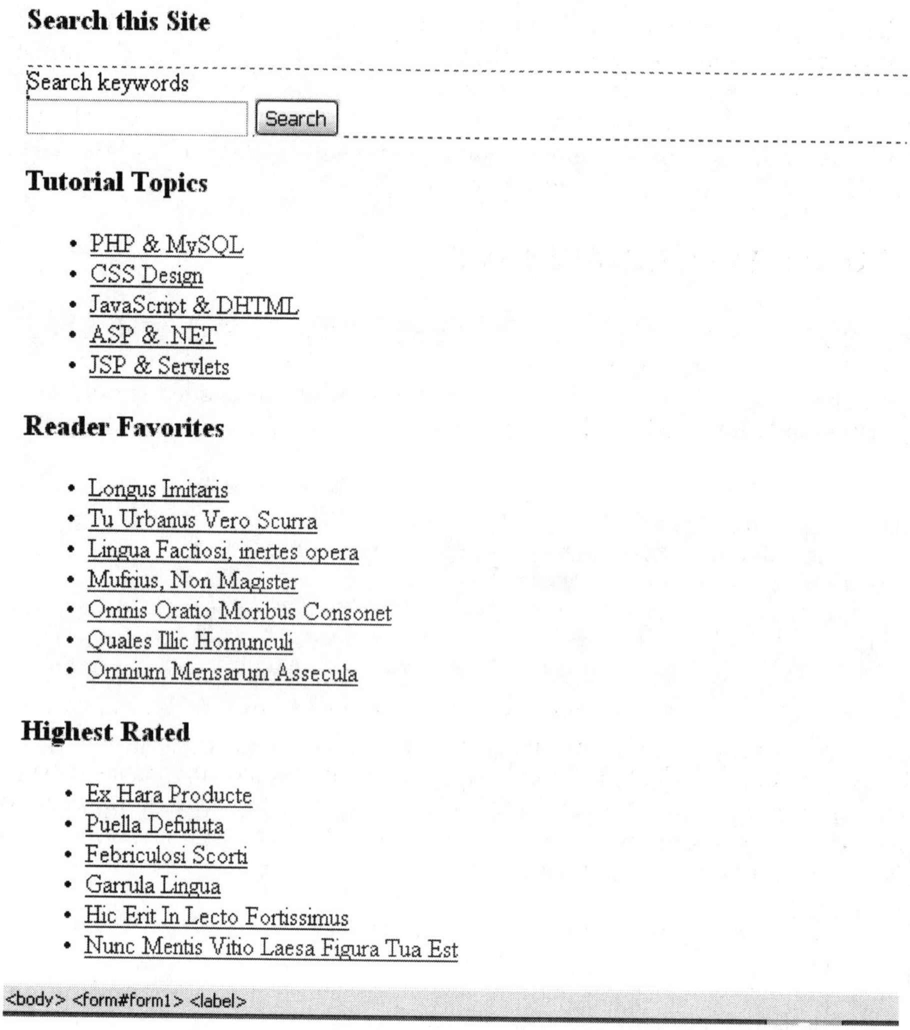

**Search this Site**

Search keywords

[                    ]  [ Search ]

**Tutorial Topics**

- PHP & MySQL
- CSS Design
- JavaScript & DHTML
- ASP & .NET
- JSP & Servlets

**Reader Favorites**

- Longus Imitaris
- Tu Urbanus Vero Scurra
- Lingua Factiosi, inertes opera
- Mufrius, Non Magister
- Omnis Oratio Moribus Consonet
- Quales Illic Homunculi
- Omnium Mensarum Assecula

**Highest Rated**

- Ex Hara Producte
- Puella Defututa
- Febriculosi Scorti
- Garrula Lingua
- Hic Erit In Lecto Fortissimus
- Nunc Mentis Vitio Laesa Figura Tua Est

`<body> <form#form1> <label>`

We can now add another heading. Insert "Reader Favorites" as a level three heading and, again, use a list with dummy links to mark up the favorite tutorials presented on the site. Figure 4.23 shows this section in Design View after the three lists are added.

# Validating your XHTML

We've completed our basic XHTML document. Later, we'll need to add to this document some grouping elements that will enable us to style the document. However, by first considering how the content should be structured, we've done a lot to ensure that our document is semantically structured, and accessible at its most basic level. The final task we should undertake is to validate our document to ensure that it constitutes correct XHTML.

## Validation in Dreamweaver

To validate your document, click the Validate markup button at the top of the document window, and select Validate Current Document, as shown in Figure 4.24.

**Figure 4.24. Validating the current document.**

ernatur aut odit aut fugit.

If you're lucky, the message "No Errors or Warnings Found" will display in the panel. However, while Dreamweaver will let you create a document with an XHTML Strict DOCTYPE, it sometimes misses required elements, or adds attributes that are not allowed by this DOCTYPE. Luckily, these are pretty easy to find and remove: any problems are listed in the Results Panel after Dreamweaver's validator is run, as shown in Figure 4.25.

One of the errors you're likely to see reads as follows:

> The tag:"label" is not allowed within: "form" It is only allowed within: a, abbr, acronym, address, b, …

## Figure 4.25. Reviewing errors presented in the Results panel.

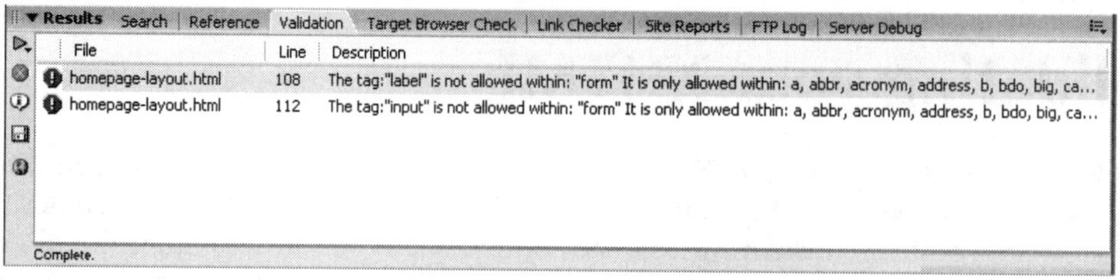

This error indicates that the `label` element needs to be contained within some other element (not just `form`). XHTML Strict—as the name implies—is very strict about which elements can be contained within which other elements. We can address this issue by wrapping the whole section in `<p>` and `</p>` tags, like so:

File: **homepage-layout-strict.html** (excerpt)
```
<p><label>Search keywords<br />
  <input name="keywords" type="text" id="keywords" />
  <input type="submit" name="Submit" value="Search" />
  </label></p>
```

Now, revalidate your document to see if it's error-free. If not, step through the list of errors, and fix them one by one. Pretty soon, your work should be free of errors, and ready to roll! Save the file as `homepage-layout-strict.html`.

The more you work with Dreamweaver, the more you'll start to understand its eccentricities, and the better you'll become at correcting its markup. XHTML can become quite complex at times, and Dreamweaver 8 does a fairly good job of getting the markup right most of the time, so do try and cut it some slack.

# Summary

In this chapter, we've taken what might be seen as a slightly unconventional way of beginning our page layout. We concentrated almost solely on the structure of the document, and how the actual content is to be marked up, bearing in mind our goal of standards compliance.

In the next two chapters, we'll move on to look at CSS. We'll see how we can take this structured, valid document and use CSS to create a visually attractive layout without compromising its accessibility or semantic structure.

# 5

# CSS and Dreamweaver

Now that we've written a well-structured XHTML document, we'll be able to use CSS throughout the remainder of this book to style text, lay out our site, and create effects that wouldn't be possible using HTML alone. Whether you're a CSS beginner or a seasoned developer, you'll find that Dreamweaver's tools can make CSS development easier. As we're about to see, Dreamweaver 8 offers a huge amount of CSS functionality. As you use it, you'll soon work out which tools best suit your way of working.

This chapter starts with an overview of CSS, then goes on to explain how we can use Dreamweaver to make working with CSS easier. If you've already used CSS, but you're new to Dreamweaver's CSS tools, you might want to skip over the first section and get straight into the details of working with CSS in Dreamweaver.

## Why CSS?

If you're a longtime Dreamweaver user, you're probably used to styling text with the Property Inspector. Dreamweaver has always allowed us to select text and apply a font, size, or color to it easily. Prior to the release of Dreamweaver MX 2004, HTML <font> tags were used to achieve these styles, but in the latest versions of the program, the Properties Inspector applies styles using CSS. Though functional, Dreamweaver's application of styles is not necessarily the best way to implement CSS in your site. We'll see why a little later in this chapter.

That Dreamweaver has chosen to use CSS instead of `<font>` tags to style text is indicative of the way in which most Web designers and developers now work. `<font>` is one of a number of elements that, while originally developed to control style and layout, have since been deprecated in the HTML specification in favor of the use of style sheets.

CSS offers many benefits over HTML when it comes to styling your pages:

❑ It supports increased accessibility: styling tags and attributes are no longer needed, which makes the HTML easier for alternative devices to read.

❑ Alternative large print or high-contrast style sheets may be provided for users with specific disabilities; users can even apply their own style sheets to a page.

❑ Smaller file sizes are produced, as one file is able to control the look and feel of many pages.

❑ Development time is reduced, and the maintenance burden is eased; CSS makes site-wide changes as easy as changing one property in one CSS file.

# CSS Basics

In this chapter—and throughout the rest of this book—we'll be using basic CSS terminology. If you're not already familiar with CSS, this section is for you: here, I'll run through the basics of CSS. The beauty of working with Dreamweaver is that you really *can* learn how to use CSS as you go along, so I'll not spend too much time on this discussion. If you already have an understanding of basic CSS, feel free to skip to the section called "Your Basic Toolkit", where we look at the specific CSS functionality available in Dreamweaver 8.

## How to Use CSS

When you use `<font>` tags to style a chunk of text, you end up with something that looks like this:

```
<h1><font color="#336699" size="4">Hello World!</font></h1>
```

In its simplest form, CSS can be applied to text via the `style` attribute, which is set on the HTML element that you wish to style, like so:

```
<h1 style="color: #336699; font-size: 130%">Hello World!</h1>
```

This is called an **inline style**. The CSS within the `style` attribute will apply only to this `h1` element—not to anything else on the page—in much the same way that a font element would apply only to the content found within the element's opening and closing tags.

When we discussed the benefits of CSS earlier, I explained how you can use CSS to set up styles that are applied to every instance of an element on a page, or throughout a site. To do this, we need to move our CSS out of the element's tag, and instead create the definition either in the header of the document—an **embedded** style sheet—or in a separate file that's referenced from all pages of the site as a **linked** or **imported** style sheet.

To create an embedded style sheet we simply add the CSS property definitions and the element's tag name (or selector) to the head of the document; we place this information between `<style>` tags, which lets the browser know that it's dealing with CSS. The styles will then be applied to every instance of the specified element within the document.

As an example, here's the XHTML document `hello.html`, which uses an embedded style sheet:

File: **hello.html**

```
<!DOCTYPE html PUBLIC "-//W3C//DTD XHTML 1.0 Strict//EN"
    "http://www.w3.org/TR/xhtml1/DTD/xhtml1-strict.dtd">
<html xmlns="http://www.w3.org/1999/xhtml">
<head>
<title>Example embedded style sheet</title>
<style type="text/css" media="all">
h1 {
  font-size: 130%;
  color: #336699;
}
</style>
</head>
<body>
<h1>Hello World!</h1>
<p>It's a lovely day.</p>
<h1>Notice the Big, Colored Headings?</h1>
<p>That's because this page contains an embedded style sheet!</p>
</body>
</html>
```

To create a linked style sheet, place the rules into a separate file (without any `<style>` tags surrounding them), then add a link to the head of the document.

Consider this style sheet, `mystyles.css`, which is ready to be linked from another file:

File: **mystyles.css**

```
h1 {
  font-size: 130%;
  color: #336699;
}
```

Here's the head of `hello.html`, which links to the `mystyles.css` style sheet:

File: **hello.html (excerpt)**

```
<head>
<title>Example linked style sheet</title>
<link rel="stylesheet" href="mystyles.css" type="text/css" />
</head>
```

Importing an external style sheet is very similar to this linking approach. However, instead of using a `<link>` tag, we use `<style>` tags, placing an `@import` statement between them. Here's the head section of `hello.html` again, this time referencing an imported style sheet:

File: **hello.html (excerpt)**

```
<head>
<title>Example imported style sheet</title>
<style type="text/css">
@import url("mystyles.css");
</style>
</head>
```

Styles in linked or imported style sheets will apply to elements in any of the pages from which they're referenced, which means that, to change the color of your `h1` element, you need only change it in one style sheet file.

# Tags

As we've already seen, we can create for any given HTML element styles that will then redefine how the browser displays that element. In comparison to `<font>` tags, using embedded or external style sheets removes a huge amount of presentational markup from your pages, making them easier to maintain and to keep consistent across the site.

# Media Types

We can also change the way elements appear when they're printed by specifying the media type to which a particular style sheet applies. Consider this example:

```
<style type="text/css">
p {
  font-family: Verdana, Arial, sans-serif;
}
</style>
<style type="text/css" media="print">
p {
  font-family: Times, serif;
}
</style>
```

This markup will cause <p> tags to be printed in Times, but to display on-screen in Verdana.

You can also specify a media type when you're linking or importing style sheets.

```
<link rel="stylesheet" href="mystyles.css" type="text/css"
    media="all" />
<link rel="stylesheet" href="printstyles.css" type="text/css"
    media="print" />
<style type="text/css">
@import url("screen.css") screen;
</style>
```

Dreamweaver includes support for screen, print, handheld, projection and TV media types, allowing you to develop Websites that are accessible from a large number of devices.

# Classes

Changing the way elements look isn't the only application of CSS. Sometimes, you might want to style a particular HTML element differently than other elements of the same type. In such cases, you can create a CSS class to be applied to the elements that you want to change. Consider this class:

```
.hilite {
  background-color: #F7F2C3;
}
```

You could apply the hilite class to any element on the page, like so:

```
<p class="hilite">Hello world</p>
```

Only the elements to which the class is applied will adopt this style. Note that you create a CSS class rule in the much same way that you'd create a rule for an element, with the exception that the selector must begin with a period.

We'll be returning to these concepts as we use Dreamweaver throughout the rest of this book.

# Your Basic Toolkit

In this section, we'll look at the tools available for working with CSS in Dreamweaver 8, and see how they're used in practice. We'll refer back to these tools as we apply them in later chapters.

## Setting Preferences for CSS

To launch the Preferences dialog, select Edit > Preferences. Select the CSS Styles category, as illustrated in Figure 5.1.

You can use shorthand or longhand syntax to write your CSS: it's really a question of personal preference. Shorthand CSS looks like this:

```
h1 {
    font: bold 10pt/12pt Verdana
}
```

Here's the same rule in longhand CSS:

```
h1 {
    font-weight: bold;
    font-size: 10pt;
    line-height: 12pt;
    font-family: Verdana;
}
```

If you already prefer one syntax over the other, you can select and use those styles accordingly. In this book, I'll use shorthand syntax.

## Figure 5.1. The CSS Styles Category of the Preferences dialog.

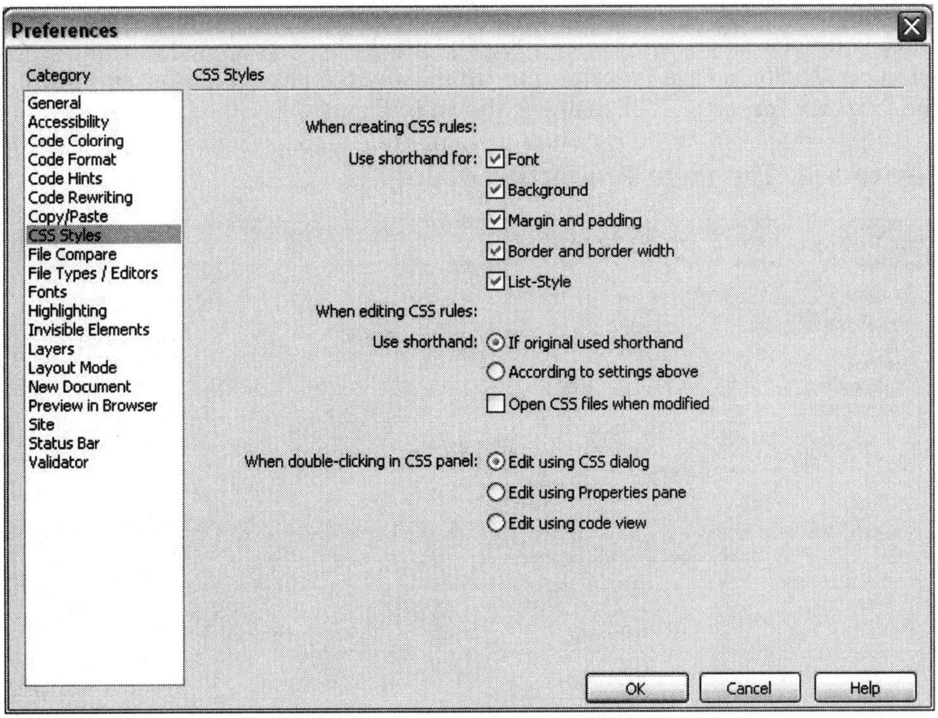

Possibly more important to note are the Use shorthand if original used shorthand and Use shorthand according to settings above options. If you're opening and editing existing CSS documents in Dreamweaver, you will most likely want Dreamweaver to avoid changing that code unless you make changes yourself. By checking the first radio button, Dreamweaver will honor the way in which the style sheet you open was written.

This screen's Open CSS files when modified checkbox allows you to keep an eye on the CSS code that the software adds to your style sheet.

You can also choose how to work with and edit your CSS files in Dreamweaver. By default, if you double-click a rule or property in the CSS panel, Dreamweaver will open the CSS Rule Definition dialog so that you can edit the style rules. If you would prefer to edit the CSS in the Properties pane of the CSS panel, then select the Edit using Properties pane option. If you'd rather Dreamweaver opened the CSS file in Code View, select the Edit using code view option.

# The Page Properties Dialog Box

Once you open a new document, you can launch the Page Properties dialog by selecting Modify > Page Properties, or by clicking the Page Properties button on the Property Inspector. The dialog is shown in Figure 5.2.

## Figure 5.2. The Page Properties dialog.

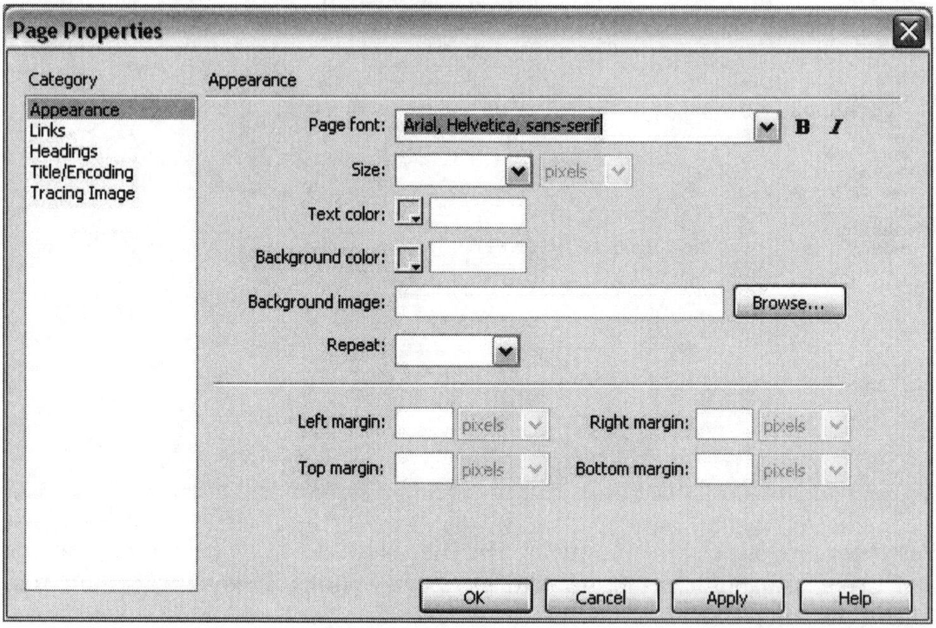

If you've used previous versions of Dreamweaver, the Page Properties dialog will be familiar to you. Since the release of Dreamweaver MX, this dialog has inserted CSS, instead of using the now deprecated attributes of the body element, to control basic page styling information.

The first category in this dialog—Appearance—enables you to set the basic font for the page, as well as its size and color. You can also set a background color and image for the page, and control how that background repeats. The boxes underneath for the left, right, top and bottom margins affect the space between the edge of the browser window and that of your layout. Play with these settings on a document to see their effects both in Design View, and in the code.

Other categories enable you to set styles for links and headings; whether you do so here, or later in the development of your style sheet, is entirely up to you.

# The CSS Panel

Much of your work with CSS is done through the CSS Panel, shown in Figure 5.3. In Dreamweaver 8, this panel has been revised to provide a single, unified location in which you can work with CSS in Dreamweaver.

## Figure 5.3. The New CSS Panel in Dreamweaver 8

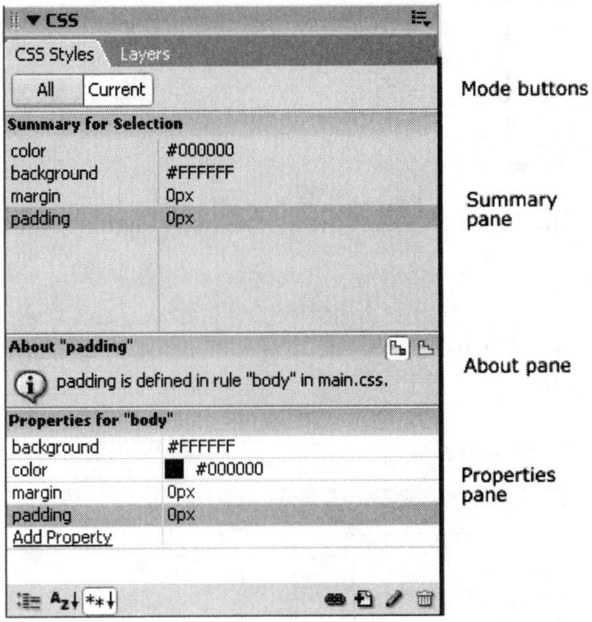

Any styles you have defined, whether in an external style sheet or in the head of your document, will appear in the CSS panel.

# Creating a New CSS Rule

### Figure 5.4. The New CSS Rule button.

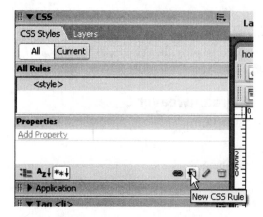

To create a new CSS rule, click the New CSS Rule button shown in Figure 5.4 at the bottom of the CSS Panel.

If, in the dialog that appears, you select Tag under Selector Type, you can then make a selection from a list of element names in the drop-down list at the top of the box. Figure 5.5 shows the selection of the h1 element through this menu.

### Figure 5.5. Selecting the h1 element.

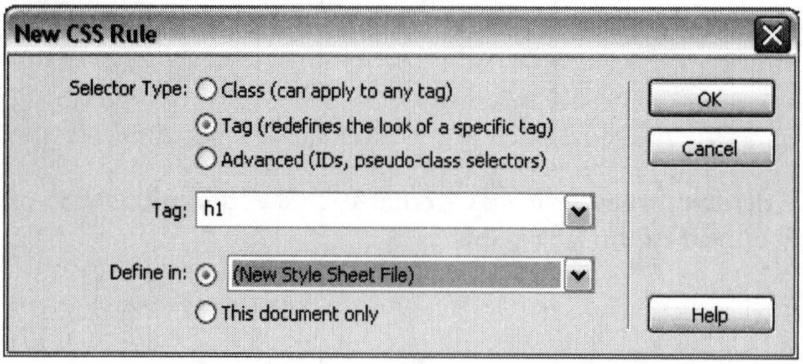

At the bottom of the dialog, you can choose whether to define the style in an existing style sheet (if one is already attached to the document), or in a new style sheet file (in which case you will be asked to save the file). Alternatively, you can create it for this document only, which will put the CSS into the head of the document.

You can also create a class using this dialog: simply choose the Class selector type, then type a class name into the text input box at the top of the dialog. You'll notice that there's a third selector type: Advanced. We'll discuss the usage of these selectors in the next chapter.

Whatever selector you use, clicking OK will launch the CSS Rule Definition dialog, shown in Figure 5.6.

## Figure 5.6. The CSS Rule Definition dialog.

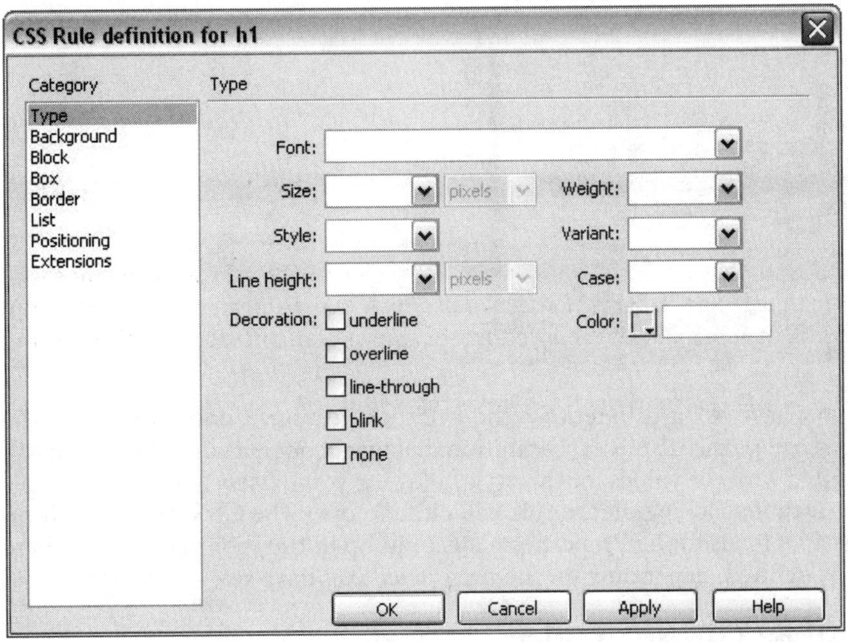

This dialog enables you to set the different properties for the selector you've chosen. We'll explore the various properties in coming chapters, as we create our CSS design. One of the best ways to find out what a property does is to try it out, so do have a play around and create a few styles to see how this dialog works.

After setting the styles that you want for your selector, click OK to create the style, which will appear in the CSS Panel.

# Editing a CSS Style

To edit a style that you have created either in Dreamweaver, or by hand or in another application, select it in the CSS Panel, then click the Edit Style button, as shown in Figure 5.7.

### Figure 5.7. Clicking the Edit Style button.

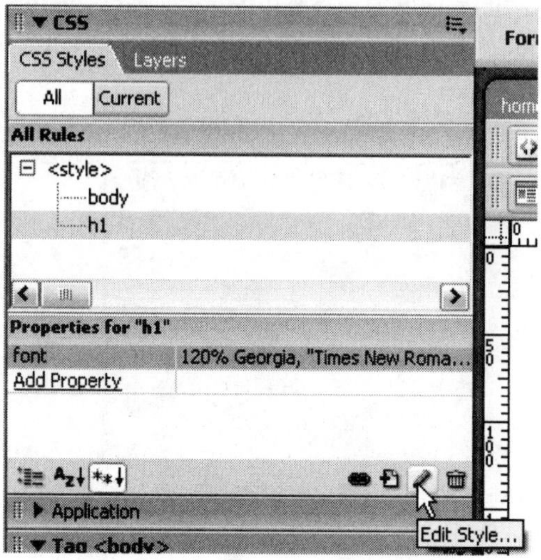

Unless you have set a different method (either through Code View or in the Properties pane), the CSS Rule Definition dialog will open again. The dialog will be populated with the values for this style, allowing you to view and make changes to them. Double-clicking on the rule will either reopen the CSS Rule Definition dialog, switch focus to the Properties pane, or jump to the spot in the code where the rule is defined, depending on the preference you have set.

# Viewing All or Current Styles

Use the Mode buttons at the top of the CSS Panel, as shown in Figure 5.8, to view all of the styles in your document, or just the current styles—those that apply to the element you've selected in the document window.

**Figure 5.8. Select to view All Styles or just those that apply to the selected element.**

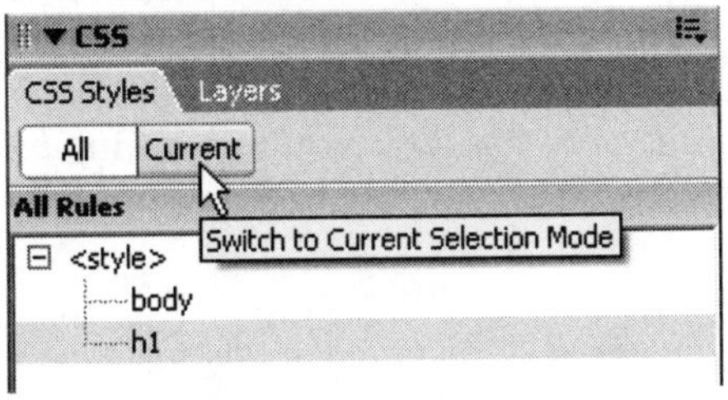

Once you have defined some CSS style rules in your document, you can use the extra functionality of Dreamweaver's CSS Panel to make working with CSS easier and faster.

## The CSS Properties Pane

At the bottom of the CSS Panel, you'll find the new CSS Properties Pane. This powerful tool helps speed up CSS development by giving you quick access to the CSS rules and properties that are already defined in your document. If you're in All Mode, clicking on any CSS rule in the top pane will display its properties in the CSS Properties Pane. As Figure 5.9 shows, you can edit the properties directly in that pane.

**Figure 5.9. Editing a CSS rule in the Properties Pane.**

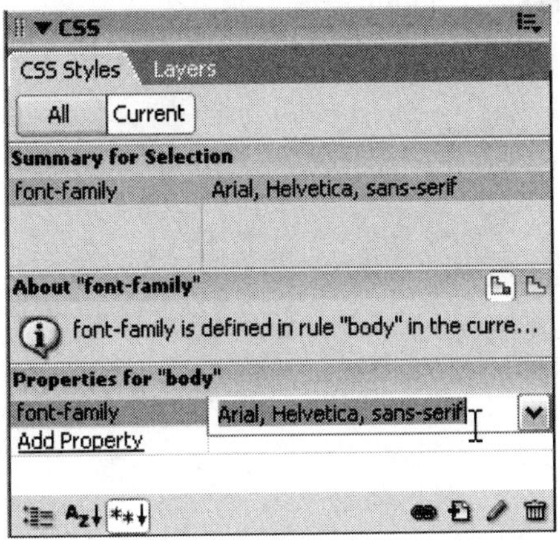

# The About Pane

In Current Mode, the top part of the CSS Panel displays the CSS properties that apply to the current selection. If you click on any of these properties, the About Pane, illustrated in Figure 5.10, will identify the rule in which this property is set, and where that rule is defined. This can be very handy if you're working on a page that uses a lot of different style sheets, and you're trying to figure out why your headings are green.

### Figure 5.10. The About Pane.

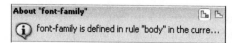

Below the About Pane, the CSS Properties Pane will let you view or edit the properties for the selected rule.

# Attaching a Style Sheet

You can use the CSS Panel to attach an external style sheet to a document. If you've created an embedded style sheet with the CSS Panel or Page Properties dialog, you can move it into an external style sheet for reuse in other pages. Switch into Code View and select all of the CSS between the <style> and </style> tags, as shown in Figure 5.11. Copy this to the clipboard.

### Figure 5.11. Selecting the CSS Styles.

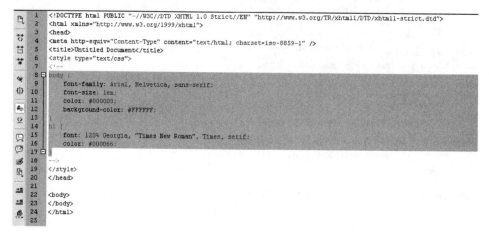

In Dreamweaver, select File > New. In the New Document dialog shown in Figure 5.12, select Basic page, then CSS.

## Figure 5.12. Creating a new CSS file.

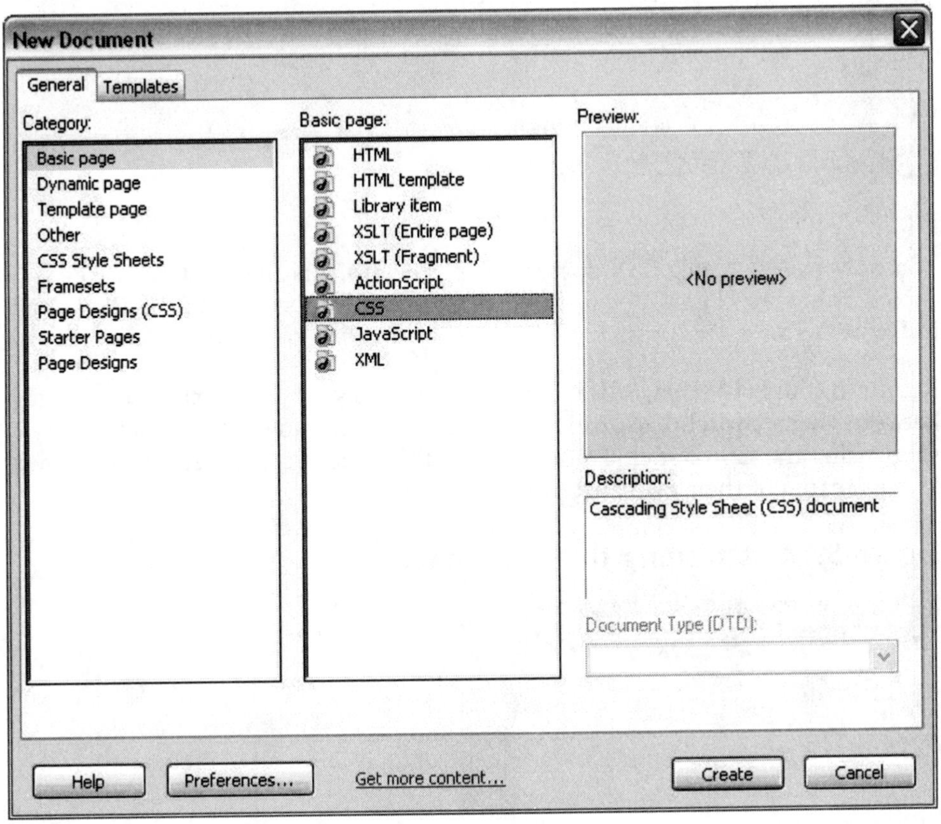

## Figure 5.13. The CSS file `style.css`.

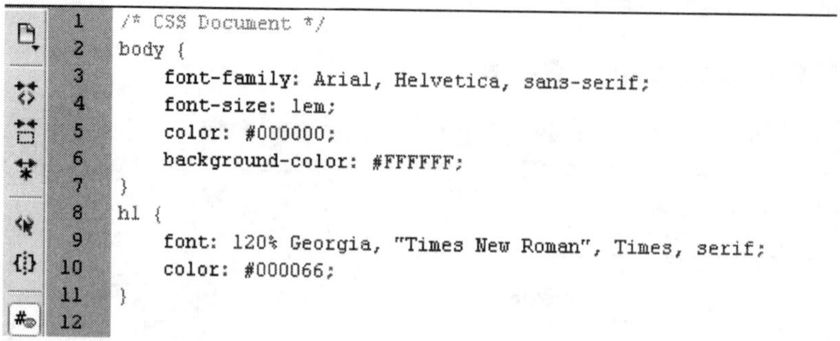

```
1    /* CSS Document */
2    body {
3        font-family: Arial, Helvetica, sans-serif;
4        font-size: 1em;
5        color: #000000;
6        background-color: #FFFFFF;
7    }
8    h1 {
9        font: 120% Georgia, "Times New Roman", Times, serif;
10       color: #000066;
11   }
12
```

You now have a blank CSS document; paste into this file the CSS styles you copied from your HTML document, and save the file as `style.css`, as illustrated in Figure 5.13.

Return to your HTML page; delete the `<style>` and `</style>` tags and everything between them. Switch back to Design View. We can now attach our new style sheet using the CSS Panel. To do so, click the Attach Style Sheet button shown at the bottom of the CSS Panel in Figure 5.14.

## Figure 5.14. Attaching the style sheet.

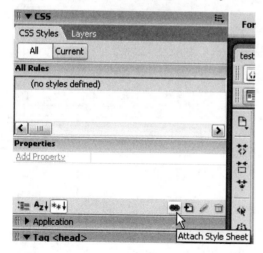

The Attach External Style Sheet dialog will open as shown in Figure 5.15; browse for the file `style.css`. You can add this style sheet using the link or import methods. We briefly discussed these methods earlier, and will return to them in the next chapter, but for now, it doesn't matter too much which approach you choose.

### Figure 5.15. Using the Attach External Style Sheet dialog.

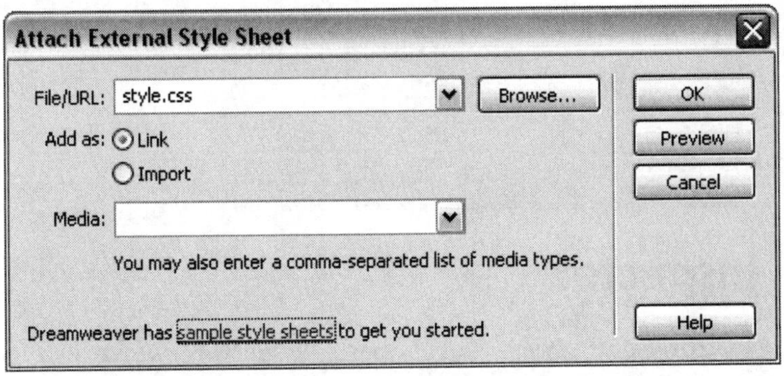

If you select Link, Dreamweaver will add the following line to the head of your document:

```
<link href="style.css" rel="stylesheet" type="text/css" />
```

Select Import, and you will end up with the following:

```
<style type="text/css">
<!--
@import url("style.css");
-->
</style>
```

Whichever method you use to attach your style sheet, once you've done so, you should see your style sheet and rules appear in the All Mode of the CSS Panel. To add new CSS rules to this style sheet, select the style sheet from the Define in drop-down list, as shown in Figure 5.16. You can add style rules to the embedded style sheet by selecting This document only.

**Figure 5.16. Defining a new style in the `styles.css` style sheet.**

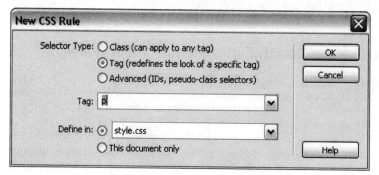

## The Property Inspector

In Dreamweaver MX 2004 and above, the Property Inspector, shown in Figure 5.17, uses CSS by default, instead of `<font>` tags. You'll likely find that you use the Property Inspector a great deal as you work in Dreamweaver, as it provides convenient control over element properties as you work on them.

**Figure 5.17. The Property Inspector.**

If you type some text into the document window, you can style it using the Property Inspector. You can choose whether an element is a paragraph or a heading using the Format drop-down list, as shown in Figure 5.18; buttons allow you to style the text as a list. These choices affect the structural markup of your document: they don't add any CSS to it.

## Figure 5.18. Creating a level one heading using the Property Inspector.

However, if you decide to change the font, size, or color of an element, the Property Inspector will apply those changes using CSS, and inserting the appropriate rules into the head of the document. This can be very useful for "mocking up" pages: whenever you want to create new pages for your design, simply select all the newly created styles and place them into an external style sheet, as we did earlier.

If you've already defined CSS rules for a document, the Property Inspector will allow you to view the CSS for any of the elements in that document. Select an element in the document window, then click CSS; the CSS for that element will display in the CSS Panel's Current Mode. If the CSS Panel is already in Current Mode, the CSS button will be grayed out. The CSS will automatically display in the CSS Panel as you select elements within the document.

# Selecting Styles

A very useful feature of the Property Inspector is the Style drop-down list, which allows you to apply the CSS classes you've created to specific page elements. The classes defined in a document's embedded or external style sheets are located; they're then added to the Property Inspector's Style drop-down list, complete with a preview of how text will display once the style is applied. To apply one of these classes, select the element you wish to style through the document window, then select the appropriate class from the Style menu. This process is depicted in Figure 5.19.

## Figure 5.19. Applying a class from the Property Inspector.

At the bottom of the list of classes is the Attach Style entry—another shortcut to add a linked or imported style sheet to the current document.

# Editing CSS in Code View

Another way to edit CSS is via Code View, through which you can edit the CSS code itself. You can obviously type CSS directly into your style sheet via Code View, but additional help is also available here.

Open your style sheet in Code View and start to type a CSS property in one of your selectors. After you type a few letters, a list of properties will display; the property that's most likely to match the attribute name you've typed will be highlighted, as shown in Figure 5.20. You can select this property, or continue to type. This helpful feature is called "code hinting."

**Figure 5.20. Editing CSS in Code View.**

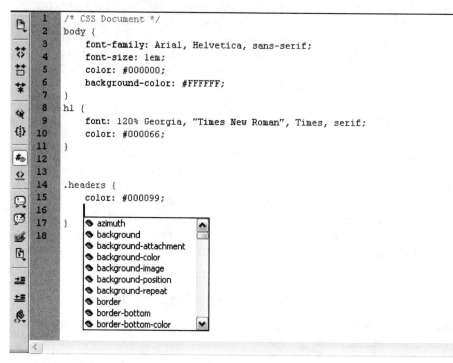

Once you've typed a property's full name, and finished it with a colon, Dream-weaver will again come to your aid with a list of suggested values for the property (or a color picker if you're setting a color). You can press **Escape** to dismiss the list; **Ctrl-Space** will make the list reappear.

# Sample CSS Styles

Dreamweaver 8 comes with some sample style sheets that range from simple starting points (defining some of the most commonly used elements in a document), to full CSS layouts.

You can use the CSS Panel to attach a sample style sheet to your document. Instead of browsing for your own style sheet, click the sample style sheets link at the bottom of the Attach External Style Sheet dialog, as shown in Figure 5.21.

### Figure 5.21. The Attach External Style Sheet dialog.

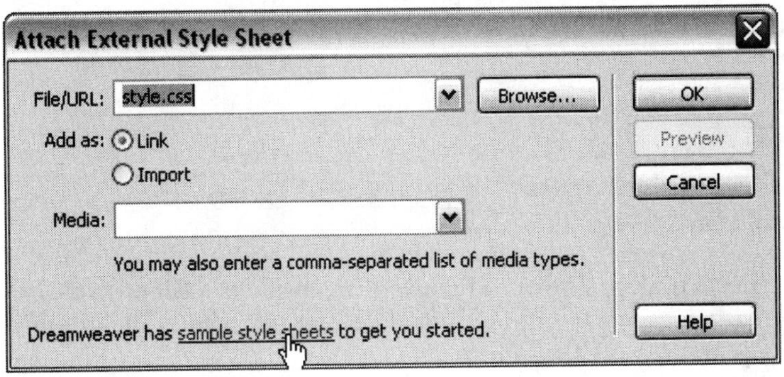

**Figure 5.22. Choosing a sample style sheet.**

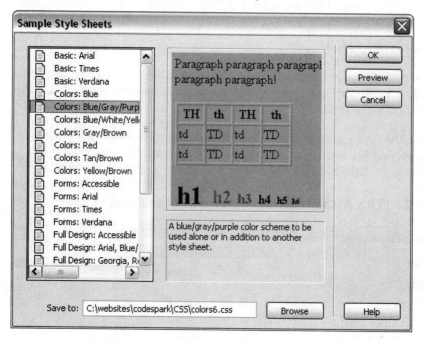

The Sample Style Sheets dialog, shown in Figure 5.22, displays a list of available style sheets, along with a preview window that lets you see what's included in each style sheet.

To attach a style sheet to your page, use the Browse button at the bottom of the dialog to select the directory to which you'd like to save the style sheet, then click OK. The style sheet will be saved to the directory you identified, and will be linked to your document. You can also preview how your document will look once the style sheet is applied by clicking the Preview button on the right side of the dialog. This Preview functionality won't make any permanent changes to your document.

# CSS Page Designs

Dreamweaver also contains some starting-point page designs that provide basic CSS layouts. To use a CSS Page Design, select File > New > Page Designs (CSS). After you've looked through the previews, and you've decided which one you'd like to use, click Create. You'll be prompted to save the file; after you've done so, you can edit the design to suit your needs. Changing the created design does not alter the Page Design in Dreamweaver itself, so you can always start over again, or use the same design as a starting point for several different layouts.

# Design Time Style Sheets

The Design Time Style Sheets feature allows you to apply at "design time" (that is, while you're working on the site in Dreamweaver) a CSS file that will not be attached to the document when it is live. This might seem like a strange thing to do, but, as we'll discover later, Design Time Style Sheets can be a very useful feature when you're working with print or other alternative style sheets.

This feature seems rather hidden away in Dreamweaver; to access it, select Text > CSS Styles > Design Time... or right-click within the CSS Panel and select Design-time.... The dialog shown in Figure 5.23 will appear.

**Figure 5.23. The Design Time Style Sheets dialog.**

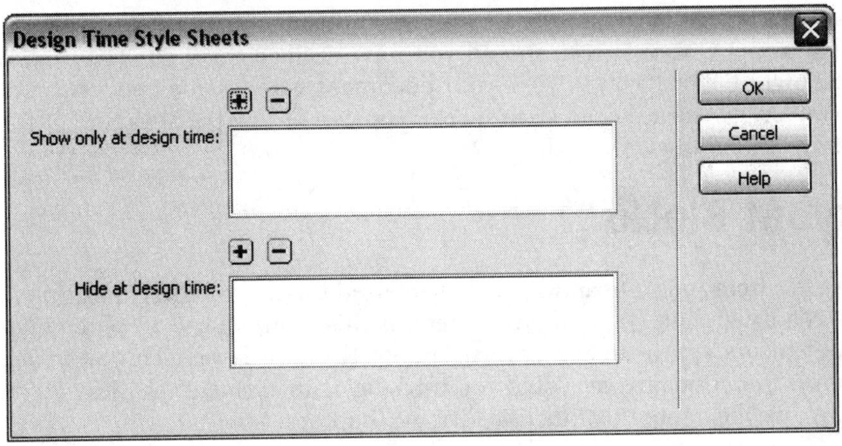

Clicking on the + symbol will allow you to browse for style sheets associated with your site, and select those that you'd like to Show only at design time (in the top box) or Hide at design time (in the bottom box). We'll be looking at this feature in more depth a little later on.

# The Style Rendering Toolbar

The Style Rendering toolbar lets you see how your design will look following the application of alternative style sheets that are designed to display the document effectively in different media types, such as in print, on handheld devices, or on Web TV.

Once you've created a style sheet for a given media type, you can use the Style Rendering toolbar to see how your document will display once that style sheet is applied. Open the toolbar by selecting View > Toolbars > Style Rendering; it displays above the document window, as shown in Figure 5.24.

**Figure 5.24. Displaying the Style Rendering toolbar.**

You can use the toolbar's buttons to toggle through screen, print, handheld, projection, and TV style sheets, should you have defined them all. The button on the far right enables you to view your document without the application of styles from any of the attached style sheets: you can review the structure of the document without any CSS at all.

# CSS "Layout Blocks"

In its last few iterations, Dreamweaver has referred to any absolutely positioned element as a Layer, and Dreamweaver 8 retains this terminology: absolutely positioned elements appear in the Layers Pane of the CSS Panel. This approach makes more functionality available for working with elements positioned in other ways; we'll explore this functionality in Chapter 6.

Dreamweaver 8 refers to positioned elements as Layout Blocks, and highlights these in your document so that you can easily select and edit the content that's contained within a positioned element, as shown in Figure 5.25. If you hold your mouse over a Layout Block, its outline will be highlighted; you can click this outline to select the whole block. Content may be added to the block in the same way you'd normally add content to a document in Dreamweaver.

## Figure 5.25. Selecting a Layout Block.

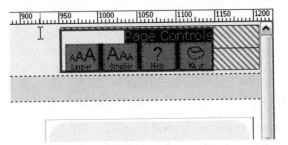

# Layout Block Visual Aids

Dreamweaver provides visual aids to help you to understand your layouts, and to see how the differently positioned elements work together. To turn on the Visual Aids, select View > Visual Aids, then select all items in the list that begins with Layout Block.... If you turn on the background colors, as shown in Figure 5.26, you'll immediately see a clear representation of the way in which the different elements of your document have been positioned with CSS.

## Figure 5.26. Layout blocks displaying with background colors turned on.

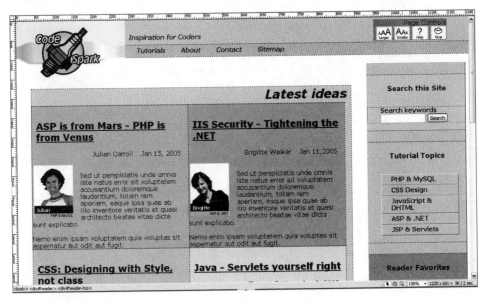

# Summary

This chapter has provided a broad overview of the Dreamweaver tools that can help you as you develop documents with CSS. If you're new to Dreamweaver, and this all seems very confusing, don't worry! You'll find that, as we start to work with this functionality, it becomes more understandable. You'll also get a feel for the tools that you like to use—those that suit your workflow.

As is often the case with Dreamweaver, there are several routes by which you can achieve the same end result. Part of the process of becoming comfortable with the product is identifying which tools you find helpful, and which ones you don't want to use—there's no "right" or "wrong."

# 6

# Constructing the Layout with CSS

In this chapter, we'll use Dreamweaver's CSS tools to develop a CSS layout for the document we created in Chapter 4.

While Dreamweaver offers good CSS support, be aware that some elements don't display in Dreamweaver exactly as they will in the browser. Don't get caught in a trap of trying to design for Dreamweaver! Check your work regularly in your browser as you move through the steps explained here—this will help you to identify and understand the differences that are inherent in the program.

Later in this chapter, we'll see how you can test your work in various browsers, and validate those CSS files.

## The Homepage Document

We start this chapter where we left off in Chapter 4: with the basic, barebones homepage document shown in Figure 6.1.

## Figure 6.1. Displaying the unstyled homepage document in a Web browser.

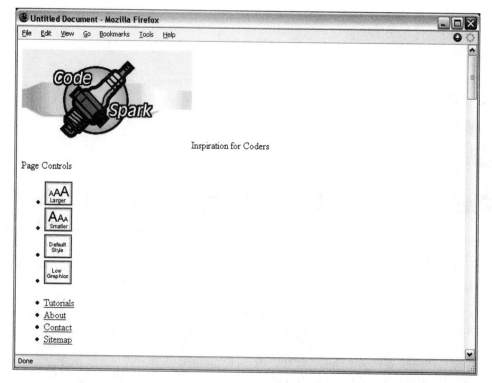

We created this document using semantic XHTML, having considered which XHTML elements would best describe each part of the page content. This provides a solid framework on which we can now base our design.

We will need to add to this document—we'll need to put containers around the main sections of the page so that we can position them easily with CSS—but we'll take care to do so in a way that doesn't compromise the structure and accessibility of the document.

# Defining the Basic Layout

Our layout comprises three sections: the heading area with the logo, accessibility links, and main navigation; the main content area; and a sidebar containing sub-navigation and search. Our first task will be to set up the basic areas of the page in the markup; then, we'll use CSS to position these sections so that they display roughly in the locations in which we want them to appear, instead of displaying one after the other as they do now.

Open the document `homepage-layout-strict.html` in Dreamweaver. This is the XHTML document that we converted to XHTML Strict at the end of Chapter 4.

# The Header

Let's start by creating a container around our header area. The container will allow us to create style rules specifically for this area, and address it separately from other parts of the document.

We can define a given area of our document by wrapping it in `<div>` tags. The `div` can then be given a class or an ID, which allows us to style that part of the document using CSS. A class is normally applied when we want to apply a given style rule to multiple elements of the page; an ID can only be used for one tag in any given page. Since we're only going to have one header, we'll give this `div` an ID, rather than a class.

To wrap all the elements that belong to the header area in a `div`, switch to Design View and select the header section: the logo, accessibility images, and main navigation list. Now, switch to the Layout panel of the Insert toolbar, and click the Insert Div Tag button.

## Figure 6.2. Selecting all of the page elements that belong to the header.

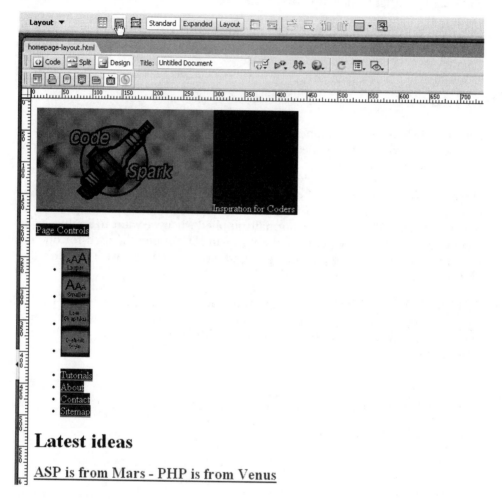

Once you've clicked the Insert Div Tag button, the Insert Div Tag dialog, shown in Figure 6.3, will appear. The Insert drop-down list contains a list of all the places in which the div can be inserted, including Wrap around selection, which can be used if some content or element is selected in the document. Select Wrap around selection from the Insert drop-down, and type **header** into the ID field to give the div an ID of header. Click OK to insert the div.

## Figure 6.3. The Insert Div Tag dialog.

**Insert Div Tag**

Insert: Wrap around selection

Class:

ID: header

New CSS Style

OK
Cancel
Help

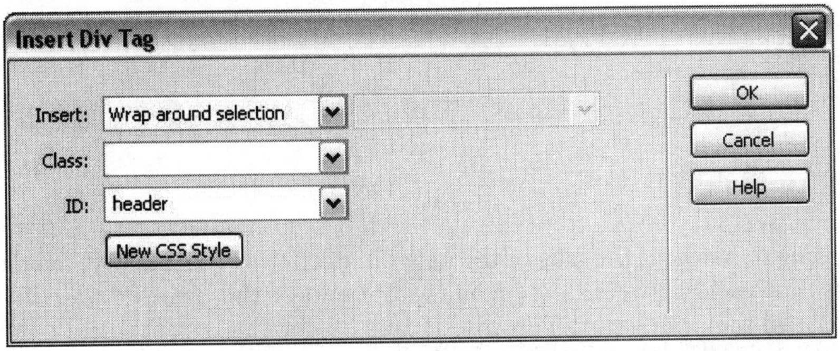

### Classes, IDs, and the Insert Div Tag Dialog

If you have already created CSS rules for any classes or unused IDs, they will appear in the Class and ID drop-down lists, so you can choose to select them when you insert a div. IDs can only be used once per document, so, once you've used an ID, it won't show up in the list. Classes can be used multiple times, so they will always be displayed here, ready to be selected.

A dotted line should now surround the area that will become the header. If you switch into Code View, you can see the opening <div> right before the logo's <p> tag, and the closing </div> tag after the close of the navigation list, similar to that shown below:

File: **homepage-layout-strict.html (excerpt)**

```
<div id="header">
  <p><img src="img/logo.gif" alt="Code Spark" width="290"
     height="160" />Inspiration for Coders </p>
  <p>Page Controls</p>
  <ul>
    <li> <a href="#"><img src="img/control_larger.gif"
        alt="Increase Text Size" width="43" height="35" />
        </a></li>
    <li><a href="#"><img src="img/control_smaller.gif"
        alt="Decrease Text Size" width="43" height="35" />
        </a></li>
    <li><a href="#"><img src="img/control_low_graphics.gif"
        alt="Low Graphics" width="43" height="35" /></a></li>
    <li><a href="#"><img src="img/control_default_style.gif"
        alt="Default Style" width="43" height="35" /></a></li>
  </ul>
  <ul>
```

```
    <li><a href="">Tutorials</a></li>
    <li><a href="">About</a></li>
    <li><a href="">Contact</a></li>
    <li><a href="">Sitemap</a></li>
  </ul>
</div>
```

# The Content Area

We're now going to mark up the part of the page that contains our content. Select everything from the heading "Latest ideas" to the end of the browser statistics section just above the search box. You can do this by clicking at the start of the selection, scrolling to the end the selection, then holding down **Shift** as you click at the end of the selection. Click the Insert Div Tag button, again selecting Wrap around selection. This time, type **content** into the ID box. Click OK and the dotted line should appear around the area of the page that you had selected, as shown in Figure 6.4.

### Figure 6.4. The dotted lines show the areas of the `divs`.

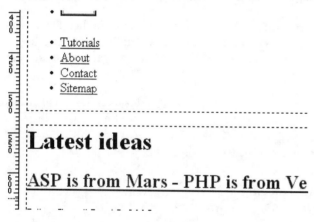

### On your Selection

It's not always easy to select content accurately in Dreamweaver's Design View—often, tags that you don't want to include are selected, while some desired tags are left out. One way to check whether the correct tags are selected is to use the tag selector at the bottom of the document window, but an accurate and quick way to ensure that you have all the content and tags you need is briefly to switch into Code View: your selection will be highlighted there.

## The Navigation Area

The final container that we'll insert at this point will wrap the navigation area of the page. Select everything from the search box down to the end of the page. Then, use the Insert Div Tag button to wrap this selection in a div with the ID nav.

You have now marked out the three main areas of the page using divs; this will form the foundation of our layout. We can now move on to style these areas with CSS.

# Creating CSS Rules

We are going to start by adding to the body element some style rules that will affect the document as a whole. After that, we'll move on to style the individual areas of the page that we've marked out.

## The Body Area

Locate the CSS Panel and click the New CSS Rule button, as shown in Figure 6.5, to open the New CSS Rule dialog.

**Figure 6.5. Clicking the New CSS Rule button in the CSS Styles Panel.**

We'll start by creating some styles for the <body> tag; these styles will be saved into a new style sheet file that will become our site's main CSS file. In the section Selector Type, choose the Tag radio button and select body from the Tag drop-down list. Finally, in the Define in section, select (New Style Sheet File). The dialog should look like the one shown in Figure 6.6.

## Figure 6.6. Creating a CSS rule for the body.

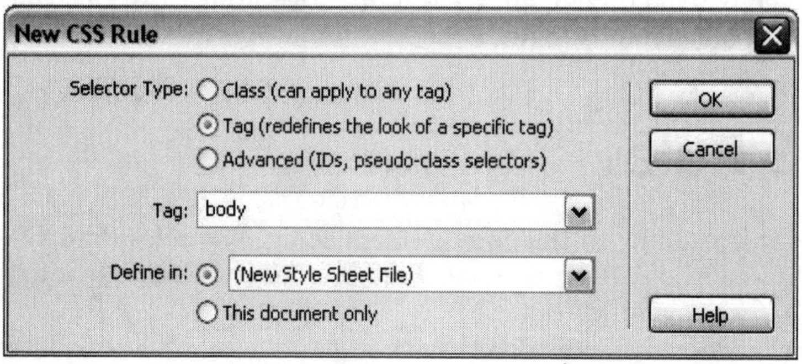

Because you've chosen to define this CSS rule in a new style sheet file, Dreamweaver will prompt you to save the file when you click OK. In the Save Style Sheet File As dialog, click the Create New Folder button and create a new folder named inc (for includes). Save the style sheet as main.css in that folder. Once you've saved your style sheet, the CSS Rule Definition dialog will open and you can begin to create styles for the <body> tag. First, select the Background category and give the page a white (#FFFFFF) background color, as illustrated in Figure 6.7.

### Controlling Color

Don't forget to set the background and text colors for your pages. If you don't, your pages may display very strangely for users who have their default backgrounds set to unusual colors: your page's background will default to the colors those users have set.

## Figure 6.7. Applying styles to the body element to give the page a white background.

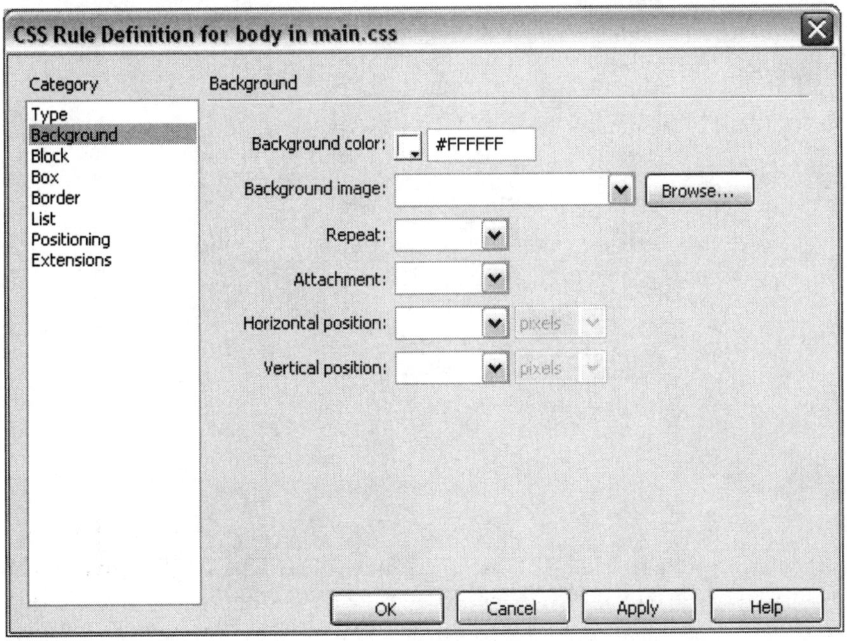

**CSS Rule Definition for body in main.css** ☒

Category | Background
---

Type
**Background**
Block
Box
Border
List
Positioning
Extensions

Background color: ☐ #FFFFFF

Background image: [        ] ⌄ [Browse...]

Repeat: [   ] ⌄

Attachment: [   ] ⌄

Horizontal position: [   ] ⌄ pixels ⌄

Vertical position: [   ] ⌄ pixels ⌄

[ OK ] [ Cancel ] [ Apply ] [ Help ]

Next, select the Type category. Here, we can set our text color to black (**#000000**), and set a base font size of 1em, as depicted in Figure 6.8.

### Font Size Setting Secrets

A common method used to set font sizes is to use pixels (px) or points (pt). However, this approach can prevent your site visitors from resizing page text in their browsers. The method I typically use is to set a base size of 1em, then size individual elements, such as <p> and <h1>, as percentages (%) or ems (em) relative to this base size. This helps ensure that all elements scale in relation to each other.

## Figure 6.8. Setting the font color and size for the body.

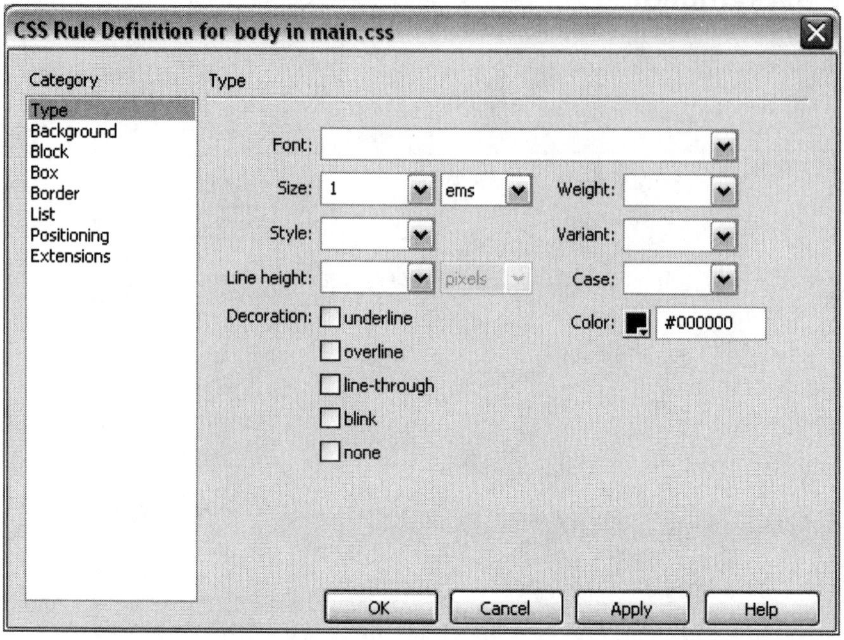

Finally, access the Box category, and set the padding and margins on the body to 0 pixels, as shown in Figure 6.9. This will ensure that your layout sits flush against the edge of the browser window, and doesn't display the default padding or margins that the browser applies. Leave Same for all checked: this will apply the margin and padding to the top, right, bottom and left of the body element.

Click OK to apply these CSS rules to your style sheet, and see the effect on your document. The only noticeable difference at this point is that your logo image and text should display flush with the left edge of the document window in Dreamweaver. If you switch into Code View, you'll see that Dreamweaver has added this link to the style sheet in the head of your document:

File: **homepage-layout-strict.html** (excerpt)

```
<link href="inc/main.css" rel="stylesheet" type="text/css" />
```

## Figure 6.9. Setting margin and padding to 0.

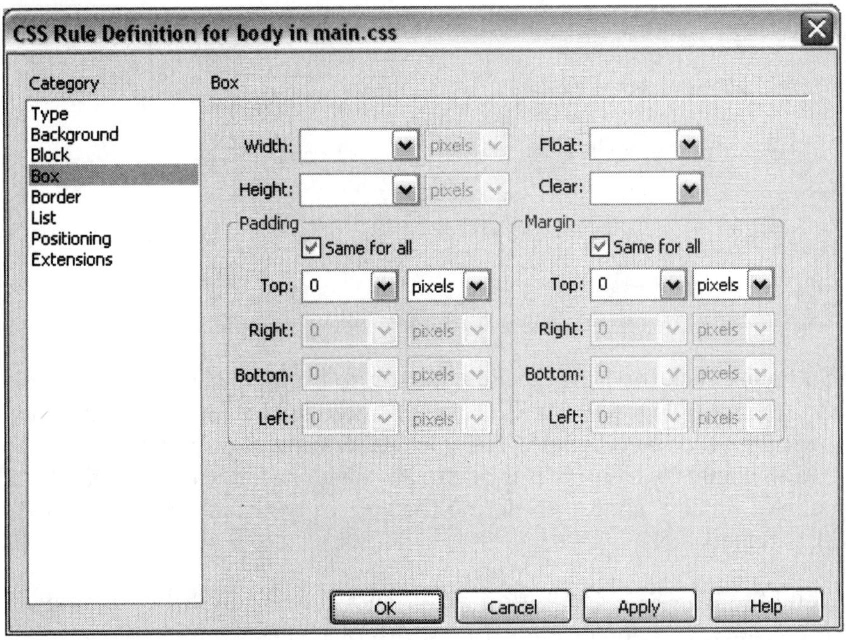

Open the style sheet `main.css` in Dreamweaver, and you should see that your work in the CSS Rule Definition dialog has produced the following CSS for the `<body>` element.

File: **inc/main.css (excerpt)**

```
body {
  font-size: 1em;
  color: #000000;
  background-color: #FFFFFF;
  margin: 0px;
  padding: 0px;
}
```

# Styling the Header `div`

Now, let's use CSS to style the "header" area that we wrapped with a `<div>` tag, as well as some of the elements within it.

## Figure 6.10. Creating a new CSS rule for the "header" div header.

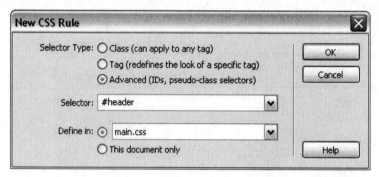

In the CSS Panel, click the New CSS Rule button to bring up the New CSS Rule dialog that appears in Figure 6.10. Choose Advanced as the Selector Type, then type **#header** into the Selector field. The # lets CSS know that "header" is an ID; otherwise, CSS would try to apply this rule to all <header> tags (of which XHTML contains none). Finally, choose to define the rule in main.css: the style sheet that we just created.

Click OK, and the CSS Rule Definition dialog shown in Figure 6.11 will appear. In the Box category, give the header div a width of 100%.

It's common practice to temporarily give a div a background color so that we can make sure that the new CSS rule applies to the element we expect it to. If you like, go to the Background category, set the background color to **#FFFF66**, and click OK to create the CSS rule. The header area becomes yellow, meaning that the style has taken effect. You'll want to remove this background color again before proceeding any further, so make sure the CSS Panel is in All mode and select the #header rule in the All Rules list. Right-click on the background-color line under Properties for "#header" and select Delete to remove that property definition.

Now, we're going to concentrate on the elements inside the header div, positioning them so that they start to resemble our layout image. Our first step will be to position the logo so that the rest of the header area can be aligned with it.

Create a new CSS rule in Dreamweaver. Once again, choose the Advanced Selector Type and type **#logo** into the Selector field.

Within the CSS Rule Definition dialog, switch to the Positioning category, which is illustrated in Figure 6.12. Select absolute from the Type drop-down, and place the logo in the top left-hand corner by setting Top to 0 pixels and Left to 0 pixels.

## Figure 6.11. Giving the header a width of 100%.

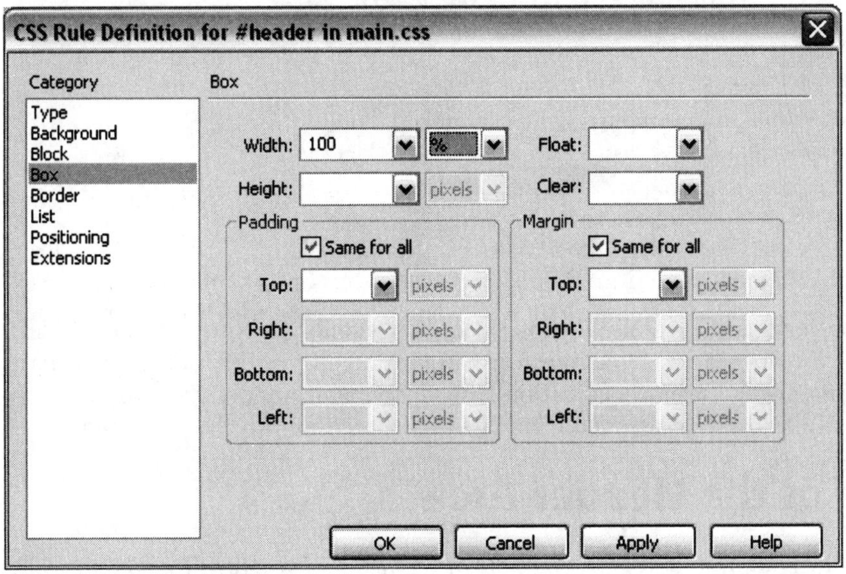

## Figure 6.12. Positioning the logo.

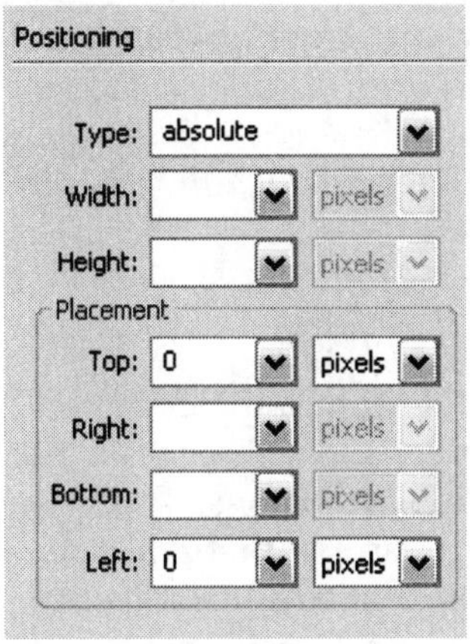

Click OK to close the dialog. You won't see any change right away, because we still need to give the logo the ID we've just created. Click on the image and then, using the Tag Selector at the bottom of the document window, right-click on the `<img>` tag. Select Set ID and then select logo, as in Figure 6.13.

### Figure 6.13. Applying the ID to the logo.

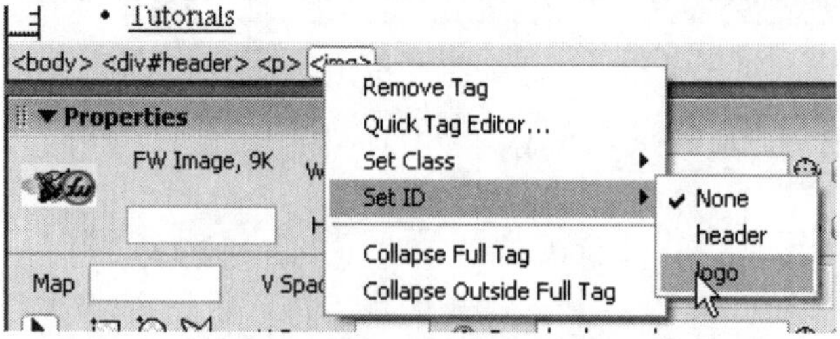

Once you have applied your ID to the logo, it should jump up to the top left corner of the document. Dreamweaver will also highlight the image; this is part of Dreamweaver's Layer visualization feature set, which is designed to help you see where absolutely positioned elements are located within the document.

# The Top of the Header Area

Next, we'll create a style for the top part of the header, which will match up with the top half of the logo image. Create another CSS rule using the Advanced Selector Type and the Selector **#header-top**.

1.  In the Background category, give this rule a background color of **#E9ECE4** to match that of the logo image.

2.  In the Block category, set Vertical Alignment to bottom, which will align the content of this element to the bottom of its content area.

3.  In the Box category, set the height of the area to 65 pixels.

Click OK. We now need to add a `div` with the ID `header-top` to the document. This will create the lighter colored stripe in the header, and will contain the tagline, "Inspiration for coders," as well as the accessibility buttons. To do so, you'll need to switch into Code View, for a couple of reasons: firstly because, when you view the page in Design View, the logo is positioned over some of the elements that you'll need to select, and secondly, because Dreamweaver may have added some additional paragraph tags that you'll need to remove before you continue.

Find the logo image in the code; if `<p>` and `</p>` tags wrap the image and the tagline, remove them. This section of code should look like this:

File: **homepage-layout-strict.html** (excerpt)

```
<img src="img/logo.gif" alt="Code Spark" width="290"
    height="160" id="logo" />Inspiration for Coders
<p>Page Controls</p>
<ul>
  <li> <a href="#"><img src="img/control_larger.gif"
      alt="Increase Text Size" width="43" height="35" />
      </a></li>
  <li><a href="#"><img src="img/control_smaller.gif"
      alt="Decrease Text Size" width="43" height="35" />
      </a></li>
  <li><a href="#"><img src="img/control_low_graphics.gif"
      alt="Low Graphics" width="43" height="35" />
      </a></li>
  <li><a href="#"><img src="img/control_default_style.gif"
      alt="Default Style" width="43" height="35" /></a></li>
</ul>
```

Select the code from the point immediately before the `<img/>` tag through to the end of the `</ul>` tag, then click the Insert Div Tag button in the toolbar. This command works in Code View in the same way that it does in Design View. When the Insert Div Tag dialog appears, as shown in Figure 6.14, select the ID header-top from the drop-down, click OK, and return to Design View.

## Figure 6.14. Accessing the Insert Div Tag dialog in Code View.

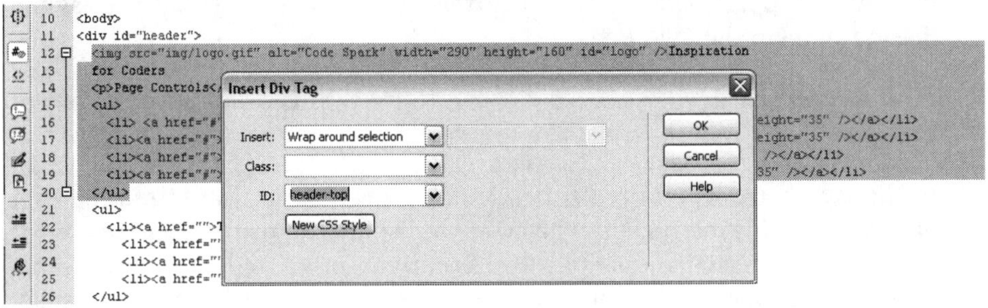

Design View may start to look strange in at this point; we're manipulating one part of the document using CSS, while leaving others untouched. Don't worry: things will look better as we continue.

The `header-top div` contains the tagline and accessibility buttons. We'll start by working on the tagline, which is currently hiding behind the logo image. Let's use CSS to position it within the header, where it can be seen. Create a new CSS rule, this time choosing to create a Class, and name it `.tagline`, as depicted in Figure 6.15.

## Figure 6.15. Creating a CSS class named `.tagline`.

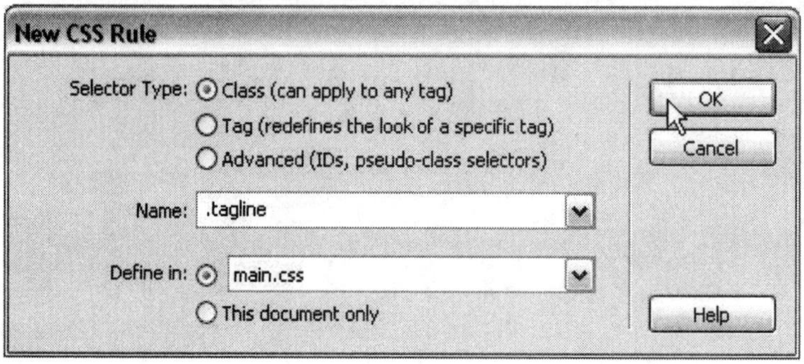

Now, complete the following steps within the CSS Rule Definition dialog, as depicted in Figure 6.16:

1. In the Box category, give the class a top padding of 2 ems, making sure that you uncheck the Same for all checkbox.

2. While you're in the Box category, set the top, right and bottom margins to 0, and set the left padding to 300 pixels. This will ensure that the tagline doesn't overlap the logo image.

3. Still in the Box category, set Float to left to move this element to the left of the page.

4. In the Type category, select Verdana, Arial, Helvetica, sans-serif from the Font drop-down. This instructs the browser to display the text in Verdana, or, if Verdana isn't available, one of the alternative fonts listed. Note that "sans-serif" is not actually a font, but a way for us to instruct any browser to display its default sans-serif font.

5. Also in the Type category, set Size to 100%, Weight to bold, Style to italic, and Color to **#3C582F**.

6. Click OK to create the rule.

## Figure 6.16. Setting the type properties for the tagline.

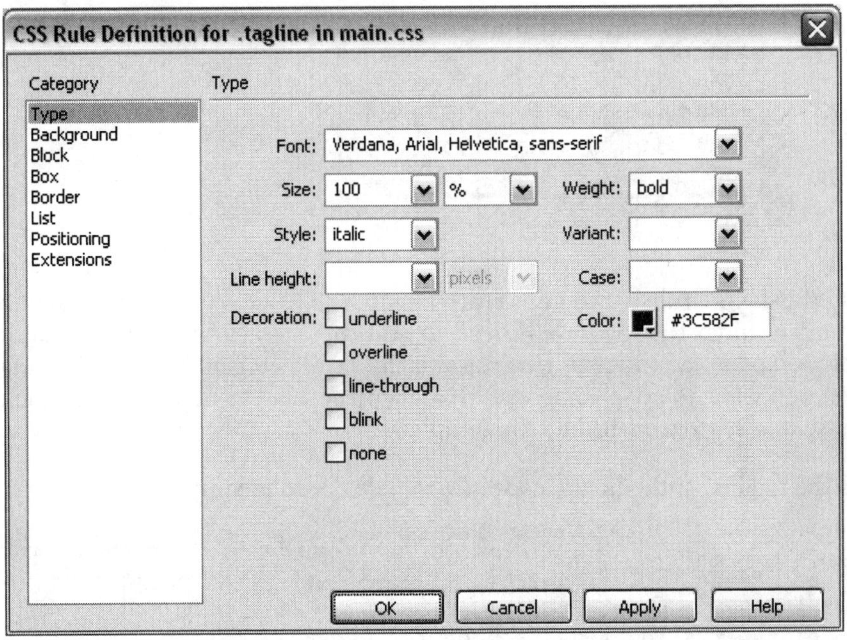

**CSS Rule Definition for .tagline in main.css**

Category: Type, Background, Block, Box, Border, List, Positioning, Extensions

Type

Font: Verdana, Arial, Helvetica, sans-serif

Size: 100 %    Weight: bold

Style: italic    Variant:

Line height: pixels    Case:

Decoration: ☐ underline    Color: #3C582F
☐ overline
☐ line-through
☐ blink
☐ none

[ OK ]  [ Cancel ]  [ Apply ]  [ Help ]

## Making Whitespace with Padding and Margins

If you're just starting out with CSS, you may get confused as to the difference between "padding" and "margins." They both seem to do the same thing: create whitespace around an element. However, there is a subtle difference, and understanding it will help you to deal with your own complex CSS layouts.

❏ **Padding** is the space between the content of the element and its border. You can think of padding as being "inside" the element.

❏ **Margin** is the minimum space between the element's border and the border of the nearest element on each side, so margin can be thought of as being "outside" the element.

A good way of visualizing this is to create an element with some padding, a border, and some margin, and to then set a background color for that element. You should see the padding display as the colored area inside the border, while the margin is the uncolored area outside the border, as shown in Figure 6.17.

## Figure 6.17. Displaying padding inside the border.

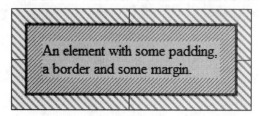

To apply the tagline rule we've just created, switch to Code View. As the tagline is still hidden under the logo, we'll need to add the class to the code by hand. We'll use a <span> tag to apply this class to the text. You can use a <span> tag whenever you want to style some text that's part of a larger block of text, such as a phrase or a sentence within a paragraph.

So, find the tagline, and edit the code to produce the following:

File: **homepage-layout-strict.html (excerpt)**

```
<div id="header-top"><img src="img/logo.gif" alt="Code Spark"
    width="290" height="160" id="logo" />
<span class="tagline">Inspiration for Coders</span>
  <p>Page Controls</p>
```

Switch back to Design View, and the tagline should display to the right of the logo image.

# The Accessibility Buttons

The final part of the top section of the heading includes the accessibility buttons. Create a new CSS rule with the Advanced Selector Type and the Selector **#controls**. Then, access the CSS Rule Definition dialog:

1.  In the Type category, select Verdana, Arial, Helvetica, sans-serif from the Font drop-down. Set the size to 70%, and the color to #72746D.

2. In the Block category, select right from the Text align drop-down to align the controls to the right of the display.

3. In the Box category, set the top margin to 0.2 ems and the right margin to 60 pixels, and select right from the Float drop-down. This will move the controls to the right of the page, while giving them a margin of 60 pixels, so that they're not up against the edge of the window.

Click OK. In Code View, select the section of markup that deals with the accessibility buttons:

File: **homepage-layout-strict.html (excerpt)**

```
<p>Page Controls</p>
<ul>
  <li><a href="#"><img src="img/control_larger.gif"
      alt="Increase Text Size" width="43" height="35" />
    </a></li>
  <li><a href="#"><img src="img/control_smaller.gif"
      alt="Decrease Text Size" width="43" height="35" />
    </a></li>
  <li><a href="#"><img src="img/control_low_graphics.gif"
      alt="Low Graphics" width="43" height="35" /></a></li>
  <li><a href="#"><img src="img/control_default_style.gif"
      alt="Default Style" width="43" height="35" /></a></li>
</ul>
```

Use the Insert Div Tag button to wrap this section in a `div` with the `controls` ID.

If you view your page in Design View, you can see that our positioning of the page elements is coming together. By using the CSS `float` property to float the tagline and controls left and right respectively, we have enabled them to display at opposite ends of the header space that remained after we added the logo: the 300 pixels of left margin that we placed on the tagline moves this element clear of the logo.

In Design View, the page controls should be outlined with a dashed line, as Dreamweaver now recognizes these as a single positioned element. If you click on the dashed line, the right margin we added will display as a crosshatched area, as shown in Figure 6.18.

## Figure 6.18. The margin on the controls `div`.

The last thing that we need to do with this top part of the header is to have the accessibility buttons display horizontally, rather than looking like a bulleted list.

Create a new CSS rule with the Advanced Selector **#controls ul**, which will style any <ul> tag inside the `controls` div. This is called a descendant selector, and is the most common type of **contextual selector**. Give this rule a margin and padding of 0 pixels on all sides within the Box category; then, do exactly the same for **#header p**. Next, create a CSS rule for **#controls li**. In the Block category, select inline from the Display drop-down, as shown in Figure 6.19.

## Figure 6.19. Selecting inline form the Display drop-down.

Display: inline

 **A Note on Syntax**

We'll use syntax similar to #controls li throughout this chapter. This selector applies styles to any li element that's contained within an element that has the ID of controls. However, it won't affect other li elements found elsewhere within the document.

Click OK, and your accessibility buttons should display on a single line. Did you notice that we didn't need to assign an ID to the div, as we have previously? We had already applied the ID controls to a div in the page, and the last three styles dealt with any ul, p or li elements located inside the controls element, so the styles are applied without our needing to apply any additional markup.

Your layout should look similar to Figure 6.20 at this point.

**Figure 6.20. The layout after the top heading area is styled.**

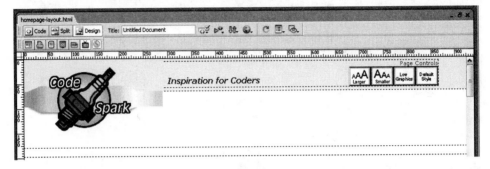

Have a look at that layout in a browser, too: Dreamweaver displays CSS fairly well, but there will likely be differences between the Dreamweaver display and the document's appearance in a Web browser. You should check your work in a browser regularly; we'll discuss browser support for CSS towards the end of this chapter.

# The Main Navigation

We can now finish off the header by styling its bottom portions, including the main navigation: that's currently hiding somewhere behind the logo.

Create a new CSS rule with the selector **#header-bottom**. Give this rule a background color of **#D9DDCF** and a height of 31 pixels to match the bottom part of the logo. Click OK.

As you've probably realized, we'll need to wrap the contents of the bottom part of the header with a div. In Code View, select the list that contains the main navigation, including the <ul> and </ul> tags, click the Insert Div Tag button and select the #header-bottom ID, as shown in Figure 6.21.

## Figure 6.21. Wrapping the main navigation.

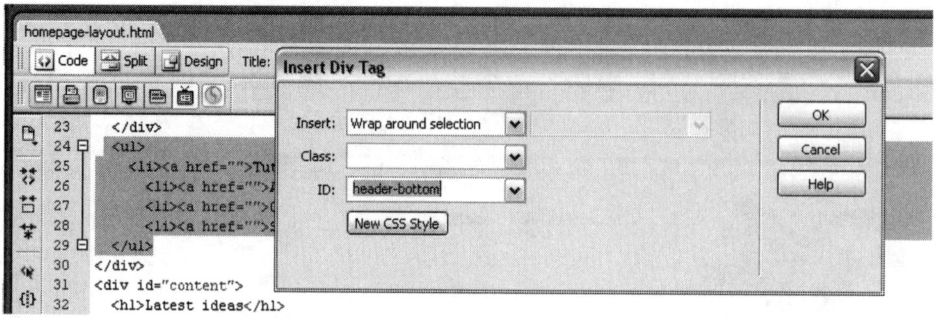

We can now address the unordered list that's being used for the main navigational elements. As with the accessibility buttons, we'll want to display these list items horizontally, rather than as a list in the default style of the browser.

First, we need to style the ul element itself. As before, we can address this ul by using a selector that defines a CSS rule for every ul within header-bottom; this saves us from adding unnecessary markup to the document. Create a new CSS rule for the selector **#header-bottom ul**.

In the Box category, give this element a margin of 0 pixels; then set the padding to 5 pixels on the top, 320 pixel on the left, and 0 pixels on the right and bottom, as shown in Figure 6.22. The left padding will push the navigation elements along, giving them clearance from the logo image.

## Figure 6.22. Using padding to clear the navigation links from the image.

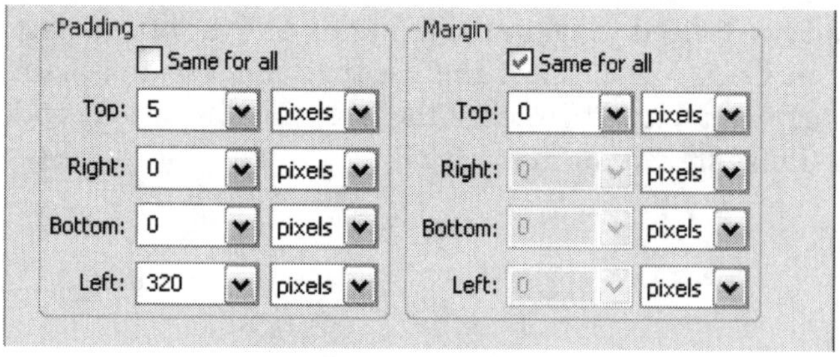

Now, create a new CSS rule for **#header-bottom li**.

Under Type, set the Font to Verdana, Arial, Helvetica, sans-serif; set the Size to 90%, the Weight to bold, and the Style to italic. Under Block, set Display to inline, which will cause the list to display horizontally. Under Box, give the li a right margin of 2.4 ems. This will space the links out across the display. Click OK. Your list of navigation links should now display horizontally within the bottom part of the header.

# Styling the Navigation Links

Next, let's tidy up the header by changing the color of our navigational links. To do this, we'll style the **pseudo-classes** of the links. Links have a number of states that can be styled, including link (a link to a page that you haven't visited yet), visited (a link to a page you have visited), hover (which occurs when you mouse over the link), and active (which occurs when you click on the link, but before the browser loads the next page). Since more than one of these may apply at once, you don't have to style all of them to style a link; in this case, we need to style just the two mutually exclusive states: link and visited.

Let's start with link. Create a new CSS rule in Dreamweaver, select Advanced as the Selector Type and enter the Selector **#header-bottom li a:link**, as illustrated in Figure 6.23. This will style any a element in its link state (a:link) within any li element that is inside header-bottom; the style won't affect any other links on the site.

**Figure 6.23. Styling the header navigational links.**

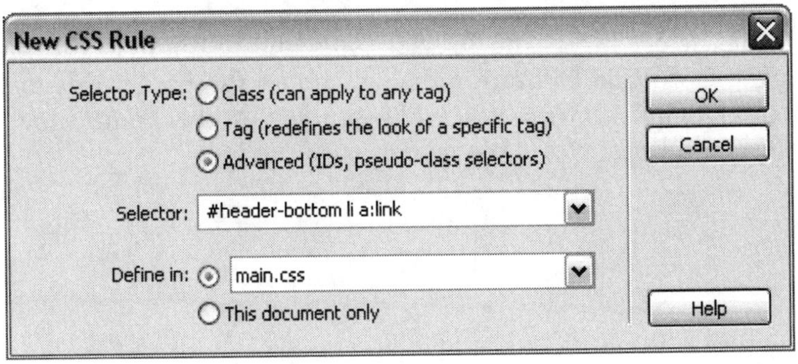

In the CSS Rule Definition dialog, select the Type category, give the links a color of **#3C582F**, and check the none checkbox in Decoration, as shown in Figure 6.24: this removes the underline that most browsers display on links.

## Figure 6.24. Setting `text-decoration` to none.

Decoration: ☐ underline
☐ overline
☐ line-through
☐ blink
☑ none

## The Question of Link Usability

In this case, the links are quite obviously a navigation element, so, even though we've removed the links' underlines, people should still instantly recognize them as links. It's a bad idea, from a usability viewpoint, to remove the underlines from non-navigational links, and to rely on some other feature to differentiate those links from the rest of the text. Many people find it difficult to differentiate between colors, and may not see the links at all; alternatively, they may think the links are simply highlighted text. The convention of using underlines to identify links is widely understood.

After clicking OK to create this style, repeat the process for **#header-bottom li a:visited**.

We'll finish off the header by removing the blue borders around the accessibility buttons. Before the advent of CSS, you may have done this by adding border="0" to every <img/> tag in the document, but with CSS we can quickly and easily remove these blue borders from every linked image in the document.

Create a new CSS rule, select Tag as the Selector Type, and find img in the Tag drop-down list. In the CSS Rule Definition dialog, choose the Border category and set Width to 0 pixels. This will turn off the blue borders. At this point, shown in Figure 6.25, you should begin to see the layout taking shape.

## Figure 6.25. The layout displaying in Firefox.

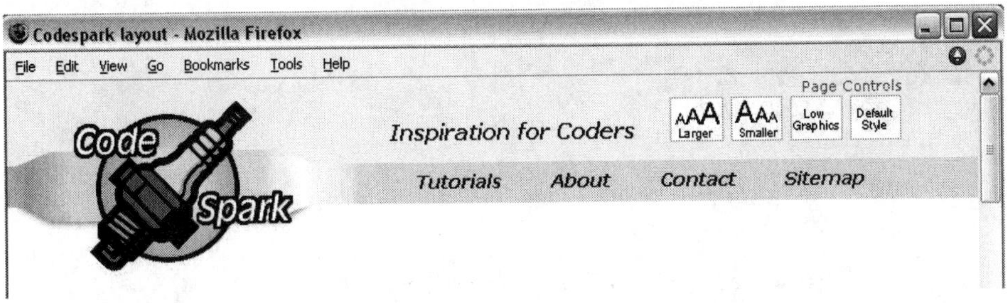

Although we have added to the document by way of wrapping certain sections in divs and spans, and giving them IDs and classes, we have not in any way affected the basic semantic structure of the document: how it will be read out in a screen reader, or displayed on a text-only device.

At this point, your style sheet should look something like the code shown below. If you're using longhand, rather than shorthand styles, it might be somewhat lengthier!

File: **inc/main.css**

```css
body {
  font-size: 1em;
  color: #000000;
  background: #FFFFFF;
  margin: 0px;
  padding: 0px;
}
#header {
  width: 100%;
}
#content {
  margin-top: 80px;
  margin-right: 320px;
  margin-left: 40px;
}
#nav {
  position: absolute;
  width: 266px;
  top: 120px;
  right: 10px;
}
#logo {
  position: absolute;
```

```
    left: Opx;
    top: Opx;
}
#header-top {
    background: #E9ECE4;
    vertical-align: bottom;
    height: 65px;
}
.tagline {
    margin: Opx Opx Opx 300px;
    float: left;
    padding-top: 2em;
    font: italic bold 100% Verdana, Arial, Helvetica, sans-serif;
    color: #3C582F;
}
#controls {
    font: 70% Verdana, Arial, Helvetica, sans-serif;
    color: #72746D;
    text-align: right;
    float: right;
    margin-top: 0.2em;
    margin-right: 60px;
}
#controls ul {
    margin: Opx;
    padding: Opx;
}
#controls p {
    margin: Opx;
    padding: Opx;
}
#controls li {
    display: inline;
}
#header-bottom {
    background: #D9DDCF;
    height: 31px;
}
#header-bottom ul {
    margin: Opx;
    padding: 5px Opx Opx 320px;
}
#header-bottom li {
    font: italic bold 90% Verdana, Arial, Helvetica, sans-serif;
    display: inline;
    margin-right: 2.4em;
```

```
}
#header-bottom li a:link {
  color: #3C582F;
  text-decoration: none;
}
#header-bottom li a:visited {
  color: #3C582F;
  text-decoration: none;
}
img {
  border: 0px;
}
```

You should be able to identify the different selectors, and see how Dreamweaver has created the style sheet using the values you've entered into the CSS dialogs. If you make any changes directly to the style sheet file itself, Dreamweaver will recognize them.

# The Properties Pane of the CSS Panel

You can also edit your CSS using the Properties Pane of the new unified CSS Panel in Dreamweaver 8, as shown in Figure 6.26. As you created your layout, you may have noticed the CSS rules that you created were displayed in the top half of the CSS Panel. If it's not already selected, select All at the top of the CSS Panel. A list of the CSS rules that you created as you styled the header area should appear in the top part of the CSS Panel. If you select any of these rules, the properties that make up that rule will display in the bottom half of the panel.

If you edit any of the properties in the panel, that change will immediately be reflected in Design View, and in your CSS file; you can also add new properties via this panel. The Properties Pane is a very useful tool for editing CSS, particularly when you've already created CSS rules, and you just want to try tweaking colors, margins, or padding: the Properties Pane lets you avoid opening up the CSS Rule Definition dialog.

**Figure 6.26. The Properties Pane of the CSS Panel.**

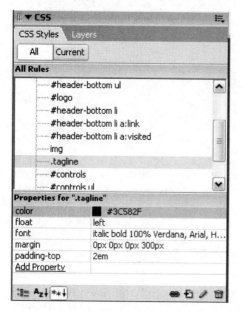

# The Content Area

It's now time to start creating rules for the main content area of the page, which we've already wrapped in a `div` with an ID of `content`. Back in Design View, create another new CSS rule just as you did for `#header`, naming this one **#content**.

In the CSS Rule Definition dialog, choose the Box category. Under Margin, deselect the Same for all checkbox, and set a top margin of 80 pixels, to provide 80 pixels of space between the top of the content and the bottom of the header. Give it a right margin of 320 pixels, which will leave space for the navigation menu, and a left margin of 40 pixels, to provide 40 pixels of space between the content and the left-hand edge of the browser window. These measurements are applied to the dialog in Figure 6.27.

Select the Type category and select Verdana, Arial, Helvetica, sans-serif as the font, giving it a size of 80%. When you click OK, this change will take effect immediately, as we've already got a `div` with the ID `content`. If you select the `content` `div` in Design View by clicking on its dotted border, as shown in Figure 6.28, the content area is outlined, and the margins that we created display clearly as crosshatched areas.

## Figure 6.27. Setting the margins for #content.

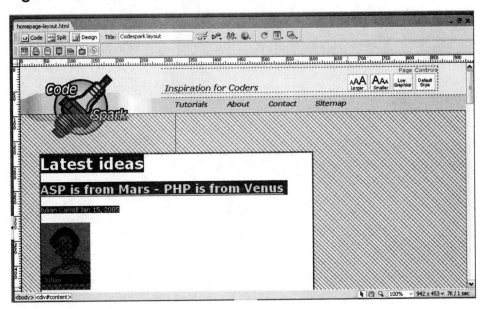

## Figure 6.28. content selected in Design View

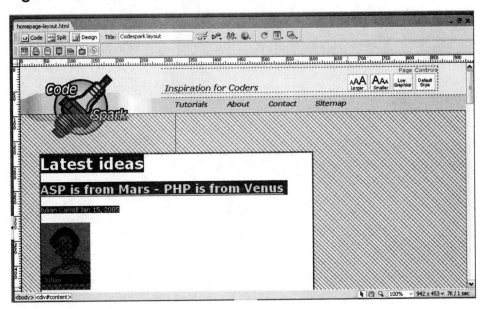

# The Content Sections

The page content is divided into article boxes, as shown in Figure 6.29. Our next job is to create these blocks of content; then, we'll style their contents.

## Figure 6.29. Four of the six article boxes.

*Latest Ideas*

### ASP is from Mars - PHP is from Venus

Julian Carroll          Jan 15, 2005

Praesent sagittis est. Sed massa sapien, ultrices auctor, facilisis nec, posuere a, wisi. Fusce diam lacus, semper sed, euismod interdum, varius quis, odio. Maecenas lobortis.

Nunc pretium, sapien eu mollis pellentesque,

### IIS Security - Tightening the .Net

Brigitte Walker          Jan 11, 2005

Praesent sagittis est. Sed massa sapien, ultrices auctor, facilisis nec, posuere a, wisi. Fusce diam lacus, semper sed, euismod interdum, varius quis, odio. Maecenas lobortis.

Nunc pretium, sapien eu mollis pellentesque,

### CSS: Designing with Style, not Class

Georgina Laidlaw          Jan 7, 2005

Praesent sagittis est. Sed massa sapien, ultrices auctor, facilisis nec, posuere a, wisi. Fusce diam lacus, semper sed, euismod interdum, varius quis, odio. Maecenas lobortis.

Nunc pretium, sapien eu mollis pellentesque,

### Java - Servlets yourself right

Thomas Rutter          Jan 3, 2005

Praesent sagittis est. Sed massa sapien, ultrices auctor, facilisis nec, posuere a, wisi. Fusce diam lacus, semper sed, euismod interdum, varius quis, odio. Maecenas lobortis.

Nunc pretium, sapien eu mollis pellentesque,

Using the Advanced Selector Type, create a new CSS rule for the selector `#content .homepage-box`. This descendant selector will apply to anything with the class `homepage-box` inside a `div` with the ID `content`. In the Box category, set the value of Float to left and set a width of 49%. In the Border category, uncheck all of the Same for all checkboxes, and add a solid, 1 pixel top border with a light green color of **#8A9877**. Click OK. We now need to apply the class to the blocks on our homepage.

Select the contents of the first box from the heading, "ASP is from Mars - PHP is from Venus," right down to the end of the paragraph before the next heading.

If you do this in Design View, flick into Code View to make sure you've selected all of the tags.

Click the Insert Div Tag button, and from the Class drop-down select homepage-box, as shown in Figure 6.30.

## Figure 6.30. Inserting a `div` tag with the class `homepage-box`.

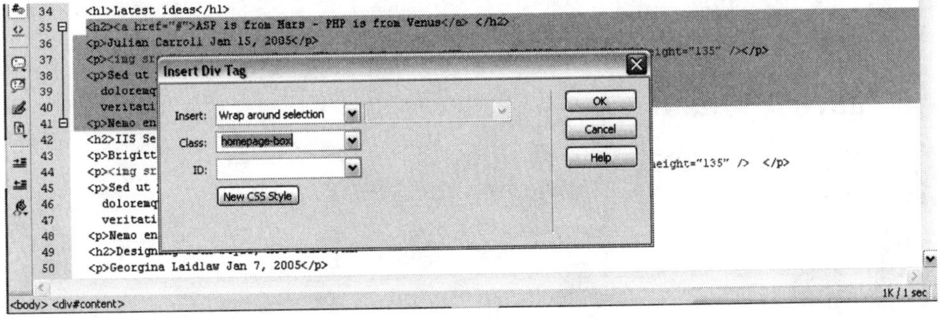

Click OK to wrap the selection in a `div` tag. Now, select the next box's contents and repeat the process. As we have created a class for our homepage boxes, we can apply it multiple times to as many boxes as we have; if we'd used an ID, we could only apply it once. Continue to apply this class to each of the six sections of the homepage content.

Once that's done, in Design View you should see that you have two columns of content within the content area. We have achieved this by using the CSS `float` property. Floating the boxes left in a confined area with a width of 49%[1] means that we can fit two boxes into the full width of the content area, as shown in Figure 6.31.

If you open the page in a browser, you'll see that our layout is coming along nicely! But, if you resize the window, you may well spot a small problem with this layout. Sometimes the boxes will seem to jump around: sometimes only one will display on a line, while at other times, three or four may display.

---

[1] Why not 50%? Some current browsers like to round up fractional pixel dimensions, so 50% plus 50% can sometimes mean more than 100%, which would break our layout.

## Figure 6.31. Viewing the floated article boxes.

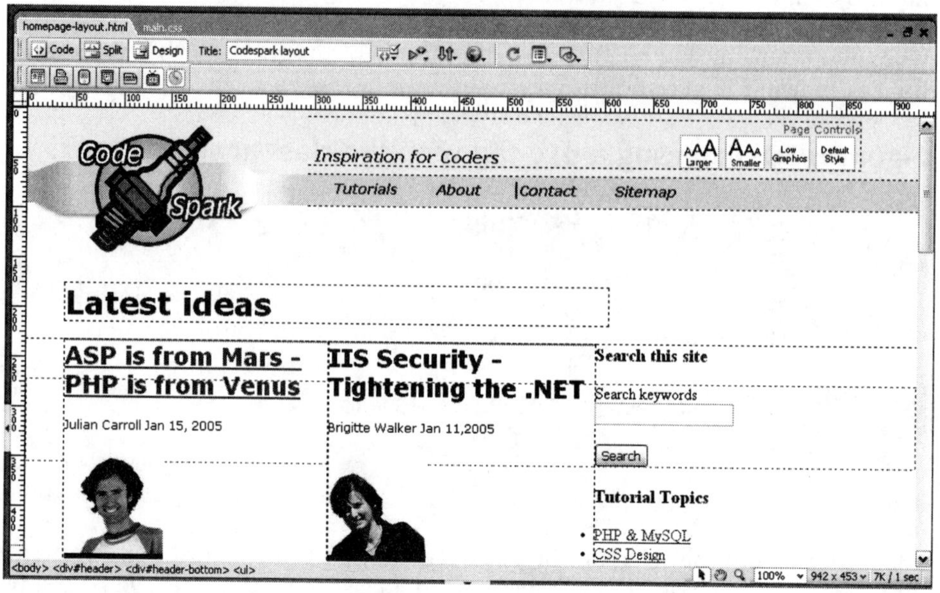

We can cure this browser bug by adding an empty `div` between the rows of homepage boxes (i.e. after every two boxes). Adding unnecessary markup does constitute a hack that we'll use to get the browser to behave exactly as we want it to; however, importantly, this additional code will not damage the accessibility of our carefully crafted document: `divs` and `spans` are generally ignored by alternative devices. This empty `div` is assigned the `clear` CSS property to make sure that no more content appears in the current row.

When using floats, you'll often need to do this clearing of the next element. In fact, we'll need to do so again later, when we style some more of the content. So, let's make a reusable `clear` class.

### The Clear Effect

*Tip*

You don't always need to add a redundant element in order to get the clearing effect: sometimes, you can instead add the `clear` property to the CSS rules for the element that follows the floated section.

Create a new CSS rule with a class selector of `.clear`, and in the Box section of the CSS Rule Definition dialog, set Clear to both.

Then, back in your document, switch into Code View. Place your cursor after the closing `div` of the second homepage box, and before the opening `div` of the third.

Click the Insert Div Tag button, select the class clear, ensure that At Insertion point is selected, and click OK. Dreamweaver will insert the tag along with some dummy text. Delete this text, so that all you're left with is the following:

File: **homepage-layout-strict.html (excerpt)**

```
<div class="clear"></div>
```

Repeat this process in between the fourth and fifth homepage boxes. The problem of the boxes jumping about should now be resolved in all browsers.

# Using Dreamweaver Visual Aids

To help see how these boxes relate to each other, you can switch on Dreamweaver's Layout Block Background visual aid. To turn it on or off, select View > Visual Aids > Layout Block Background. This displays each element with a different background color, as shown in Figure 6.32—not the prettiest of effects, but very helpful in visualizing how your CSS is positioning the various page elements.

## Figure 6.32. Layout Block Backgrounds turned on.

With a basic structure in place for this section, we can concentrate on how we want the elements to look.

# The Headings

Let's style the headings that appear on this page. Here, we have a level one heading, "Latest Ideas," as well as level two and three headings contained within the boxes. We'll start with the level one heading, creating a new CSS rule using the selector **#content h1**; this rule will style all **h1** elements within the **content div**.

1.  In the Type category, set Weight to bold, Style to italic, Size to 120% and the Color to **#3C582F**.

2.  In the Block category, set Text align to right.

3.  In the Box category, set the bottom padding to 0.2 ems. Set all other padding to 0 pixels, and all of the margins to 0 pixels as well (you can use the Same for all checkbox if you wish).

Click OK, and the styles should automatically apply.

To style the level two headings, create a new CSS rule for **#content h2**.

1.  In the Type category, set the value of Weight to bold, Size to 120%, and Color to **#3C582F**.

2.  In the Box category, set Padding to Top 0 pixels, Right 0 pixels, Bottom 0.1 ems and Left 0 pixels. Set Margin to Top 1.5 ems, Right 0.5 ems, Bottom 0 pixels, and Left 0.5 ems.

Our linked headings now display with the default link color. We can now create for links a style that will affect any links within the **content div**, including these headings. To do so, create a CSS rule for the selector **#content a:link** and simply set the color to **#3C582F** in the Type category. Repeat for **#content a:visited**. Finally, create a CSS rule for the selector **#content h3**. In the Type category, set the Size to 100%, the Color to **#000000**, and click OK.

# The Contents of the Homepage Boxes

Our boxes contain various elements that need to be styled with CSS. I'm going to start with the boxes that detail the latest articles; I want the author picture to display alongside the text about the author, instead of above it. We can achieve this using the `float` property.

Create a new CSS rule for the selector **#content .homepage-box .author-pic**:

1.  In the Box category, set the value of Float to left.

2.  Set your Margins: the right margin to 20 pixels, and the left to 4 pixels.

3.  Set Width to 104 pixels.

Having created this class, we need to apply it to the author images. Select the first of the four author images, and use the Property Inspector to apply the class, as shown in Figure 6.33.

## Figure 6.33. Using the Property Inspector to apply the class author-pic.

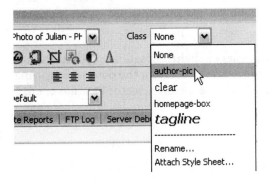

Apply this class to all four of the author images.

The article boxes are really starting to take shape now, but the article text doesn't look so great: the text of an article on the left runs right up to the article on the right. Let's add a margin to the right-hand edge of any paragraph within a homepage box. Create a new CSS rule for the selector **#content .homepage-box p**, and in the Box category, apply a right margin of 20 pixels. To highlight the author credit and article date, let's establish a separate class. Create a new CSS rule for **#content p.authorcredit**.

1.  In the Type category, set a Color of **#8A9877**.

2.  In the Block category, set the value of Text align to right.

Apply this class to the author credits by selecting each credit and, using the Property Inspector as illustrated in Figure 6.34, applying the `authorcredit` class to it. Make sure you select the entire author credit: you can do this by clicking the <p> in the Tag Selector at the bottom of the document window.

### Figure 6.34. Applying the `authorcredit` class to the author credit line.

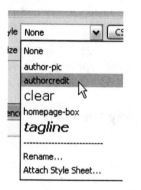

In our original page design, the date appears in slightly smaller text than the author name. We can achieve this tweak by creating a class for the date and applying it with the help of a `span`. Create a new CSS rule for the selector `.authorcredit .date`, then:

1.  In Type, set the Font Size to 80%.

2.  In Block, set Vertical Alignment to top.

3.  In Box, set the left Margin to 1 em.

Click OK, then select the date text in the first article box. One way to apply this class using a `span` is to right-click on the selection, and choose Quick Tag Editor.... This process is depicted in Figure 6.35.

**Figure 6.35. Selecting** Quick Tag Editor....

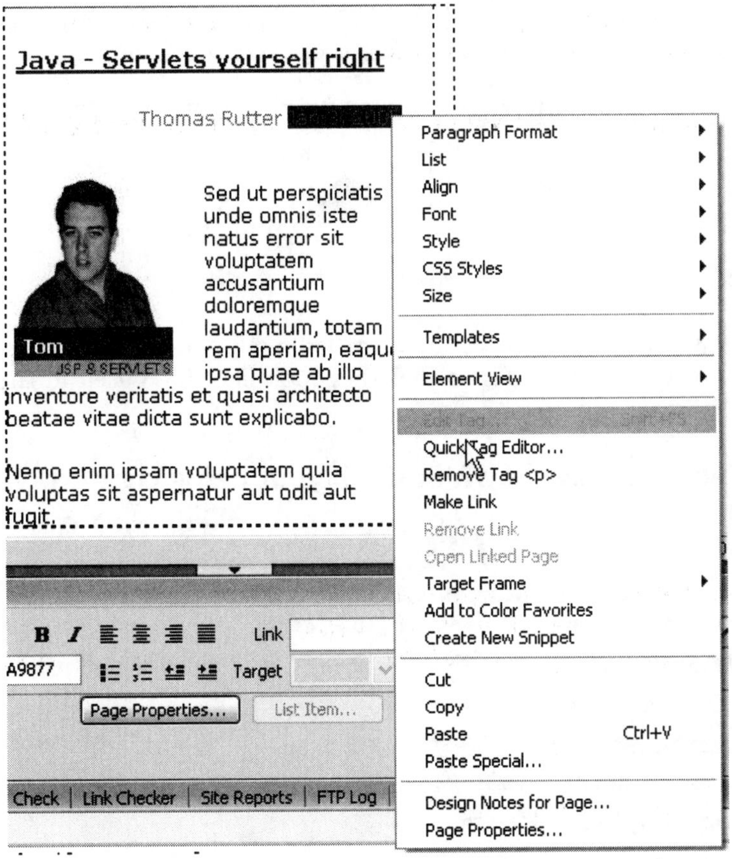

A box will open; here, you can enter the opening tag of the element that you wish to wrap around the selection. Into this box, type **&lt;span class="date"&gt;**, as shown in Figure 6.36.

You can either repeat this process to apply the `date` class to the other article dates on the page, or take a handy shortcut: after selecting each date, simply select date from the Style menu in the Property Inspector. Automatically, Dreamweaver will create for you the `span` required to apply the class.

### Figure 6.36. Using the Quick Tag Editor to add a span to the date.

Designing with Style,
Wrap tag: <span class="date">
Georgina Laidlaw
Thomas Rutter Jan 3, 2005
Sed ut perspiciatis
Sed ut perspiciatis

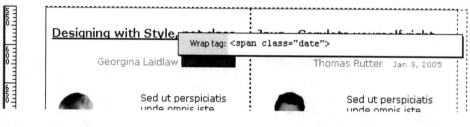

## Styling Tables

We have a table that displays a list of the latest articles in one of our article boxes. We can use CSS to style these tables so that they look like those used in the design layout, as shown in Figure 6.37.

### Figure 6.37. The tables as shown in the layout being created.

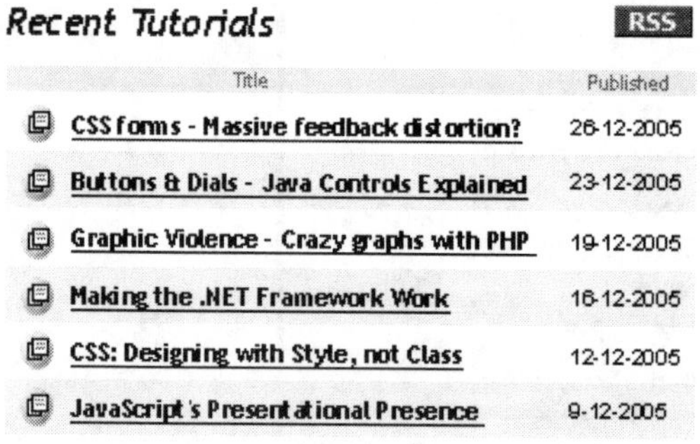

Recent Tutorials
RSS
Title
Published
CSS forms - Massive feedback distortion?
26-12-2005
Buttons & Dials - Java Controls Explained
23-12-2005
Graphic Violence - Crazy graphs with PHP
19-12-2005
Making the .NET Framework Work
16-12-2005
CSS: Designing with Style, not Class
12-12-2005
JavaScript's Presentational Presence
9-12-2005

The "Recent Tutorials" header has already been styled, along with the other level two headings on the page. In order to make this section look like the example in the layout, we need to add a button that can eventually be used to link to an RSS feed.

Place the cursor just before the leading R in "Recent Tutorials," and hit **Enter** to create a line above the header. This new line will be created as a heading, so use the Property Inspector to make it a paragraph. Insert into this line the `rss.gif` button image using the Insert Image button in the toolbar; the results are shown in Figure 6.38.

## Figure 6.38. The `rss.gif` image appearing.

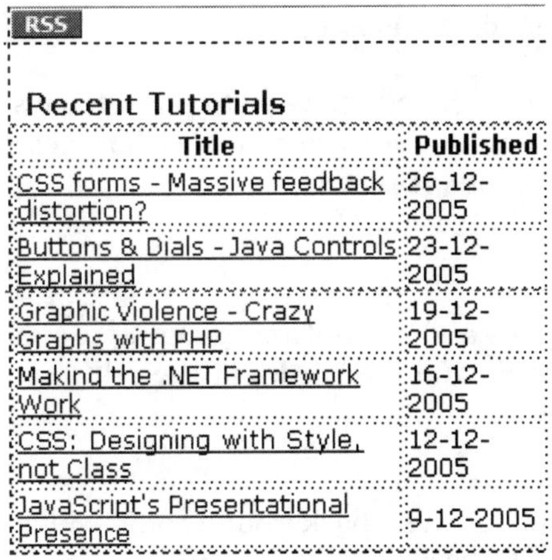

To position this button to the right of the heading, we can float it right. Create a new CSS rule, choose the Advanced selector type, and type a selector of **.homepage-box .rss**. In the Box category, simply set Float to right, and the Width to 40 pixels; then click OK.

In Design View, select the <p> tag that wraps the RSS image, and apply the `rss` class to it. The RSS image should now display to the right of the heading.

Let's now style any tables that appear within these content boxes. Create a new CSS rule for the selector **#content .homepage-box table**. This selector specifies any table located inside any element with the class `homepage-box` that appears inside an element with the ID `content`. In the Box category, apply a width of 98% and a top margin of 1 em, to allow some space between this element and the one above it. Click OK.

We also want to add to this selector a property that cannot be added through the CSS dialog. To add it, select the newly created #content .homepage-box table selector in the All Rules list of the CSS Panel; the rule's properties will be listed. Click Add Property, and type **border-collapse** into the drop-down list that appears. In the Value field to the right, select collapse from the drop-down list. This property will remove the space between the cells in the table when they display in the browser. Save and close `main.css`.

We can now style the column headings: the <th> tags. Create a new CSS rule for **#content .homepage-box th**.

1.   Under Type, set Color to **#72746D**, and Size to 70%.

2.   Under Background, set the background color to **#EAEAE2**.

Click OK: the above changes should take effect immediately, styling the table's header row. We can now create some basic rules for the td elements within these tables. Create a new CSS rule for **#content .homepage-box td**.

1.   Under Type, set Size to 90%.

2.   Under Box, set the top padding to 0.3 ems and the bottom padding to 0.3 ems, so that space appears between the text and the border of the cell.

Click OK to see the rule applied.

In this design, we wish to style alternating rows to have a background color, which makes the table easier to read. We can add this row color by creating a special class for every second row. Create a new CSS rule for the selector **#content .homepage-box tr.even**. The tr.even part of this selector restricts this style rule to tr elements with the class even. Under Background, specify a background color of **#F4F4F0**.

Apply this class to the even rows of both tables by selecting the <tr> tag using the Tag Selector at the bottom of the document window, and applying the class using the Style drop-down in the Property Inspector. At this point, you should have a table that looks something like Figure 6.39.

## Figure 6.39. The tables after styling the alternate row colors.

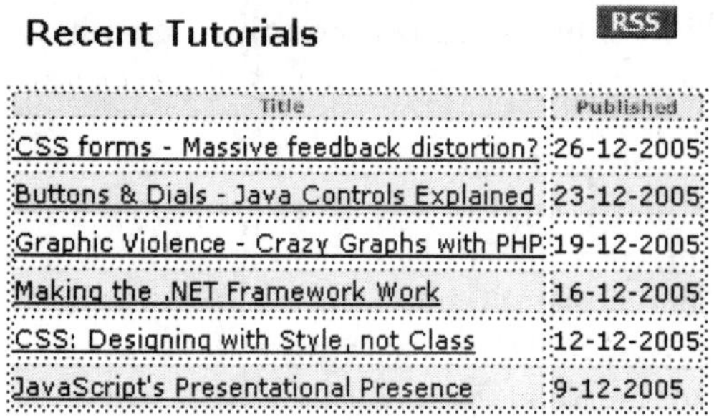

Our final step will be to add the small images that appear to the left of each row; we'll do so using specially designed classes. First, let's create a basic bullet class.

Create a new CSS rule for the selector **#content .homepage-box td.bullet**.

1. In the Background category, browse for a background image by clicking the Browse button. Select **tbl_bullet.gif** from the code archive.

2. Also in the Background category, select no repeat from the Repeat drop-down, and set Horizontal position to 3 pixels.

3. In the Box category, set Padding left to 28 pixels. This will move the text along so that it does not display on top of the background image we've just added.

Apply this class to the first cell in each row of the table by selecting the <td> using the Tag Inspector, and setting the class using the Property Inspector.

After applying the class to all the rows, you'll probably notice that on the even rows, the white background color of the bullet will display as shown in Figure 6.40.

## Figure 6.40. The bullet's white background showing on even rows.

With such a pale background color, you could probably fix this issue simply by recreating the bullet with a transparent background in your graphics application. However, if your table rows had very different background colors (for example, white and deep blue) you would probably need to create images for each row.

Rather than applying different classes to the td in each row, we can use the fact that the even tr already has a different class applied to display a different image (with the correct background color) in even rows.

Create a new CSS rule for **#content .homepage-box tr.even td.bullet**.

1. In Background, select the image for the backgrounds of the even rows: **tbl_bullet_even.gif**. Once again, set this to no repeat, and set its Horizontal position to 3 pixels.

2. While you're in Background, set the background color to **#F4F4F0**.

3.  In the Block category, set the left padding to 28 pixels. This will move the text along so that it doesn't overlap the background image we just added.

Click OK. This style will apply automatically because the complex selector that we're using for this rule relies on the classes we have already set up in the document: we have defined it for any `td` with a class of `bullet` within a `tr` with a class of `even`.

# The Browser Statistics Section

The end is almost in sight! We just need to style the section of the content area that displays browser statistics, as illustrated in Figure 6.41.

## Figure 6.41. The browser stats section of our design layout.

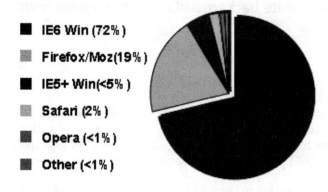

*Browser Stats - December - 04*

- IE6 Win (72%)
- Firefox/Moz(19%)
- IE5+ Win(<5%)
- Safari (2%)
- Opera (<1%)
- Other (<1%)

December saw Firefox's market share jump 1% across all major site categories, presumably on the back of it's 1.0 launch push. Increases of as much as 3% were observed in some technically-oriented categories.

Overall, though IE6 continued the gradual decrease in market share it has endured since it held 92% in November 2003, it since enjoys 4 times greater usage than any other browser.

The heading should already be styled, as we've styled all `h2` headings within `content`. So, the first thing we'll want to do is to move the pie chart image to display to the right of the list. We do this using the `float` property.

1. Create a new CSS rule for **`#content .homepage-box .browser-stats-image`**.

2. In the Box category, set the value of Float to right and give it a top margin of 10 pixels, a bottom margin of 20 pixels, and a width of 180 pixels.

3. Click OK.

4. Apply the `browser-stats-image` class by selecting the pie chart image and using the class drop-down in the Property Inspector.

After applying this class, you'll note that the paragraph below the list moves up to display alongside the image, because the image has been floated.

To stop this from happening, we can use the `clear` CSS property. Create a new CSS rule for the selector **`#content .homepage-box .browser-stats-discussion`**, and under Box set Clear to right. Click OK. Then, to apply the rule, select the two paragraphs of discussion following the list (switch into Code View if necessary to ensure that you've got both pairs of `<p>` and `</p>` tags fully selected), and then click the Insert Div Tag button in the Layout section of the Insert Toolbar. With Wrap around selection selected, pick browser-stats-discussion from the Class drop-down list. Our discussion paragraphs will now clear the image, to begin on a new line below it.

To style the list, create a new CSS rule for the selector **`#content .homepage-box .browser-stats-list`**, and, under Type, set Weight to bold. Click OK, then select the `<ul>` tag within the Tag Selector and apply the new `browser-stats-list` class. Each of the list's bullet points has a different colored block as its bullet: these correspond to the colors on the pie chart. To create this effect, we will need to establish a class for each browser represented in the stats, and apply those classes to the individual `<li>` tags.

1. Start with the IE6 list item, creating a new CSS rule for the selector **`#content .homepage-box .browser-stats-list li.ie6`**.

2. In the List category, browse for the bullet image `ie6-bullet.gif`.

3. Click OK.

4. Select the first list item and apply the `ie6` class.

5.  Repeat for the rest of the list items: match `moz` with `moz-bullet.gif`; `ie5` with `ie5-bullet.gif`; `opera` with `opera-bullet.gif`; `safari` with `safari-bullet.gif`; and `other` with `otherbrowser-bullet.gif`.

The results are shown in Figure 6.42.

## Figure 6.42. The tables and browser stats in Firefox.

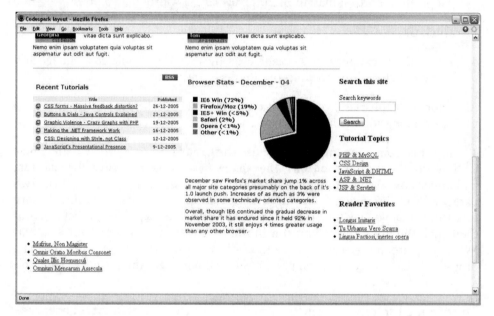

# The Sidebar

We can now move on to the final section of our layout: the sidebar. In Design View, you can clearly see that the content leaves a margin down the right-hand side of the page. We're going to position the sidebar within this space.

Create a new CSS rule with the advanced selector **#nav**. In the CSS Rule Definition dialog, select the Positioning category. Set Type to absolute, and set Width to 266 pixels—the width of the sidebar. In the Placement section, set Top to 120 pixels, and Right to 10 pixels, which will position the navigation bar into the space left by the margin of the content area, as shown in Figure 6.43.

## Figure 6.43. Setting the position for nav.

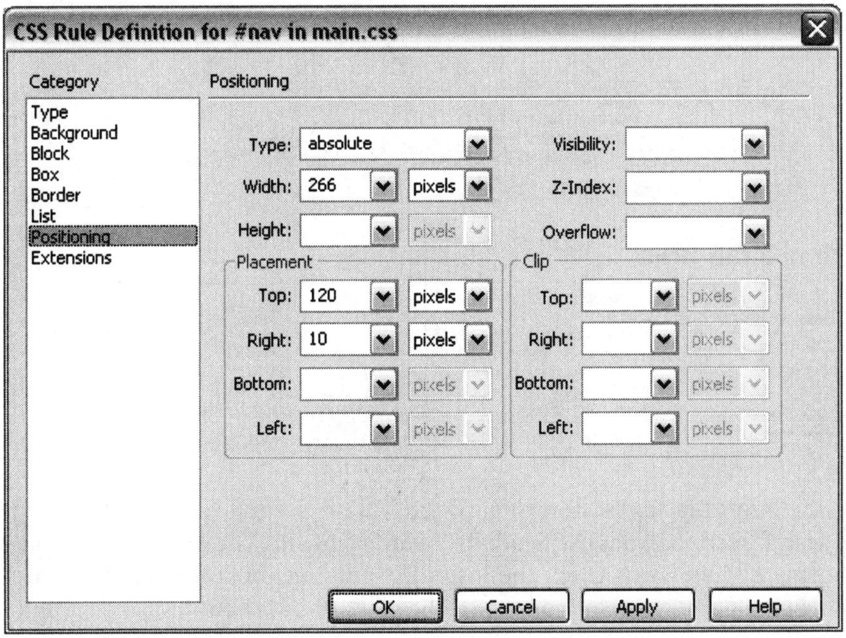

Select the Background category. We're going to add the top image of this panel using a background image. Select the image nav_top.gif, then set Repeat to no repeat and the background color to **#EAEAE2**. Click OK.

A background with a curved top should appear on the sidebar, as shown in Figure 6.44. The curved top is achieved by the background image, which is a simple curved rectangle top with a color that's the same as the background.

The sidebar is split into sections, each of which has a heading. To create these sections, make a new CSS rule for **#nav .section**.

1.  In Background, select the background image nav_headings.gif and set Repeat to no repeat.

2.  In Box, set top padding to 20 pixels and top margin to 30 pixels.

3.  Click OK.

**Figure 6.44. The sidebar after the background color and image are added.**

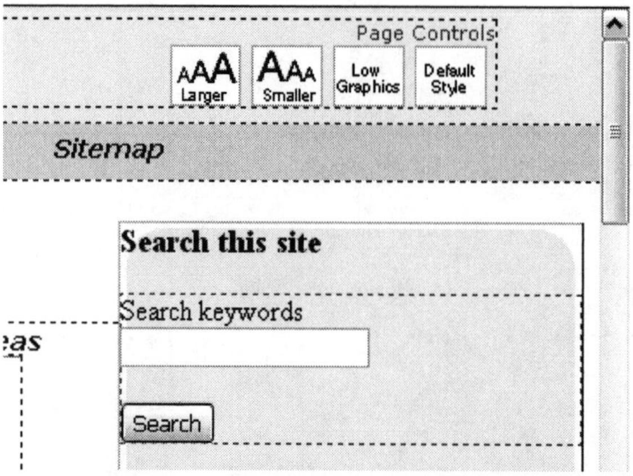

We'll use the Insert Div Tag button to apply this class. Switch to Code View and select the search section, from the heading "Search this site," down to and including the closing `</form>` tag. Click the Insert Div Tag button and select the class `section` to wrap the selection in a `div` with the class of `section`.

Repeat this for the other sections of the sidebar. The background image bar should display roughly underneath the level three headings.

We can now style the headings by creating a new CSS rule for **#nav h3**.

1.  Under Type, set Size to 120%, Font to Verdana, Arial, Helvetica, sans-serif, and Color to **#3C582F**.

2.  Under Block, set Text align to center.

3.  Under Box, set padding to 0 pixels, top margin to 0.2 ems, and bottom margin to 2 ems.

4.  Click OK.

We now need to look at some more specific styles for the different sections of the sidebar. Let's look at the search box first.

# The Search Box

Create a new CSS rule for **#nav p** to style the p element that wraps our search form field and its label.

### No <p>?

If you chose to create the design using the XHTML Transitional layout, you might not have a paragraph element wrapping your text box and its label. Add one now to follow these steps as they are described.

We need only create one property for this rule: go to the Box category and set the left margin to 35 pixels, then click OK.

Next, create a new CSS rule for **#nav label**, to style the label of the search box.

1. In the Type category, set Size to 70%, Font to Verdana, Arial, Helvetica, sans-serif, Weight to bold and Color to **#3C582F**.

2. Click OK.

The last thing that we need to do in this area is to make a new CSS rule for **#nav .searchtxt**. This will style the form field itself.

1. In the Type category, set Font to Verdana, Arial, Helvetica, sans-serif.

2. In the Box category, set Width to 120 pixels.

3. In the Border category, apply a solid, 1 pixel border with a color of **#7F9DB9**.

4. Click OK.

## Figure 6.45. The search section of the sidebar after styling the form.

![Search this Site form with Search keywords label and Search button]

Select the search form field and apply the `searchtxt` class using the Property Inspector. Your results should replicate those shown in Figure 6.45.

# The Topics List

The next thing we need to do is to style the list of topics. This is the section that appears after the search box, giving users a quick route to the topics of their choice.

1. Create a new CSS rule named **#nav ul.topics**.

2. In the Box category, set Padding to 0 pixels, the right margin to 20 pixels, and the left margin to 35 pixels.

3. In the List category, set Type to none to remove the bullets from the list.

4. Click OK.

5. Apply the `topics` class to the topics list by selecting the `<ul>` tag using the Tag Selector, then applying the class with the Property Inspector.

Let's style the individual `li` elements within this list.

1. Create a new CSS rule named **#nav ul.topics li**.

2. Under Type, set Font to Verdana, Arial, Helvetica, sans-serif, Size to 90%, and Color to **#3C582F**.

3. Under Background, set the background color to **#D9DDCF**. Browse for the image `nav-topics-bullet.gif`, set Repeat to no repeat, set Horizontal position to 4 pixels, and Vertical position to center.

4. Under Box, set top padding to 0.2 ems, right padding to 0.4 ems, bottom padding to 0.3 ems, and left padding to 26 pixels.

5. Under Border, the top and left borders should be 1 pixel, solid, with a color of **#EAEAE2**; the right and bottom borders should be 1 pixel, solid, with a color of **#72746D**.

6. Click OK to create the list styles shown in Figure 6.46.

## Figure 6.46. The border settings for the list items.

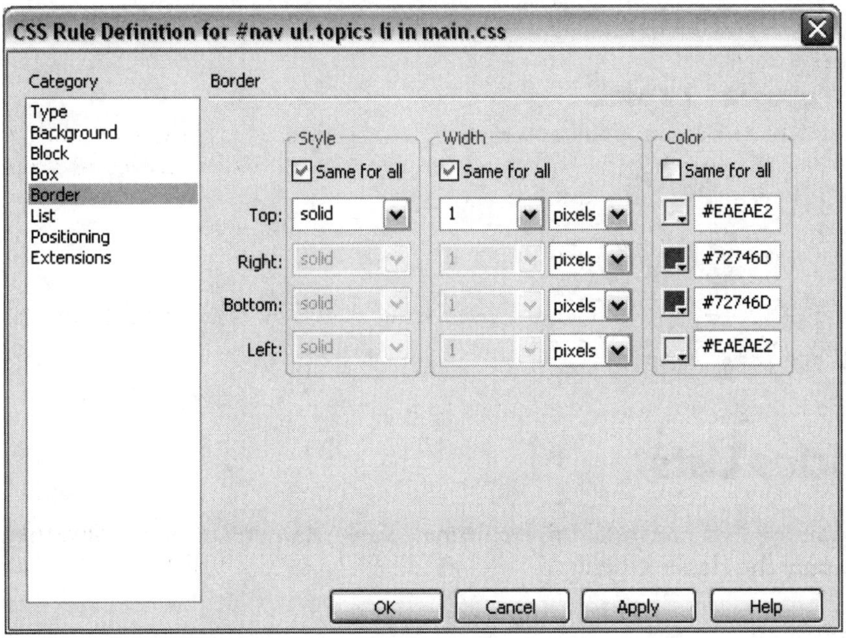

The final step with this list is to style the links within it. Create a new CSS rule for the selector **#nav ul.topics li a:link**.

1.  Set Weight to bold, Color to **#3C582F**, and Text decoration to none.

2.  Click OK.

Repeat this for **#nav ul.topics li a:visited**. The results should display as shown in Figure 6.47.

**Figure 6.47. The completed topics list.**

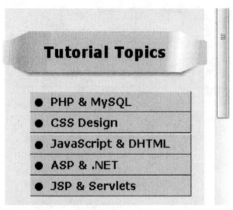

# The Articles Lists

The remaining lists are in a simpler format, so we can create our styles, then simply apply the class to the list.

1.  Create a new CSS rule for **#nav ul.list**.

2.  In the Box category, set the padding to 0 pixels, the right margin to 20 pixels, and the left margin to 60 pixels.

3.  In the List category, browse for the image nav-list-bullet.gif.

4.  Click OK.

5.  Select each of the <ul> tags of the lists and apply the list class.

6.  Create a new CSS rule for **#nav ul.list a:link**.

7.  In the Type category select Font Verdana, Arial, Helvetica, sans-serif; set Size to 80% and Color to **#3C582F**.

8.  Click OK.

9.  Repeat the links styling for **#nav ul.list a:visited**.

# Rounding Out the Sidebar

The very final step for our sidebar is to add the bottom, curved image. To do this, place your cursor outside of the final `</div>` tag that matches the last opening `<div class="section">`. This should be the `</div>` that immediately follows the last `</ul>`. You may need to switch into Code View to do this, as you don't want the image to end up inside a list item.

Insert an image and browse for `nav_bottom.gif`. In the Image Tag Accessibility dialog that displays, select `<empty>` for Alternate text: this is a layout image,[2] so screen reader and text browser users don't need to know that it's there. Leave Long description as it is, and click OK.

If you preview this page in Internet Explorer and take a look at the bottom of the sidebar, you should see part of the background color showing through the curved bottom image, as in Figure 6.48.

## Figure 6.48. The background color showing below the image.

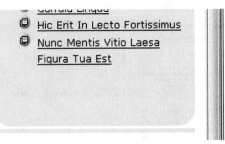

We can solve this problem by setting the image to display as a block level element. To do this, create a new CSS rule for the selector `.displayblock`. The only thing we need to do in this rule is go to the Block category and set the value of Display to block. Click OK, select the bottom image and apply the `displayblock` class to it.

---

[2]Yes, this is an example of non-semantic markup. The image will exist in the HTML document for no reason other than to provide decoration when the document displays in visual browsers. The draft CSS3 specification allows for multiple backgrounds for a single element, which would allow us to achieve this effect with purely semantic markup, but as of this writing, Safari is the only browser to support this specification. In the meantime, we'll do our best to prevent this presentational markup from impacting the document's accessibility.

If you now refresh your page in the browser, you'll find that the line of background color has disappeared.

# CSS Validation and Browser Testing

Your layout is now complete! You should hopefully see something like the screenshot in Figure 6.49 in Dreamweaver. The next step is to check your work in a variety of browsers, and to validate the markup and the CSS to make sure you haven't introduced any problems.

## Figure 6.49. The completed layout.

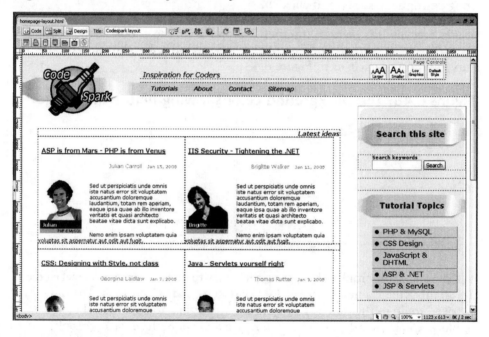

## Validating the Code

The first step is to validate your XHTML document. We checked the basic document at the end of the last chapter, before we began work on the CSS, but it is possible that we have introduced a problem, perhaps incorrectly nesting a `div`, or making use of a deprecated element. Validate the document as you did in Chapter 4. If errors are returned, locate and fix them.

The next step is to validate the CSS. Unfortunately, Dreamweaver does not have an inbuilt CSS validator, but we can use the W3C's online validator[3]. As our file is not online as yet, the easiest way to validate it is simply to paste its contents into the box on the validation page. Open main.css, copy the entire contents of the file to the clipboard, and paste them into the large text box in the validator section Validate by direct input, as shown in Figure 6.50.

## Figure 6.50. The CSS Validator.

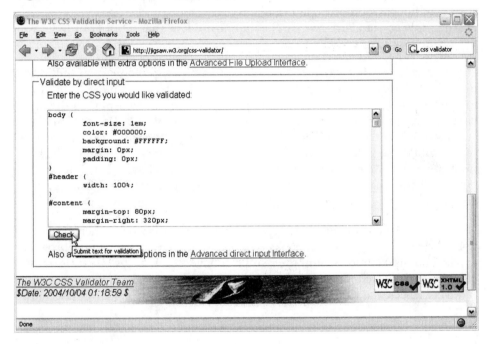

Click the Check button, and the validator will return a page that indicates whether or not your CSS is valid. As we have used Dreamweaver to write almost all of our CSS, the validator should return, "No error or warning found". If it does, you have a valid CSS document.

---

[3] http://jigsaw.w3.org/css-validator/

# Browser Testing

As I've built this site, I've been checking my work in the Firefox Web browser.[4] This is a good browser to use for checking, as it is one of the most standards-compliant browsers available. Just as we are working to comply with standards, browser manufacturers look to the standards when they write their browsers. Newer browsers, such as Firefox and the latest versions of Internet Explorer, Netscape and Opera, generally have better standards support than their predecessors, although Internet Explorer 6 still leaves much to be desired. As we are working to Web standards, we can be more confident that a newer browser will display our work correctly.

At the time of writing, far more people use Internet Explorer than any other browser: obviously, we can't ignore them. Bugs with Internet Explorer's interpretation of CSS tend to be well-documented, as everyone has to deal with them. By working in a standards compliant browser, then validating your CSS and markup, you stand a good chance of being able to solve any problems quickly and easily. You should be able to perform a quick Web search on any Internet Explorer problems you encounter, and find a fix. If you work to have your page display correctly in Internet Explorer first and foremost, you may well find your site is almost impossible to get working without error in any other browser!

Checking our layout in IE6 didn't give me any nasty surprises. There are a few slight differences, but nothing looks wrong. I also have various other browsers installed on my Windows computer, so I can have a look at the site in Netscape 7 and Opera 7, as well. These displays are shown in Figure 6.51. If you have access to a Mac, check the site in Safari, the browser of choice for many Mac OS X users.

---

[4] http://www.mozilla.org/products/firefox/

## Figure 6.51. The site as displayed in Opera, Netscape and Internet Explorer 6 on Windows.

### Get a Different Perspective

If you don't have access to other browsers or operating systems, an excellent way to check the display of sites in a range of browsers is through Websites such as Browsercam,[5] which offers a great number of broswers, and Browsershots,[6] which offers mainly Linux and Mac OS X-based browsers.

Since the site looks good in newer browsers, you might decide to consider a couple of dinosaurs: Internet Explorer 5.01 and 5.5. These old browsers are still used

---

[5] http://www.browsercam.com/
[6] http://browsershots.org/

by many people, though their CSS support is very spotty. Previously, users couldn't run more than one version of IE on their computers, which meant that testing Websites for use on older versions of IE was very difficult. Thankfully, a workaround has been found: you can now download and install older versions of Internet Explorer[7] alongside your current version.

On viewing our site in IE 5.5, I see immediately that there's a problem. If you look at the screenshot in Figure 6.52, you'll see that the homepage boxes are displayed one after the other, instead of appearing in two columns.

## Figure 6.52. The homepage as rendered by Internet Explorer 5.5.

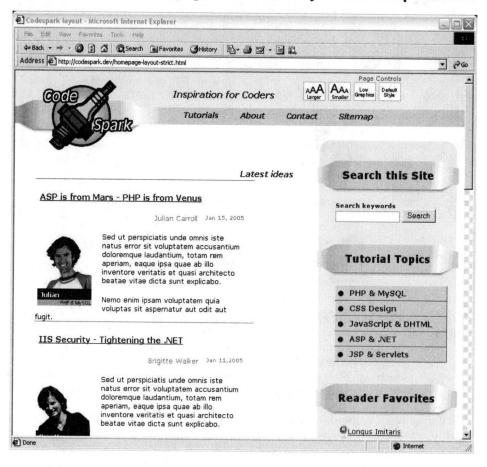

---

[7] http://www.skyzyx.com/downloads/

You might think that, for a site aimed at Web designers who are likely to have the most up-to-date browsers, this doesn't really matter. However, the bug that causes this problem is very common, so let's have a look at how we can deal with it.

# Fixing the Site for IE 5.x

The bug arises because IE 5.5 doesn't respect the width of the container in which the homepage box `divs` sit: it thinks that the 49% width of the homepage box is 49% of the *browser*, not 49% of the `content div`. We could fix this for IE 5.5 by giving `content` a width of 100%, but that would cause the page to be too wide in standards compliant browsers.

What we can do to fix the problem is to use a CSS "filter" that will only apply 100% width on `content` if the browser is Internet Explorer 5 or 5.5. To do this, open your `main.css` style sheet and find the `#content` rule (which should be near the top).

Add the following CSS code below the existing rule:

File: **inc/main.css (excerpt)**

```
/* Hack for IE5.* which misinterprets the width */
* #content {
 width: 100%;
 w\idth: auto;
}
/* end hack */
```

A CSS filter is a technique that you can use to hide certain CSS rules or properties from older browsers. It relies on the older browser not implementing some feature of CSS (in this case, the fact that the browser is supposed to interpret \i as i). When Internet Explorer 5 reads the above rule, it understands the `width: 100%;` property, but ignores `w\idth: auto;` because it doesn't understand the slash. Other browsers that do understand the slash will see both `width` properties, and the second one will override the first.

*Tip*

## Have any Comments?

The note between the `/*` and `*/` is a comment in the CSS file; it serves to remind us later on why this code is included. It's a good idea to comment any CSS hacks and filters you use so that, when you come back to the code at a later date, you know what you've done and why.

Save the style sheet and check the page again in Internet Explorer 5; it should now render very similarly to other browsers. If you check the page in your other browsers, you'll see that nothing has changed.

There really isn't enough space here to go into a lot of detail about fixing browser incompatibilities. For a detailed look at how to troubleshoot CSS, you might like to read over Chapter 7, *Browser and Device Support*, of my book, *The CSS Anthology: 101 Tips, Tricks, & Hacks*, also published by SitePoint.

# Summary

This has been a long chapter covering a lot of ground. If you were new to CSS or CSS positioning at the start of this book, I hope this chapter has demonstrated the power of working with CSS to create a page layout, and given you some understanding of how the different properties can be used to change the page display without compromising the document's structure.

The layout that we have created in this chapter will be used as the basis of the site; the heading and sidebar are common to the other pages on the site. While we will be creating additional CSS as needed for other pages, we have now done the bulk of the work that's required to create our layout.

# 7 Accessibility

We've already explored accessibility in some detail, but we haven't yet looked at what it means to build an accessible site. In meeting our objectives, it's important that we develop the site in adherence to the appropriate accessibility guidelines. In this chapter, we'll expand on what we've already discussed, and look more closely at the guidelines.

Many people argue that building accessible sites is difficult, expensive, and not something with which average Web designers should concern themselves. But the fact remains that making accessible sites is a very easy way to communicate your message to an audience that often finds it difficult to get hold of quality information. Imagine you owned a traditional, bricks-and-mortar gift store. If you wanted to make your products accessible to all potential customers, you might create wider aisles, and add ramps and elevators, so that visitors with restricted mobility could move around the store easily. Visually impaired shoppers would need to have your products described to them, so that they could understand what they were buying.

The online gift shop makes viewing products far easier for users with limited mobility. By considering users who, because of the difficulty they experience using a mouse, navigate using their keyboards, we can ensure that even those with greatly limited mobility can move through our store and select products. By ensuring that our document is easily read by screen readers, we can offer an excellent experience to visually impaired users, providing full product descriptions for those who cannot see images clearly, and thereby delivering a better shopping experience than may be achieved in a physical store.

In this chapter, we'll find out more about the different types of users who access our site, and consider how accessibility benefits them. We'll then look at the Web Content Accessibility Guidelines in detail: this document, created by an initiative within the W3C, represents the "standard" to which we work when considering accessibility. We need to understand what the guidelines mean, so that we're able to put them into practice as we develop Websites that are to remain accessible in the future.

# Will Considering Accessibility Stop us Creating Exciting Designs?

It's a common misconception that an accessible Website is one that displays large text on a plain background, and is completely devoid of imagery. This is not the case at all. In fact, in the course of our work to date, we've already taken large steps toward the creation of an accessible site. For example, we've used standards-compliant, structurally semantic XHTML, and we've kept our visual formatting to the CSS style sheet, ensuring that our images and styles don't affect the semantic structure of the document itself. This approach, along with the creation of an easy-to-understand interface that doesn't require the perception of color or images in order to be navigated, is sufficient to comply with the most basic level of accessibility: WCAG Level A.

# Which Users Benefit?

When considering accessibility, we often think of visually impaired users and, in particular, those who use screen readers: devices that read aloud the text that displays on the Web page. However, these are not the only users who will benefit from accessible design, nor are they the only visitors we should consider as we develop an accessible site.

Visually impaired users can have any of a range of specific needs. They may need to use a screen reader; they might view the site using software that allows them to zoom in on certain sections of the display; they could simply want to make the site's text larger using their browsers' settings. A user who is unable to distinguish between colors might otherwise have perfectly good sight. This user's requirements will be very different from those with other visual impairments.

Web users may experience a variety of mobility problems: if they have difficulty using a mouse they may, instead, navigate the Web using their keyboards or other devices. If you assume that everyone can point and click, your site will be inaccessible to these users. Similarly, if your site uses sound, you should consider the needs of deaf users: is the audio content you offer also provided in a text-based format?

Finally, we must consider users with a variety of cognitive disabilities. To help visitors with dyslexia, or disabilities that make it difficult to understand a complex Website, we should make design decisions that make the site as easy to understand as possible.

# Which Guidelines are we Working to?

We're Web designers and developers, not disability experts. How are we supposed to create sites that can be accessible to all these diverse groups? Thankfully, we don't have to work out a solution alone. The guidelines issued by the W3C, and governments around the world, provide guidance as to how we can create accessible sites. A host of additional assistance is available freely on the Web, and is built into Dreamweaver 8.

## The Web Accessibility Initiative (WAI)

The WAI is a group within the W3C that creates the Web Content Accessibility Guidelines (WCAG) that we'll follow here. The latest version of these guidelines is WCAG 1.0, although, at the time of writing, version 2.0 of the guidelines is in working draft format.

The guidelines have been developed to provide clear specifications for the creation of accessible Websites. The current specification contains fourteen guidelines that deal with specific issues relating to a variety of disabilities. These guidelines are accompanied by checkpoints that allow us to confirm whether or not our sites conform to each of the specifications. Later in this chapter, we'll work through these checkpoints to see which apply to our site, and whether our work conforms to the specifications.

## WACG Checkpoint Priorities

Each checkpoint in the WCAG has been assigned a priority level of 1, 2 or 3. These priority levels help us to understand how important that checkpoint is, and can be used to measure the "conformance level" of a document. There are three conformance levels: A, Double-A (AA) and Triple-A (AAA). Let's look at them in more detail now.

## Priority 1

> A Web content developer *must* satisfy this checkpoint. Otherwise, one or more groups will find it impossible to access information in the document. Satisfying this checkpoint is a basic requirement for some groups to be able to use Web documents.
>
> —WCAG 1.0[1]

These Priority 1 checkpoints identify the basic, fundamental steps you should take to ensure that most people can access your site. As we'll see, most of these issues are very simple to address but, in meeting the specification, you do a lot to create an accessible site. If your site satisfies all Priority 1 checkpoints, you're able to claim Level A conformance with the WCAG, and you can display the Level A logo, shown in Figure 7.1, on your site.

### Figure 7.1. The WAI Level A logo.

## Priority 2

> A Web content developer *should* satisfy this checkpoint. Otherwise, one or more groups will find it difficult to access information in the document. Satisfying this checkpoint will remove significant barriers to accessing Web documents.
>
> —WCAG 1.0[2]

Conforming to the Priority 1 and 2 checkpoints is an excellent aim and should be possible, particularly for new sites that you've designed with accessibility in mind. Complying with these checkpoints will make your site far more accessible; it will also see you achieve Level Double-A conformance, the logo for which appears in Figure 7.2.

---

[1] http://www.w3.org/TR/WAI-WEBCONTENT/#wc-priority-1
[2] http://www.w3.org/TR/WAI-WEBCONTENT/#wc-priority-2

## Figure 7.2. The WAI Level Double-A logo.

# Priority 3

> A Web content developer *may* address this checkpoint. Otherwise, one or more groups will find it somewhat difficult to access information in the document. Satisfying this checkpoint will improve access to Web documents.
>
> —WCAG 1.0[3]

The Priority 3 guidelines include some checkpoints that are more difficult to address, as well as some that are relevant only to relatively small groups of people. It is always worth the effort to meet all of the relevant checkpoints, but these guidelines are, to the WAI, of lesser importance than those in the first two groups. If you address all Priority 1, 2 and 3 checkpoints, you'll have reached Level-AAA conformance. You can display the WAI's Level-AAA conformance badge, shown in Figure 7.3, on your site.

## Figure 7.3. The WAI Level Triple-A logo.

## Administering the Logo

You will sometimes see variations of the above logos displayed on Websites; for example, accessibility validator Bobby has its own set of logos, and individual designers sometimes make their own logos to fit in with the style of the Website. These logos essentially mean the same thing: that the site has achieved the level of conformance stated on the logo.

Anyone can download and use the logos if they believe that their work meets the required standard of conformance. No "officials" make checks on sites that use the logos, so they should not be considered a badge of approval from the W3C, or any other organization. However, use of the logos does show that the site owner or designer has considered accessibility issues in the

---

[3] http://www.w3.org/TR/WAI-WEBCONTENT/#wc-priority-3

process of designing the site, and reassures the visitor that they'll more than likely be able to access the site's content.

# Legislation

In addition to the WAI guidelines, many countries have now created legislation that covers Website accessibility. If you're building a site for the government of a country that has such legislation in place, you should investigate that legislation to ascertain which sections and requirements apply to you. For example, in the USA, the "Section 508" legislation deals with Websites that are developed for, or purchased by government bodies, and states that such sites should be accessible to those with disabilities. Section 508 lists 16 rules to which Websites must conform:[4]

1194.22 Web-based intranet and internet information and applications.

(a) A text equivalent for every non-text element shall be provided (e.g., via "alt", "longdesc", or in element content).

(b) Equivalent alternatives for any multimedia presentation shall be synchronized with the presentation.

(c) Web pages shall be designed so that all information conveyed with color is also available without color, for example from context or markup.

(d) Documents shall be organized so they are readable without requiring an associated style sheet.

(e) Redundant text links shall be provided for each active region of a server-side image map.

(f) Client-side image maps shall be provided instead of server-side image maps except where the regions cannot be defined with an available geometric shape.

(g) Row and column headers shall be identified for data tables.

---

[4] http://www.section508.gov/index.cfm?FuseAction=Content&ID=12#Web

(h) Markup shall be used to associate data cells and header cells for data tables that have two or more logical levels of row or column headers.

(i) Frames shall be titled with text that facilitates frame identification and navigation.

(j) Pages shall be designed to avoid causing the screen to flicker with a frequency greater than 2 Hz and lower than 55 Hz.

(k) A text-only page, with equivalent information or functionality, shall be provided to make a web site comply with the provisions of this part, when compliance cannot be accomplished in any other way. The content of the text-only page shall be updated whenever the primary page changes.

(l) When pages utilize scripting languages to display content, or to create interface elements, the information provided by the script shall be identified with functional text that can be read by assistive technology.

(m) When a web page requires that an applet, plug-in or other application be present on the client system to interpret page content, the page must provide a link to a plug-in or applet that complies with §1194.21(a) through (l).

(n) When electronic forms are designed to be completed on-line, the form shall allow people using assistive technology to access the information, field elements, and functionality required for completion and submission of the form, including all directions and cues.

(o) A method shall be provided that permits users to skip repetitive navigation links.

(p) When a timed response is required, the user shall be alerted and given sufficient time to indicate more time is required.

As we'll see when we work through the WCAG checkpoints later in this chapter, the Section 508 rules a–k are covered by the WACG Priority 1 checkpoints; rules l–p are covered in the Priority 2 and 3 checkpoints. Where countries or organizations have implemented accessibility guidelines, they tend to have based them on the WCAG 1.0, so if you have followed these official specifications, you should have covered most, if not all, of a government's requirements. Of course, it's always worthwhile to check that you haven't missed any requirements that are specific to your particular situation.

# Dreamweaver Tools for Accessibility

We've already used some of the Accessibility features that are built into Dreamweaver 8. When setting up our site, we set the Accessibility Preferences dialog, depicted in Figure 7.4, to show accessibility attributes when we inserted Forms, Frames, Media and Images.

## Figure 7.4. The Accessibility category in Preferences.

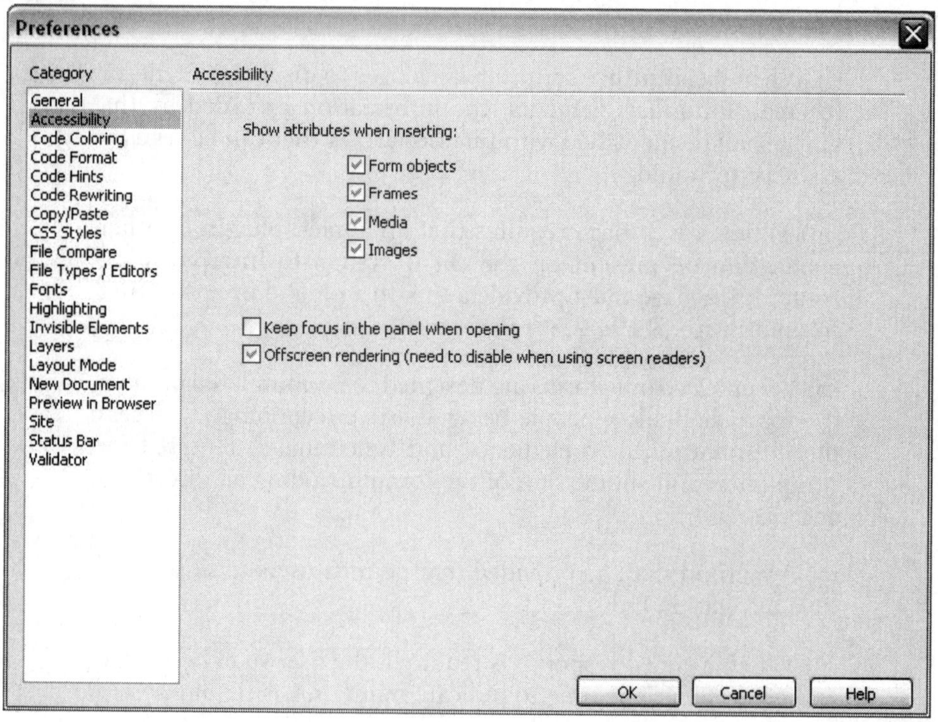

With these preferences set, we are reminded by Dreamweaver to add alternate text for images and media objects, forms and frames. In Chapter 4, we used the Accessibility attributes dialog for the image tag as we inserted images into our document.

Dreamweaver includes an accessibility validator, which we will be using later in this chapter as we validate our site for accessibility. In case you don't understand any of the points raised by the validator, Dreamweaver also includes in the Reference panel the UsableNet Accessibility Reference shown in Figure 7.5 , so that you can look up from within Dreamweaver any checkpoints that you find confusing.

**Figure 7.5. The UsableNet Accessibility Reference.**

As we now know a bit about the standards to which we're trying to work, and the kinds of problems we're hoping to prevent, let's turn to our site and see if we can meet the WCAG 1.0 checkpoints. I'm going to work through them in priority order; you can find the complete list on the W3C Website.[5]

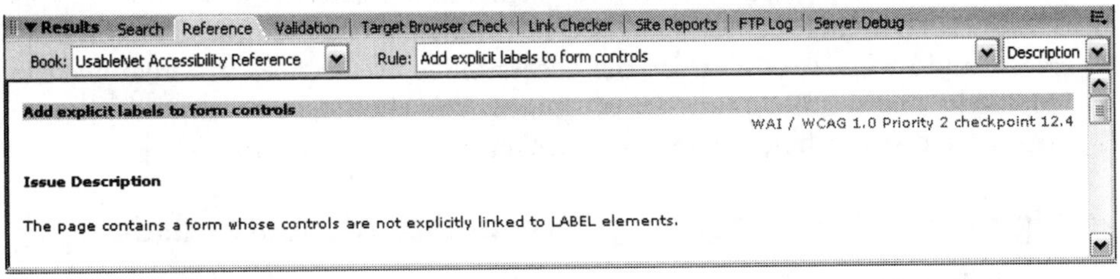

# Accessibility in Practice

In this discussion, I've concentrated more heavily on those checkpoints that affect our site. Some checkpoints deal with multimedia elements or scripting that we haven't used, and we'd need to write another book to fully explain how to make such elements accessible! Instead, I've explained those checkpoints briefly so that, if you're working on a site that includes such elements, you'll know that you need to ensure their accessibility.

Heated debate rages over whether or not some of the Priority 3 checkpoints are a good idea, and how they can best be achieved. The devices that people use to access the Web change constantly with advances in technology, so it's important to keep up-to-date with the evolving ideas and research in this area. Notes that accompany many of the checkpoints state that those checkpoints are to be followed until user agents support some particular feature, and that, in the future, the checkpoint might not be necessary. If this is the case, a future version of the guidelines may not include those checkpoints.

---

[5] http://www.w3.org/TR/WCAG10/checkpoint-list.html

# Priority 1

The following checkpoints fall within Priority 1, and should be met to ensure the Level-A basic level of conformance.

## General Issues

**1.1 Provide a text equivalent for every non-text element.**
Non-text elements include images, Flash movies, video, audio files, Java applets, and so on. If you've set the accessibility preferences in Dreamweaver correctly, every time you insert an image, you should be prompted to enter alternate text by the dialog shown in Figure 7.6.

### Figure 7.6. The Image Tag Accessibility Attributes dialog.

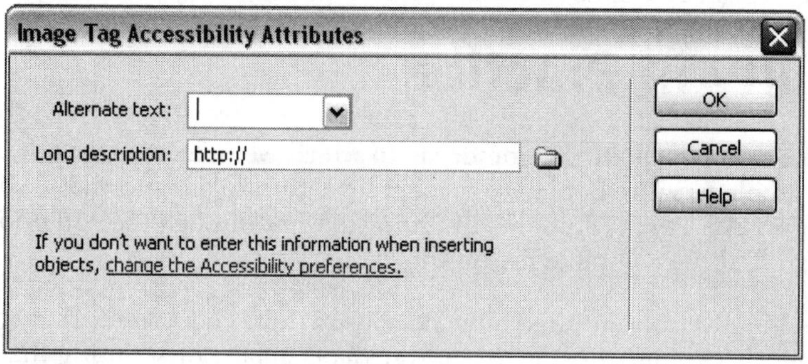

When you insert an image, you can enter a text description of that image into the Alternate text field of the dialog. This text will then be used to generate the `img` element's `alt` attribute. We haven't used Flash or any other elements that utilize the `<object>` tag; however, had we done so, a similar dialog would prompt us to insert the alternate text for each of those objects.

The Long description field provides us the opportunity to insert a link to some other page that describes the image. If you published a complex graph or chart image, for example, you might use this `longdesc` attribute to link to a page that explained the data in textual form. This would eliminate the need to include a lengthy, complicated explanation on the main page.

We can use Dreamweaver to check whether any of our images are lacking the `alt` attribute: open the Reports dialog from Site > Reports..., check Missing Alt Text, and click Run, as shown in Figure 7.7.

## Figure 7.7. Running a Report for Missing Alt Text.

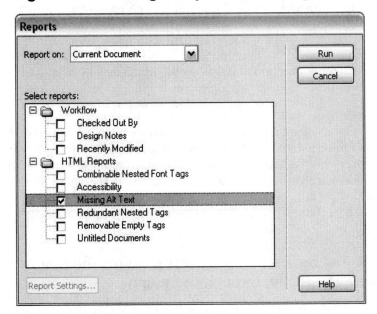

Any images that lack alternate text are listed in the Results Panel as warnings, which is handy if you're trying to make a large, existing site accessible: you can run the report over the entire local site, then simply go through the pages, adding alternate text as appropriate.

Where an image is used purely for layout purposes—the bottom of a rounded rectangle, for example—you can add an empty alternate text attribute, which tells screen readers and text browsers to ignore the image. Here's how it appears in the code:

```
<img src="img/nav-bottom.gif" alt="" />
```

If your site contained an audio or video file, you'd need to provide a text equivalent—for example, a transcript—of that content.

**2.1 Ensure that all information that's conveyed with color is also available without color, for example, from context or markup.**

This checkpoint ensures that your site can be understood by users who do not see the colors you've used in your design—perhaps because they're using a text-only device or screen reader—and those who have trouble distinguishing between colors due to color blindness.

Imagine if, in your online store, you used a red rectangular button icon to denote products that were out of stock, and a green rectangular button icon to identify in-stock products. Without a text alternative to these buttons, color-blind users and those with other forms of visual impairment could easily become confused. By inserting a text label next to the icon, you can retain the visual representation of stock levels—which may be helpful to some users—while ensuring that users who don't see the image, or don't differentiate between the colors, know which products are in or out of stock.

One potentially problematic use of color in our own design is in the chart that displays browser statistics. If we explained which part of the chart relates to each browser using only the colored icons beside the browser name, those who could not perceive the icons could not interpret the chart. We have, however, added percentage figures in text beside the name of each browser, as you can see in Figure 7.8. So, even if users don't see the chart, they can access the information about browser usage.

**Figure 7.8. The browser statistics list presents the figures in text as well as visually, through the graph.**

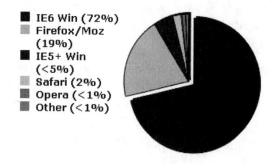

Browser Stats - December - 04

- IE6 Win (72%)
- Firefox/Moz (19%)
- IE5+ Win (<5%)
- Safari (2%)
- Opera (<1%)
- Other (<1%)

**4.1 Clearly identify changes in the natural language of a document's text and any text equivalents (e.g. captions).**

If our document contains more than one language, we should specify changes in the language used as those changes occur within the document. To do this, we insert as the lang attribute of the containing element a value that represents the code for the language being used. This enables screen readers to speak the text using the correct pronunciation.

```
<p lang="en">Do you speak English?</p>
<p lang="fr">Parlez-vous Français?</p>
<p lang="de">Sprechen Sie Deutsches?</p>
```

A comprehensive list of language codes is available online.[6] We don't need to worry about this checkpoint in our design.

**6.1 Organize documents so they may be read without style sheets. For example, when an HTML document is rendered without associated style sheets, it must still be possible to read the document.**

As we've already discussed, text-only devices ignore the style sheet and deal with only the document markup. We have been considering this checkpoint right from the start of this book, and our method of creating the semantically structured document first, then adding the style, will, we hope, have ensured that our document is completely understandable without the style sheet.

To make sure this is the case, simply remove the style sheet and view your site in a regular browser; alternatively, you could use a text-only browser such as Lynx to view the site. You might see something like the display shown in Figure 7.9.

## Figure 7.9. Viewing the site in Lynx.

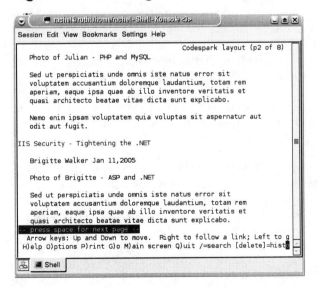

---

[6] http://www.oasis-open.org/cover/iso639a.html

You can also view your design without CSS in Dreamweaver, Select View > Style Rendering > View Styles to turn CSS on and off.

### 6.2 Ensure that equivalents for dynamic content are updated when the dynamic content changes.

"Dynamic content" refers to any content that changes over time, or changes with a different input. Search results, live stock-price applets, and graphs automatically generated from a database, are all examples of dynamic content. This checkpoint assures that any text-equivalent content on your site is an up-to-date reflection of the site's dynamic content.

For example, if the browser usage chart was generated on the server, we'd need to ensure that the percentages displayed beside it were updated whenever the chart was updated. Alternatively, the page that was linked to in that image's longdesc could include a dynamically generated table of the data displayed in the chart. A stock ticker's alternative text could link to a simple page that displayed the stock prices that were current at the time the page was loaded. However, since the image we've used is static, this checkpoint will not be an issue for our static Website.

### 7.1 Until user agents allow users to control flickering, avoid causing the screen to flicker.

Flickering is a problem to many users: those with poor vision, people with epilepsy, and even those—like this author—who suffer from migraine with visual disturbances. If I encounter any page that displays with rapid movement, I close the browser immediately! Rapidly moving page elements can also be confusing to users with cognitive disabilities.

Flickering could be caused by Flash, JavaScript, blinking or scrolling text, or by a movie playing on the page. None of these is a problem for the site that we're building.

### 14.1 Use the clearest and simplest language appropriate for a site's content.

This checkpoint relates not to our design, but to the content of the site. We should use simple, easily understood language wherever possible. For a technical site such as the one we're building, we're obviously going to use technical language. This is fine: it's appropriate for our site. However, for a site such as a medical information site aimed at the general public, or a public library Website, it would be very important to use language that didn't confuse users. This would allow users with disabilities such as dyslexia to more easily understand the information; it would also help users whose first language is not the language in which the site content is written.

Even on a technical site such as ours, consideration should be given to the language used. Many Web developers speak English as a second language, and the majority of the site's tutorials will communicate complex concepts that will be new to many users. Trying to communicate as clearly as possible will benefit everyone.

# Image Maps

Image maps are images in which different parts of the image are made into 'hot spots' that can be linked to another document. To comply with checkpoint 1.1, you must identify each of the image map's linked areas with alternate text. Dreamweaver enables you to add this `alt` attribute in the Property Inspector after you've created a hot spot on an image map, as shown in Figure 7.10.

### Figure 7.10. The Property Inspector showing the `alt` attribute for a hot spot.

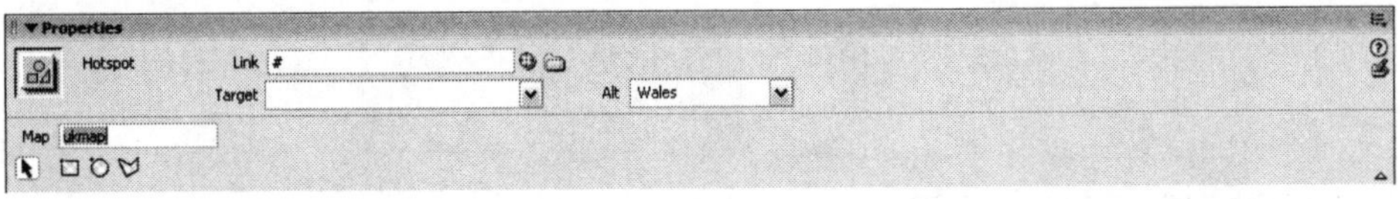

Some of the checkpoints in Priority 1 deal specifically with image maps.

**1.2 Provide redundant text links for each active region of a server-side image map.**
Dreamweaver uses client-side—not server-side—image maps. However, if you're working on a site that contains a server-side image map, you should add to the document text links that mirror the links within the image map.

**9.1 Provide client-side image maps instead of server-side image maps, except where the regions cannot be defined with an available geometric shape.**
This checkpoint indicates that client-side image maps are more accessible that server-side image maps and should be used whenever possible.

# Tables

**5.1 For data tables, identify row and column headers.**
When using tables to present data—such as that which could be displayed in a spreadsheet—we must ensure that the heading cells for each of the columns or rows are marked up as headings: we shouldn't just rely on CSS to show the user that these are headings.

Dreamweaver helps us to comply with this checkpoint. When we use the Table dialog shown in Figure 7.11, we can define whether we want the table to have no heading cells, headings on the left, headings along the top, or headings both on the left-hand side and on the top. When the table is created, it will make these elements ths rather than tds.

## Figure 7.11. The Insert Table dialog.

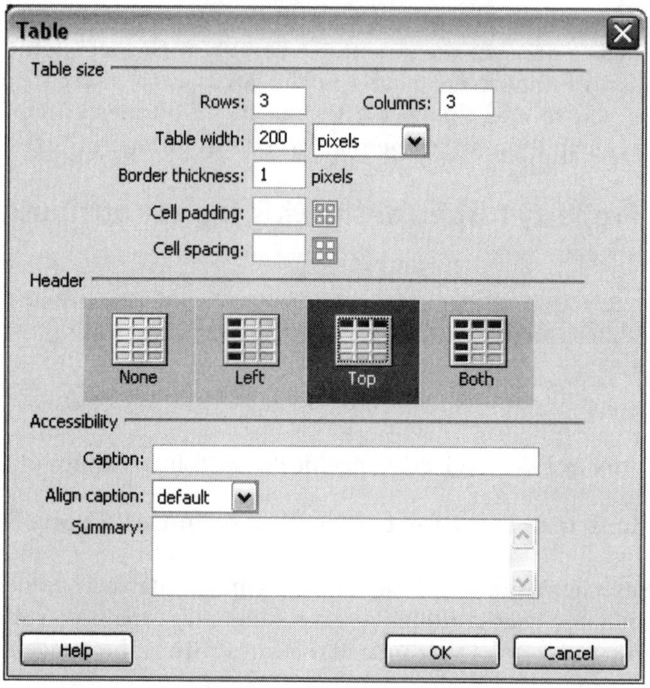

We used the Table dialog to mark up the headings when we created our Recent Tutorials table. If we view the markup for this table, we can see that the th element has been used to define the table's headings.

File: **homepage-layout-strict.html (excerpt)**

```
<table width="100%" border="0" summary="This table shows the
    most recent tutorials posted on the site and their
    publication date.">
  <tr>
    <th scope="col">Title</th>
    <th scope="col">Published</th>
  </tr>
```

```
<tr>
  <td class="bullet"><a href="#">CSS forms - Massive
      feedback distortion?</a></td>
  <td>26-12-2005</td>
</tr>
<tr class="even">
  <td class="bullet"><a href="#">Buttons &amp; Dials -
    Java Controls Explained</a></td>
  <td>23-12-2005</td>
</tr>
  ...
  </tr>
</table>
```

**5.2 For data tables that have two or more logical levels of row or column headers, use markup to associate data cells and header cells.**

The th elements in the above markup include the attribute scope, which has a value of col, indicating that these are column headings. Screen readers will know that the data in the column below each heading should be associated with that heading. To identify a row heading on the left-hand side of the table, we would use scope="row".

```
<table summary="Distances between selected cities in
    kilometers">
  <tr>
    <th scope="col"></th>
    <th scope="col">Berlin, Germany</th>
    <th scope="col">London, England</th>
    <th scope="col">New York, USA</th>
    <th scope="col">Melbourne, Australia</th>
    <th scope="col">Tokyo, Japan</th>
  </tr>
  <tr>
    <th scope="row">Berlin, Germany</th>
    <td></td>
    <td>919 kilometers</td>
    <td>6387 kilometers</td>
    <td>16000 kilometers</td>
    <td>8936 kilometers</td>
  </tr>
  <tr>
    <th scope="row">London, England</th>
    <td>919 kilometers </td>
    <td> </td>
    <td>5580 kilometers </td>
    <td>16936 kilometers </td>
```

```
      <td>9581 kilometers </td>
    </tr>
    <tr>
      <th scope="row">New York, USA</th>
      <td>6387 kilometers</td>
      <td>5580 kilometers</td>
      <td></td>
      <td>16710 kilometers</td>
      <td>10871 kilometers</td>
    </tr>
    <tr>
      <th scope="row">Melbourne, Australia</th>
      <td>16000 kilometers</td>
      <td>16936 kilometers</td>
      <td>16710 kilometers</td>
      <td></td>
      <td>8210 kilometers</td>
    </tr>
    <tr>
      <th scope="row">Tokyo, Japan</th>
      <td>8936 kilometers</td>
      <td>9581 kilometers</td>
      <td>10871 kilometers</td>
      <td>8210 kilometers</td>
      <td></td>
    </tr>
</table>
```

This markup assists screen reader users: it ensures that, as the table is read to them, these users can understand which heading is associated with the cell content of the table. As we can see, the table in our document complies with this checkpoint.

# Frames

**12.1 Title each frame to facilitate frame identification and navigation.**
Frames cause obvious issues for accessibility: users of text-only devices can view only one frame at a time, which can make navigation difficult; frames also make it difficult for users to bookmark an interesting page in the Website. We have avoided using frames in our layout, so we don't need to worry about this checkpoint.

If you use frames in a document, you must take extra steps to ensure that users of devices that don't see all these frames as a single document understand what's contained in each frame. Give each frame a descriptive title to help users identify that frame. If you have the accessibility preferences for frames turned on in your preferences, and you insert a frame into a document, Dreamweaver will display a dialog that will allow you to give that frame a title. The dialog is pictured in Figure 7.12

**Figure 7.12. Using the Frame Tag Accessibility Attributes dialog.**

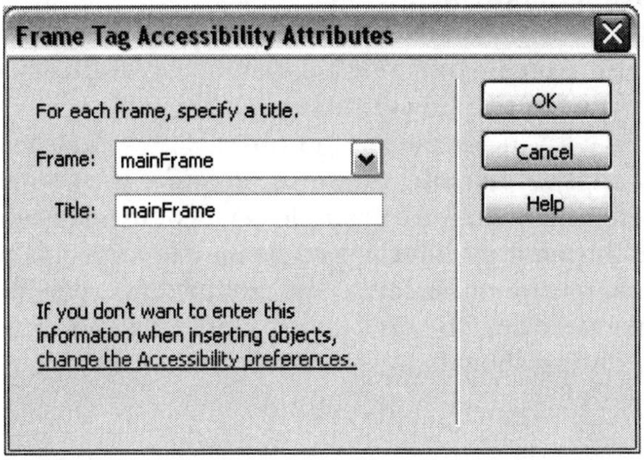

## Applets and Scripts

**6.3 Ensure that pages are usable when scripts, applets, or other programmatic objects are turned off or not supported. If this is not possible, provide equivalent information on an alternative accessible page.**

If you're using JavaScript on your site, make sure the site works when JavaScript is turned off. Many sites require the user to have JavaScript enabled in order to launch popup windows, or even to use links. This is a problem for visitors who use screen readers or other text-only devices, because these devices don't support JavaScript. It will also cause a problem for the large number of people who turn off JavaScript in their browser. We should take a similar approach to dealing with Java applets, which can be accessible in themselves, but are not available to all users.

JavaScript and Java applets aren't necessarily bad ideas—we can develop a perfectly accessible site that uses JavaScript and Java applets—but we should always ensure that all the content of our sites, including information displayed in popup windows and applets, is accessible to users for whom such features are disabled.

We haven't used any JavaScript on our site so far; however, as we further develop the site, this is something we'll need to bear in mind.

# Multimedia

**1.3 Until user agents can automatically read aloud the text equivalent of a visual track, provide an auditory description of the important information of the visual track of a multimedia presentation.**

**1.4 For any time-based multimedia presentation (e.g., a movie or animation), synchronize equivalent alternatives (e.g., captions or auditory descriptions of the visual track) with the presentation.**

These two checkpoints deal with the display of multimedia presentations on Web pages, so they don't apply to our site. However, if you're working on a site that contains multimedia elements—for example, a video tutorial—you'll need to consider how you'll make that information accessible to people who cannot hear the sound track, or cannot see the movie. For instance, you might decide to add captions, like subtitles, to a movie, or insert an audio track to describe the content that's being shown.

# Text-only Versions

**11.4 If, after best efforts, you cannot create an accessible page, provide a link to an alternative page that uses W3C technologies, is accessible, has equivalent information (or functionality), and is updated as often as the inaccessible (original) page.**

Many site owners simply create an alternative "text-only" version of their site, and assume that this means they've complied with accessibility requirements. This checkpoint states that this approach should be used only as a last resort. If you do develop a text-only version, you should ensure that the content of that version is kept up-to-date as any changes are made to the original page.

Creating a text-only version of a static Website means a lot of additional work. It's not the ideal scenario, because we're dealing with people who have numerous types of disabilities. Many of these users have no requirement for a plain text version of the site: they just need to be able to increase the text size, or understand the site despite the fact that it's difficult to tell the colors of the display apart. These users will benefit from your page design just as much as will every other user. Making their only option a plain text version degrades their experience of your site, and discriminates against them by requiring them to use a poorer version of the site.

You might want to offer "low graphics" or "high contrast" alternative style sheets for users to select as their needs dictate. This solution only works if you have an accessible site to begin with, as it doesn't affect the structure of the site: you're just replacing the style sheet with a version that's more comfortable for certain visitors.

The provision of alternative style sheets shouldn't be confused with offering a separate, text-only version of each page as a nod to accessibility. This approach should be avoided as much as possible, and used only as a last resort, perhaps to temporarily apply a degree of accessibility to a legacy site until it can be redesigned.

In the final chapter of this book, we'll create a "low graphics" version of our style sheet. Users will be able to switch to this style sheet, which will allow them to view the same XHTML pages without graphics and background colors.

# Priority 2

The following are Priority 2 checkpoints. Many of them address the semantic structure of your documents and should be familiar to you, as we discussed the correct use of elements to structure your document back in Chapter 4. If you can comply with these checkpoints, and those listed previously under Priority 1, you'll be able to claim Level Double-A conformance.

## General

**2.2 Ensure that foreground and background color combinations provide sufficient contrast when viewed by someone having color deficits or when viewed on a black and white screen.**
This checkpoint requires us to ensure that colors have sufficient contrast to enable users who confuse certain colors, or cannot distinguish between certain colors, to read the text and understand the images presented on our sites.

**3.1 When an appropriate markup language exists, use markup rather than images to convey information.**
This checkpoint advocates that we should use markup, rather than using an image or animation, to describe information wherever possible. For instance, imagine that you need to show a complicated mathematical equation in a document. You might think that the best way to show this clearly would be to display it as an image, but this would make the information inaccessible to anyone who could not see that image. A better way to deal with it would

be to use MathML—a markup language that's used to describe mathematical structures. Unfortunately, MathML is not supported by Internet Explorer, and many other browsers, without additional software, so you may decide it's not practical to use the language. We haven't used images in a way that's covered by this checkpoint, so we can move on.

### 3.2 Create documents that validate to published formal grammars.

"Formal grammar" is a term that's borrowed from computer science, and basically refers to the specification of a programming language, such as XHTML. If your document is validated by the W3C markup validator, you have passed this checkpoint.

### 3.3 Use style sheets to control layout and presentation.

To pass this checkpoint, we need to use style sheets, rather than presentational elements, to create the layout, look, and feel of our pages. We've used CSS to style our text and create the layout of our site, so we can be confident that we've satisfied this checkpoint.

### 3.4 Use relative rather than absolute units in markup language attribute values and style sheet property values.

Within CSS, we can use many different units of measurement, including ems, pixels, and percentages. These units can be broken into two categories: absolute units and relative units. Absolute units should be avoided when building sites for accessibility.

#### Relative Units

Relative units are measured in relation to some other feature of the page or device on which the element is displayed. The relative units are:

**em**  1 em is equivalent to the size of the font on the screen. 2 em is double the size of that font, while 0.5 em is half the size of the font.

**ex**  An ex corresponds to the height of the "x" character in the current font.

**px**  A pixel measurement references the number of pixels on the screen. This unit should only be used to specify sizes in relation to images and other non-scalable elements.

**%**  This unit assigns the size of the element in question as a percentage of something else. For example, `font-size: 120%;` would make the font size 120% of its usual value.

**Absolute Units**

Absolute unit measurements are those that do not change, regardless of the device they're displayed on. These are:

☐ Inches (`in`)

☐ Centimeters (`cm`)

☐ Millimeters (`mm`)

☐ Points (`pt`)

☐ Picas (`pc`)

## Avoid Using px for `font-size`

Many modern browsers enable users to resize text that has been sized using pixel measurements in the style sheet. Unfortunately, though, Internet Explorer does not, so we should not set `font-size` using pixels. If we look at the `#content` rule, we can see that the size is set to **80%**.

File: **`inc/main.css` (excerpt)**

```
#content {
    margin-top: 80px;
    margin-right: 320px;
    margin-left: 40px;
    font: 80% Verdana, Arial, Helvetica, sans-serif;
}
```

This means that the font will respect users' text size settings, even if they're using Internet Explorer.

**3.5 Use header elements to convey document structure and use them according to specification.**
**3.6 Mark up lists and list items properly.**
**3.7 Mark up quotations. Do not use quotation markup for formatting effects such as indentation.**

These checkpoints deal with semantic document structure, as we discussed in Chapter 4. The first point advocates the use of heading elements (h1–h6) instead of using CSS alone: don't just make the text *look* like a heading, *make it a heading.*

The second checkpoint considers the use of the ul, ol and dl elements to mark up lists. The third checkpoint explains the appropriate use of the `blockquote` element. Consider it the W3C's way of telling you to not use Dreamweaver's Text Indent button, shown in Figure 7.13, to indent text.

## Figure 7.13. Indenting text the wrong way, according to the WCAG 1.0.

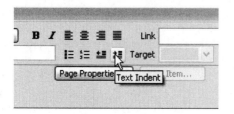

As we've built our document on good semantic foundations, we pass this checkpoint easily.

**6.5 Ensure that dynamic content is accessible or provide an alternative presentation or page.**

Dynamic content that's usually generated through user interaction with a script, or typically requires users to have a particular client-side technology installed, should also be accessible if the user cannot interact with the script, or doesn't have that technology installed.

For example, you might use JavaScript to allow users to drill down through information in a list or tree-view menu. You should provide users who don't have JavaScript enabled with a display in which all the information levels are expanded, or use a server-side technology to achieve the same effect. This would probably require a page reload, but might provide a more accessible solution overall.

**7.2 Until user agents allow users to control blinking, avoid causing content to blink (i.e., change presentation at a regular rate, such as turning on and off).**

This checkpoint is fairly straightforward: to pass it, check that none of your page elements is blinking, and make sure you've avoided using the Netscape-proprietary `blink` element or `text-decoration: blink` in your CSS. If blinking text is to be created by a script, ensure that the user has the ability to turn the script off, or—better yet—change the script to stop it blinking. We haven't used anything on our page that could cause this type of problem, so our page passes this checkpoint.

**7.4 Until user agents provide the ability to stop the refresh, do not create periodically auto-refreshing pages.**

**7.5 Until user agents provide the ability to stop auto-redirect, do not use markup to redirect pages automatically. Instead, configure the server to perform redirects.**

Some sites use an auto-refresh or auto-redirect function to update content from the server. For example, Web cam sites, sites that commence downloads automatically, and sites that detail rapidly changing information such as stock market data might use this kind of technology. However, users who read slowly, due to poor eyesight or disabilities such as dyslexia, may find that the screen refreshes before they have had a chance to read through the content. Therefore, if you have a page that behaves like this, you should provide a way for the user to stop the refresh, or to load a version of the page that does not refresh. This checkpoint is not an issue with our site, though, so we pass it.

**10.1 Until user agents allow users to turn off spawned windows, do not cause popups or other windows to appear and do not change the current window without informing the user.**

Popup windows can confuse users, as the focus suddenly and unexpectedly changes to a new window. If you absolutely must use a popup window, inform the user within the link text for that window that following the link will cause a new window to be launched. This advice is valid for popup windows regardless of how they're launched, whether it's with JavaScript, or via the `target` attribute. We're not using any popup windows, so we pass this checkpoint.

**11.1 Use W3C technologies when they are available and appropriate for a task and use the latest versions when supported.**

**11.2 Avoid deprecated features of W3C technologies.**

When the W3C creates a new specification, it considers accessibility issues, and new features are built into the specifications to assist users of various kinds of devices. Updates to these specifications usually include refinements, such as the deprecation of HTML's presentational features in favor of CSS. Over time, new browsers will most likely start to use these newer features, adding value to the presentation of your document. To pass these checkpoints, you should use HTML 4.01 Strict or XHTML 1.0 Strict, and have validated your document to ensure that it meets the specification.

**12.3 Divide large blocks of information into more manageable groups where natural and appropriate.**

This checkpoint looks at the content and information on your site: information is more easily understood when it's broken into chunks. This rule of thumb also applies to large complex forms on which grouping—for example, by wrapping sections of the form with `<fieldset>` tags—can help users understand the different sections of the form.

### 13.1 Clearly identify the target of each link.

Any text that links to another document on your site, or elsewhere, should clearly explain where the link will take users who click on it. This information should make sense when read out of context, as users may "tab" through the links to navigate a page. Phrases such as "click here" should be avoided; as the example below shows, this text doesn't describe the target content at all.

```
To help ensure accessibility,
<a href="http://validator.w3.org/">click here</a> to validate
your page.
```

Read out of context, the above link simply says, "click here." We could rewrite the link as follows:

```
To help ensure accessibility,
<a href="http://validator.w3.org/">validate your page</a>.
```

This link text is understandable, and communicates successfully when read on its own. We'll need to be mindful of this checkpoint whenever we add content to the site.

### 13.2 Provide metadata to add semantic information to pages and sites.

Metadata is data that describes data; in the context of a Website, this includes the page title, the DOCTYPE, and some of the data included in `meta` and `link` elements. As each of our pages will have a title, they will pass this checkpoint. However, we could also use the `meta` tag to add information—such as keywords and the author's name—to the document.

### 13.3 Provide information about the general layout of a site (e.g., a sitemap or table of contents).

A sitemap helps users to understand the layout of the site. Sitemaps are also particularly useful for users of screen readers and text-only devices, as they provide a quick way to jump directly to relevant pages of the site without having to move through a few irrelevant pages in order to navigate to the destination content.

Our site has a sitemap link, and we'll be creating a sitemap in Chapter 8. Once we've done so, we will pass this checkpoint.

### 13.4 Use navigation mechanisms in a consistent manner.

Inconsistent navigation is confusing for many users, not just those you might consider to have a disability. Choosing a navigational structure that's easy to understand, and then sticking to it, makes it easier for everyone to get round your site. Try not to add pages that are outside this structure.

# Tables

### 5.3 Do not use tables for layout unless the table makes sense when linearized. Otherwise, if the table does not make sense, provide an alternative equivalent (which may be a linearized version).

Screen readers "linearize" tables: they read the content line-by-line, starting at the top left-hand corner, and moving across the table, in the same order in which the content appears in the markup. This is a logical way in which to deal with data tables, but it becomes completely confusing if tables are used for layout purposes.

If we read our Recent Tutorials table in this left-to-right, top-to-bottom manner, we can see that it makes sense. As we're not using tables to create layout, it's easy for us to pass this checkpoint: our only table makes sense when linearized.

### 5.4 If a table is used for layout, do not use any structural markup for the purpose of visual formatting.

This checkpoint doesn't apply to us, as we haven't used tables for layout. If you do use tables to lay out a site, you should keep them as clean as possible, and assign all visual formatting—such as column widths, borders, and background colors—to the stylesheet. This will help you to keep the layout as accessible as possible, and give you the best chance to attain Double-A conformance with a simple table-based layout.

# Frames

### 12.2 Describe the purpose of frames and how frames relate to each other if it is not obvious by frame titles alone.

If it's impossible to describe the frame's purpose using the frame's `title` attribute, you could use the `longdesc` attribute to provide additional information about the frame on a separate page. Here's an example:

```
<frame src="myframe.html" title="Organization structure"
    longdesc="orgdesc.html"/>
```

# Forms

**10.2 Until user agents support explicit associations between labels and form controls, for all form controls with implicitly associated labels, ensure that the label is properly positioned.**

**12.4 Associate labels explicitly with their controls.**

There are two methods by which we can explicitly associate a label with a form field: we can use the `label` element's `for` attribute, or we can wrap the form field in a `<label>` tag, as shown below:

```
<label for="firstname">First Name</label> <input type="text"
    id="firstname" />
<label>Family Name <input type="text id="familyname" /></label>
```

If you've set the forms accessibility preference in Dreamweaver, you'll be prompted for form labels, and you'll be asked how you want to associate the label with the field: Wrap with label tag, Attach label tag using 'for' attribute, or No label tag. Provided you selected the Wrap with label tag option (as we did when we built the search form in Chapter 4), your label will be explicitly associated with, and positioned with, your form control.

# Applets and Scripts

**6.4 For scripts and applets, ensure that event handlers are input device-independent.**

**9.2 Ensure that any element that has its own interface can be operated in a device-independent manner.**

**9.3 For scripts, specify logical event handlers rather than device-dependent event handlers.**

These checkpoints require that any script or other element on the page can be used regardless of the type of device with which the visitor has accessed the page. Many developers assume that everyone uses a mouse and can point and click. This is not always the case, so be sure to make any scripts, Flash objects, applets, and other elements usable by visitors using other devices.

**7.3 Until user agents allow users to freeze moving content, avoid movement in pages.**

Movement in Web pages can be distracting for many users, and should be avoided. This includes scrolling text and banners, and other animations that cannot be stopped by the user. If you must use moving content, provide an easy and obvious way for users to turn it off.

**8.1 Make programmatic elements such as scripts and applets directly accessible or compatible with assistive technologies**

Our site doesn't use any scripts or applets that would be inaccessible; however, it is possible to make multimedia content, such as Java applets or Flash, accessible. You would need to do so in order to achieve level Double-A conformance for a site that used any of these elements.

# Priority 3

The Priority 3 checkpoints are the strictest accessibility checkpoints, and some propose considerable compliance hurdles for some sites. Complying with all of these checkpoints, as well as those from the previous two levels, enables you to achieve Triple-A conformance. Even if you decide not to go for Triple-A compliance, it's wise to look through these checkpoints: complying with any of them will be helpful to some users, and you might just find that you're unable to satisfy a couple of the checkpoints with relative ease.

## General

**4.2 Specify the expansion of each abbreviation or acronym in a document where it first occurs.**

XHTML provides elements for the description of acronyms and abbreviations; this approach assists users who may be unfamiliar with the acronym or abbreviation. The `abbr` element should be used for abbreviations, while the `acronym` element is designed for use with acronyms.

Within our site, we're likely to use many acronyms and abbreviations, so we should try to use the correct markup to describe them, at least upon their first appearance within a document. You can add definitions in Design View by selecting the acronym or abbreviation, then right-clicking and choosing Quick Tag Editor... from the context menu. You can then type in the tag and the title attribute, as shown in Figure 7.14.

## Figure 7.14. Using the Quick Tag Editor to add the `abbr` element.

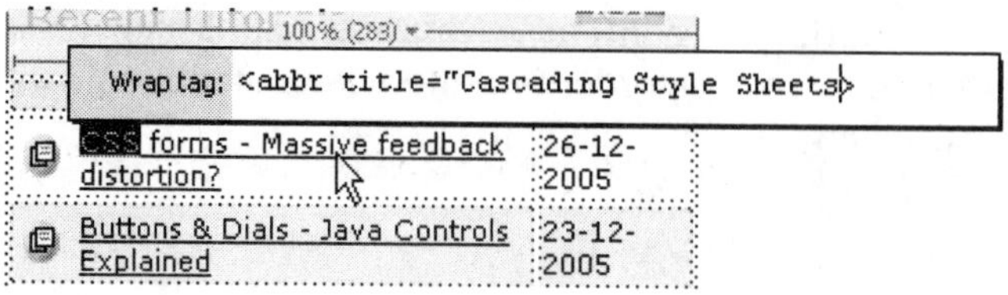

> **Tip**
>
> ## abbr vs acronym
>
> What constitutes the correct use of `abbr` and `acronym`? It's a contentious issue, but the general standard is to use `acronym` for abbreviations that are pronounced as a word—such as "NATO" or "NASA"—and `abbr` for everything else.

### 4.3 Identify the primary natural language of a document.

Identifying the primary language of a document helps screen readers to pronounce the text in the document correctly. You can identify the language in the markup by adding the `lang` attribute to the `html` element, as follows:

```
<html xmlns="http://www.w3.org/1999/xhtml" lang="en">
```

### 9.4 Create a logical tab order through links, form controls, and objects.

Users of your site who navigate using their keyboards, rather than a mouse, can use the **Tab** key to move through the links, form controls, and other items on your site. This is called "tabbing" through the page, and all major browsers support this functionality. Normally, links and form controls will be visited in the order in which they appear in the markup, but this may seem illogical in some cases—especially if you've positioned elements using CSS. You can check the logic by tabbing through your page in a Web browser yourself. If the order of links is illogical, you can use the `tabindex` attribute to force a more logical order, as shown here:

```
<label>Search: <input type="text" name="search" id="search"
    tabindex="1" /></label><br />
<input type="reset" tabindex="3" />
<input type="submit" tabindex="2" />
```

Items will be visited in the numeric order of their `tabindexes`, from the lowest `tabindex` value to the highest. In the above example, the text box is visited first, followed by the submit button, and finally, the reset button.

**9.5 Provide keyboard shortcuts to important links (including those in client-side image maps), form controls, and groups of form controls.**

It's possible to create keyboard shortcuts that allow users to jump straight to different page elements; these shortcuts are called **access keys**. We can assign an access key to an element using the `accesskey` attribute, like so:

```
<a href="http://www.sitepoint.com/" accesskey="s">SitePoint</a>
```

The above link can be activated by pressing **Alt-S** in Windows browsers.

Debate has flared around the question of whether or not access keys are actually helpful to users. The main problem with the creation of access keys is that many browsers and operating systems have already mapped certain key combinations; in creating your own access keys, you might inadvertently use a combination that's already used by another application, causing considerable user confusion.

**10.5 Until user agents (including assistive technologies) render adjacent links distinctly, include non-link, printable characters (surrounded by spaces) between adjacent links.**

This checkpoint relates to links that are positioned next to each other in the document, and may not be recognizable as separate links when viewed using a screen reader or other device. A common situation in which this problem could arise is in a navigation bar whose a elements have been styled with CSS; this styling is not applied if the end-user has disabled CSS, and, therefore, the adjacent links cannot be distinguished.

## Figure 7.15. Failing to distinguish adjacent links.

TutorialsAboutContactSitemap

We've circumvented this problem in our site by marking up our navigation as list items. If you didn't want to use list markup, the other option would be to place a non-linked character, such as a '>' or '|', between each link.

**11.3 Provide information so that users may receive documents according to their preferences (e.g., language, content type, etc.)**

This checkpoint suggests a large number of steps that can be taken to aid accessibility, for example, providing an alternative aural style sheet that details how the text in your document should be spoken, or providing alternate language versions. The suitability of the various options will depend on the type of site you're developing. However, offering users content in the most accessible format is a goal that we should all strive to achieve.

### 13.5 Provide navigation bars to highlight and give access to the navigation mechanism.

Each of the site's pages should have a consistently placed navigation bar to help users access information on the site, and understand how to return to pages they've already visited. We have created a navigation bar for our site, and intend to use it on all pages.

### 13.6 Group related links, identify the group (for user agents), and, until user agents do so, provide a way to bypass the group.

This checkpoint relates to the "skip navigation" links that are included on some sites. By grouping the links for the site's navigation, for example, it is possible to provide a mechanism that skips over these links. This is helpful for screen-reader users who would otherwise have to hear the entire navigation bar again on every page of a given site. As the bulk of our navigation links are at the end of our markup, this isn't too much of a concern for our site.

### 13.7 If search functions are provided, enable different types of searches for different skill levels and preferences.

Adding help capabilities to your search function will assist users in understanding how to use it. Describing how to use operators such as AND and OR will help people to understand how to get the best results out of their search. Searching may prove difficult for users, for example, who have a cognitive disability that makes spelling difficult. You could go so far as to add spell checking to the search function, or to provide a list of common searches. This checkpoint focuses on making it easy for users to search the information your site provides.

### 13.8 Place distinguishing information at the beginning of headings, paragraphs, lists, etc.

Screen readers read through the content of a document from top to bottom. If you can explain what a section of information is about early in that section, this will help screen reader users to know whether they want to read through all of that information. If you can describe the content accurately in a heading or short introductory paragraph, this will help not just screen-reader users, but anyone who finds reading slow or difficult. Your users can quickly move on to other content if they realize the current information is not helpful.

**13.9 Provide information about document collections (i.e., documents comprising multiple pages).**

In cases where a document spans multiple pages, using "previous" and "next" links can help users to understand where they're located within the document, and how to get to the next page. Placing these links in helpful locations—at both the top and bottom of the document—can help ensure that users can move between pages easily. The site map is another place where documents can be displayed to reflect their groupings.

**13.10 Provide a means to skip over multi-line ASCII art.**

"ASCII art" uses a collection of characters to simulate an image. Screen readers have no way of knowing what ASCII art is: they try to read out the characters, which is obviously very annoying for the user! If you use ASCII art anywhere, provide a means for screen-reader users to skip over your artwork.

**14.2 Supplement text with graphic or auditory presentations where they will facilitate comprehension of the page.**

Additional images or other content will help some users to more completely understand the page. As well as ensuring that blind users can understand the content of images, you might also consider inserting extra images or other content to assist other users to understand your pages. For those with cognitive disabilities, a visual representation of a concept may be easier to grasp than a text description. Here, once again, we need to consider the different types of disabilities that people have if we are to create usable solutions that actually help them to use our sites.

**14.3 Create a style of presentation that's consistent across pages.**

By creating a consistent look and feel across pages, you can help users to understand how they can use your site. Navigation and sub-navigation should remain in the same place and work in a consistent way. In creating our site's navigation, we've aimed to provide a consistent navigational structure and, as long as we maintain this structure on the other pages of the site, we'll pass this checkpoint.

# Image Maps

**1.5 Until user agents render text equivalents for client-side image map links, provide redundant text links for each active region of a client-side image map.**

Some devices may not describe the different areas of a client-side image map correctly. Therefore, you can help these users if, in addition to the map, you also provide links to the different sections of the map. We haven't used any image maps in this site, so we pass this checkpoint.

# Tables

### 5.5 Provide summaries for tables.

The table element has a summary attribute that can be used to summarize the information in a table. This attribute helps screen-reader users to understand the context of the table, and whether the information is relevant to them. Summaries are not displayed on-screen in browsers. As shown in Figure 7.16, Dreamweaver reminds you to add the summary attribute when you insert a table.

## Figure 7.16. Adding the summary attribute in the Table dialog.

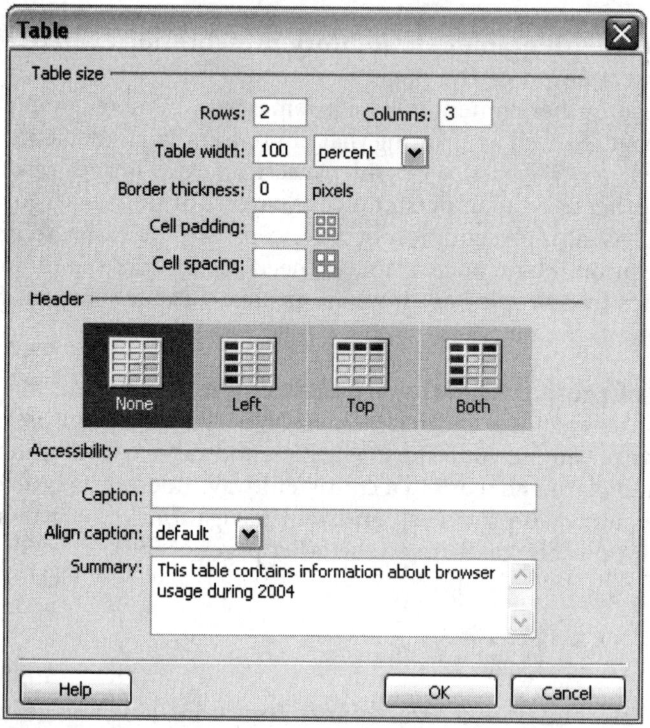

Once inserted, the summary displays in the markup as an attribute of the table element:

```
<table summary="This table contains information about browser
    usage during 2004">
```

**5.6 Provide abbreviations for header labels.**

We have already discussed table headings and their value in helping people to understand the data in a table. However, if the heading is very long, and a screen reader reads it repeatedly for each cell to which that heading applies, users could become frustrated very quickly. You can specify an abbreviated form of a heading using the abbr attribute of the th element, as shown below:

```
<th abbr="2004" scope="row">Financial year 2004</th>
```

**10.3 Until user agents (including assistive technologies) render side-by-side text correctly, provide a linear text alternative (on the current page or some other) for all tables that lay out text in parallel, word-wrapped columns.**

This checkpoint again deals with situations in which tables are used for layout. If you use a table to split a page into columns, some screen readers may read the first line of the text in the first column, then the first line of the text in the next column, and so on, rather than reading all the text in the first column, then all the text in the second. Obviously, this would make your document totally incomprehensible. To pass this checkpoint, you either need to use CSS for layout (as we have done in the Code Spark project), or provide an alternative version.

## Forms

**10.4 Until user agents handle empty controls correctly, include default, place-holding characters in edit boxes and text areas.**

Some older devices require that placeholder text be inserted into every form field, which is why this checkpoint exists. Modern browsers, screen readers, and other user agents can handle empty form fields. There is some debate as to whether placeholder text is helpful or causes more of a problem: the user needs to remove placeholder text before they enter content into the field.

# Accessibility Validation

After working through the checkpoints, I'm fairly happy that our site, in its current form, could achieve Level Double-A conformance. This is fairly good given that, while we've considered accessibility issues as we've built and structured the site, we haven't really studied the issues in depth. However, before we consider putting a Double-A badge on the site, we should check the site by validating its accessibility.

As you've probably realized, validating a site for accessibility isn't like validating its markup: many of the checkpoints don't apply to all sites, while others only apply in certain circumstances. To claim a level of conformance, you need to look at each checkpoint and decide:

1.  Does this checkpoint apply?

2.  If it applies, have I done what is needed?

For the majority of the WCAG checkpoints, the most that any accessibility validator will be able to do is remind you to check for issues that might apply to your site: the final decision will be yours. Validators are useful, however, as they highlight the points that might apply, so that you can pay special attention to those issues.

# The Dreamweaver Accessibility Validator

The simplest check is to use the Dreamweaver accessibility validator, which is available from the Results Panel: select the Site Reports tab, and click the green arrow. In the Reports dialog, shown in Figure 7.17, select Accessibility, and click Run.

## Figure 7.17. Running an accessibility report.

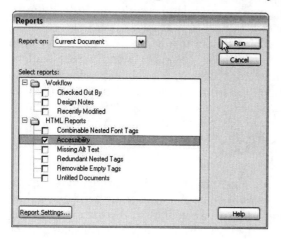

The report will appear in the Results Panel, as shown in Figure 7.18. Don't worry that a lot of points have been listed: they're not errors like those you might see in an XHTML validation report. They're issues you need to check for, and decide if they apply to your situation.

## Figure 7.18. Viewing the accessibility report in the Results panel.

| File | Line | Description |
|---|---|---|
| ? homepage-layout.html | 170 | Non spacer IMG needs LONGDESC [S508 a/WCAG 1.1 P1] -- MANUAL -- Non-spacer image may need a LONGDESC attribute. |
| ? homepage-layout.html | 2 | Color is not essential [S508 c/WCAG 2.1 P1] -- MANUAL -- |
| ? homepage-layout.html | 2 | Colors are visible [S508 c/WCAG 2.2 P1] -- MANUAL -- |
| ? homepage-layout.html | 7 | Style sheets should not be necessary [S508 d/WCAG 6.1 P1] -- MANUAL -- The page uses style sheets to present its content. Some browsers might be unable to und. |
| ? homepage-layout.html | 77 | Multiple headers should be marked in data tables [S508 h/WCAG 5.2 P1] -- MANUAL -- The page seems to contain a data table. If the table has more than one level o |
| ? homepage-layout.html | 10 | Skip repetitive links [S508 o/WCAG 13.6 P1] -- MANUAL -- Check if a textual link is present for skipping navigation links that are repeated in all the pages. |

Double-clicking on any line in this report will take you to the corresponding line of your document in Code View. Most of the lines that appeared in the report when I ran the validator on our site simply asked us to check whether the alt attribute we had provided for an image was appropriate. Double-clicking on "Non spacer IMG with equivalent ALT" jumps directly to the line at which the <img> tag is located. I find the Dreamweaver validator is useful for dealing with small documents, but for a large document or site, I tend to use an online validation service.

# Cynthia Says: Online Validation

Cynthia Says is an online validator that doesn't offer a page upload facility, so you will need to publish your document to the Internet in order to use this service. Once you've done that, visit the Cynthia Says Portal,[7] scroll down the page, and you'll find a form that allows you to check the page's accessibility. See Figure 7.19.

### Using the Web Developer Toolbar

If you use the Firefox Web browser, you can download and install the Web Developer Toolbar extension.[8] This includes handy links to validate your page with Cynthia Says, as well as useful functionality that allows you to disable JavaScript, images, and CSS.

---

[7] http://www.contentquality.com/
[8] http://chrispederick.com/work/firefox/webdeveloper/

## Figure 7.19. Using the Cynthia Says online validator.

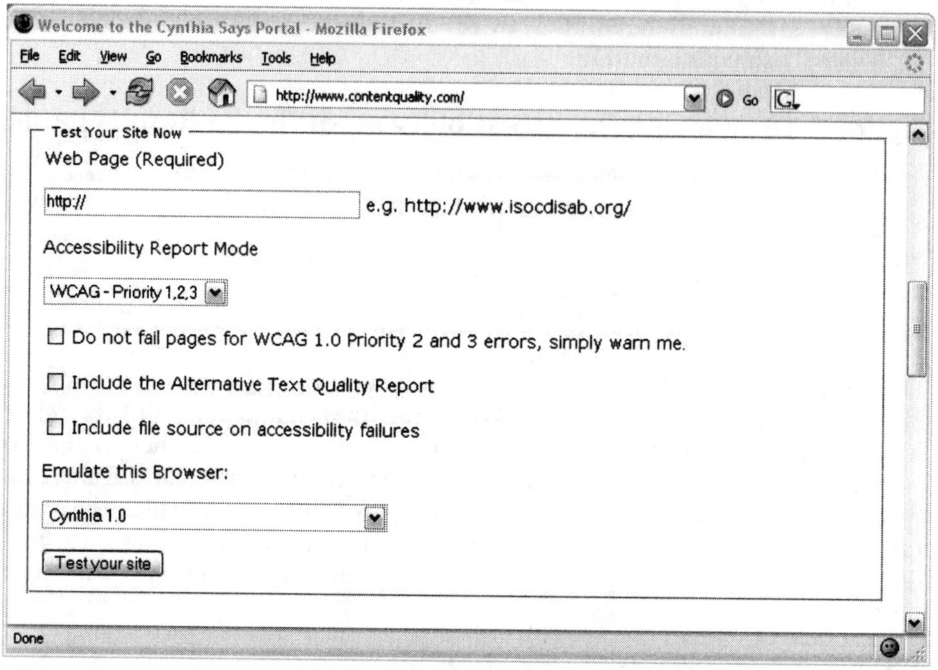

You can ask Cynthia to produce a report only for WCAG Priority 1, for Priority 1 and 2, or for Priority 1, 2, and 3 checkpoints. When you click Test your site, a report that contains all of the checkpoints that we've discussed in this chapter, as shown in Figure 7.20, will be returned.

The checkpoints are accompanied by a list of the rules Cynthia Says uses to check your documents. A Passed column is also displayed, which provides "yes" or "no" answers if the check is one that can be done automatically, and an Other column for those checkpoints for which "yes" or "no" answers are inappropriate. If these columns are left blank, the check needs to be done manually.

## Figure 7.20. Reviewing the Cynthia Says report for our document.

Cynthia Says Report - Mozilla Firefox

File  Edit  View  Go  Bookmarks  Tools  Help

http://www.contentquality.com/mynewtester/cynthia.exe

| Checkpoints | Passed | | |
|---|---|---|---|
| **Basic Settings** | Yes | No | Other |
| 1.1 / (a) Provide a text equivalent for every non-text element (e.g., via "alt", "longdesc", or in element content). *This includes*: images, graphical representations of text (including symbols), image map regions, animations (e.g., animated GIFs), applets and programmatic objects, ascii art, frames, scripts, images used as list bullets, spacers, graphical buttons, sounds (played with or without user interaction), stand-alone audio files, audio tracks of video, and video. | Yes | | |

- Rule: 1.1.1 - All IMG elements are required to contain either the alt or the longdesc attribute.
  - Warning - IMG Element found at Line: 202, Column: 9 contains the 'alt' attribute with an empty value. Please verify that this image is only used for spacing or design and has no meaning.
- Rule: 1.1.2 - All INPUT elements are required to contain the alt attribute or use a LABEL.
  - Warning - INPUT Element found at Line: 165, Column: 7 uses an implicit label, which is not recommended.
- Rule: 1.1.3 - All OBJECT elements are required to contain element content.
  - No OBJECT elements found in document body.
- Rule: 1.1.4 - All APPLET elements are required to contain both element content and the alt attribute.
  - No APPLET elements found in document body.
- Rule: 1.1.6 - All IFRAME elements are required to contain element content.
  - No IFRAME elements found in document body.
- Rule: 1.1.7 - All Anchor elements found within MAP elements are required to contain the alt attribute.
  - No MAP elements found in document body.
- Rule: 1.1.8 - All AREA elements are required to contain the alt attribute.
  - No AREA elements found in document body.
- Rule: 1.1.9 - When EMBED Elements are used, the NOEMBED element is required in the document.
  - No EMBED elements found in document body.

| | | | |
|---|---|---|---|
| 7.1 / (j) Until user agents allow users to control flickering, avoid causing the screen to flicker. | | | |

- Rule: 7.1.1 - Documents are required not to contain the BLINK element.
  - No BLINK elements found in document body.
- Rule: 7.1.2 - Documents are required not to contain the MARQUEE element.
  - No MARQUEE elements found in document body.

| | | | |
|---|---|---|---|
| 2.1 / (c) Ensure that all information conveyed with color is also available without color, for example from context or markup. | | | |
| 6.1 / (d) Organize documents so they may be read without style sheets. For example, when an HTML document is rendered without associated style sheets, it must still be possible to read the document. | | | |

- Note: Document uses external stylesheets, inline style information, or header style information.

| **Image Maps** | Yes | No | Other |
|---|---|---|---|
| 1.2 / (e) Provide redundant text links for each active region of a server-side image map. | | | N/A |

- Rule: 1.2.1 - Locate any IMG element that contains the 'ismap' attribute.
  - No IMG elements found in document body that contain the 'ismap' attribute.
- Rule: 1.2.2 - Locate any INPUT element that contains the 'ismap' attribute.

Done

By using the Cynthia Says checklist, along with the information in this chapter, you should be able to make your own decisions on the manual checks that are required, and decide whether you feel that the site has attained level Double-A conformance. As it stands, I think this page does achieve Double-A; the only "No" we receive on the Cynthia report is in the Priority 2 section in relation to form field labels: `Failure - INPUT Element, of Type TEXT, at Line: 165, Column: 7 in FORM Element at Line: 162, Column: 5`. This input element is our submit button, which does not need a label, as screen readers will read out the value of the button.

The report has also noted that the page contains "sitemap" link text, indicating that we have a sitemap. We haven't built this yet, but if we assume that we will build it, we will pass this checkpoint.

In the next chapter, we'll look at adding to our site some of the features we've already discussed—features that will bring us closer to Triple-A conformance as we build our site.

# Summary

This chapter has explained what accessibility means, discussed the specific types of users we can help by making our document accessible, and investigated how we can go about following in practice the guidelines laid down by the W3C. The fact that our document meets Level Double-A conformance without any big issues shows that accessibility doesn't have to be a difficult thing to achieve. It just takes a bit of thought to ensure that choices you make as you build your site don't make it difficult for your visitors to access your pages.

After performing these checks on a few sites, it will become second nature to you to consider these issues; after all, most of them are simply common sense, once you think about the different types of users who might want to access your site. Considering accessibility will benefit all of your users, and by going through the process of checking your site for the above issues, you are carefully considering how people will use your site, and how to make it easier for them. People you might consider as having a "disability" won't be the only ones who will benefit from the care you've taken: all users benefit from clear navigation and well-conceived site structure and content.

# Building the Site

By now, you should have an accessible, valid XHTML document complete with a valid style sheet. We can use this document as the basis for the rest of the site, knowing that we have a standards compliant framework from which we can build the rest of our pages. As we create new pages, we can be confident that, generally, the site is accessible and standards compliant. We need only worry about the new elements that we add to each page.

In this chapter, we'll lay out the main pages we need for this site:

❑ The homepage

❑ The tutorial list page

❑ An example tutorial page

❑ A sitemap

By the end of this chapter, you should be able to create as many new pages for your site as you need, and understand the techniques that are used to create a site using server-side includes.

# Creating the Includes

Our first job will be to take the page that we've built and place its reusable parts into separate files, called include files, or just includes. These include files will be included on each individual page by the server before the page is served to the browser, so you'll need to view them through the Web server we set up in Chapter 2. If you didn't set up the server then, you'll need to do it now in order to follow the examples we discuss here.

We are going to create three includes from our layout file. The first will contain the DOCTYPE and everything above the `title` element. All our pages will have unique titles—something that's important for accessibility and for search engine optimization—so we'll leave the title out of the include, instead specifying it in each page. The second include will start just after the `<body>` tag, and will contain the banner and top navigation section. The third will contain the sidebar and the end of the document.

To begin, save your `homepage-layout-strict.html` file as `index.shtml` in the root of your site folder: access File > Save As..., and select Server-Side Includes from the Save as type drop-down. We will be working in this file as we create our includes.

## The First Include: `head.html`

Open `index.shtml` in Code View and select everything from the beginning of the DOCTYPE down to `<head>`. Copy this code.

Create a new file in Dreamweaver by selecting File > New.... In the New Document dialog, select Other from the Category list, then Text from the Other list. Click OK. This process creates an empty file. Paste into it the code that you copied from `index.shtml`, and save this new document in the `inc` directory as `head.html`. The contents of `head.html` should be as follows:

File: **inc/head.html**

```
<!DOCTYPE html PUBLIC "-//W3C//DTD XHTML 1.0 Strict//EN"
    "http://www.w3.org/TR/xhtml1/DTD/xhtml1-strict.dtd">
<html xmlns="http://www.w3.org/1999/xhtml">
<head>
```

Back in `index.shtml`, we can replace the code we've just saved into `head.html`. Delete the code from `index.shtml`, and select Insert > Server Side Include. The Select File dialog will appear. Browse for `inc/head.html`, as shown in Figure 8.1.

## Figure 8.1. Selecting the `head.html` file.

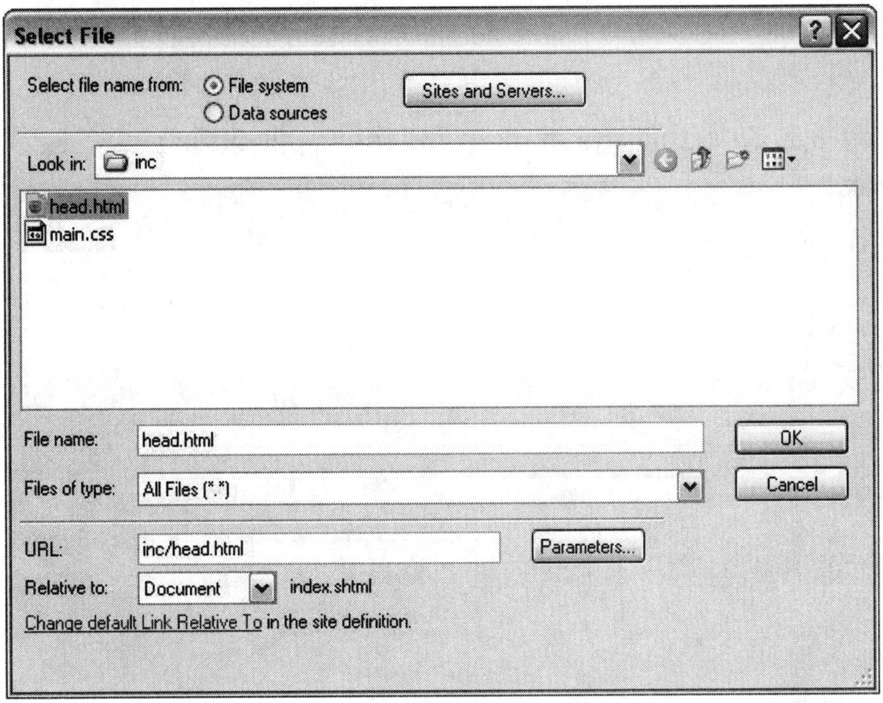

In the Relative to drop-down list, make sure Document is selected. Then, click OK. The following line should be inserted into your document:

File: **index.shtml (excerpt)**

```
<!--#include file="inc/head.html" -->
```

This instructs the Web server to insert the file `inc/head.html` at this point in the document, before it sends the document to the user's browser.

# The Second Include: `top.html`

The next include file that we need to create is the file that contains the top part of the document: the header `div` and its content, as well as some of the markup within the head of the document.

Select and copy everything from `<div id="header">` down to and including `<div id="content">`, as depicted in Figure 8.2.

## Figure 8.2. Selecting the markup for the top include.

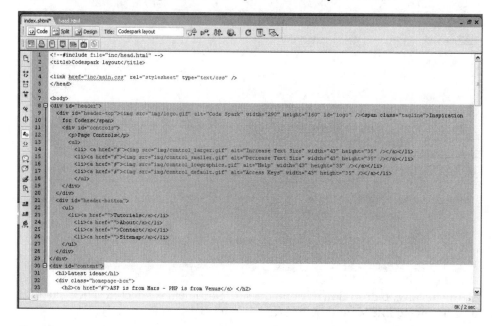

Create a new text file and paste into it the code you've copied. Save this file as `top.html`. This file should contain the following code:

File: **inc/top.html**

```
<div id="header">
  <div id="header-top">
    <img src="img/logo.gif" alt="Code Spark"
        width="290" height="160" id="logo" />
    <span class="tagline">Inspiration for Coders</span>
    <div id="controls">
      <p>Page Controls</p>
```

```
    <ul>
      <li> <a href="#"><img src="img/control_larger.gif"
          alt="Increase Text Size" width="43" height="35" /></a>
      </li>
      <li><a href="#"><img src="img/control_smaller.gif"
          alt="Decrease Text Size" width="43" height="35" /></a>
      </li>
      <li><a href="#"><img src="img/control_low_graphics.gif"
          alt="Low Graphics" width="43" height="35" /></a></li>
      <li><a href="#"><img src="img/control_default_style.gif"
          alt="Default Style" width="43" height="35" /></a></li>
    </ul>
  </div>
</div>
<div id="header-bottom">
  <ul>
    <li><a href="">Tutorials</a></li>
    <li><a href="">About</a></li>
    <li><a href="">Contact</a></li>
    <li><a href="">Sitemap</a></li>
  </ul>
</div>
</div>
<div id="content">
```

Back in `index.shtml`, delete all of the markup that you've just pasted into `top.html`, and insert a server-side include as before. This time, however, select `top.html` and insert it just after the `<body>` tag. At this point, the first few lines of `index.shtml` should appear as follows:

File: **index.shtml (excerpt)**

```
<!--#include file="inc/head.html" -->
<title>Code Spark layout</title>

<meta http-equiv="Content-Type" content="text/html;
    charset=iso-8859-1" />
<link href="inc/main.css" rel="stylesheet" type="text/css" />
</head>
<body>
<!--#include file="inc/top.html" -->
  <h1>Latest ideas </h1>
```

**Figure 8.3. Dreamweaver includes the files and displays them as they will display in the browser.**

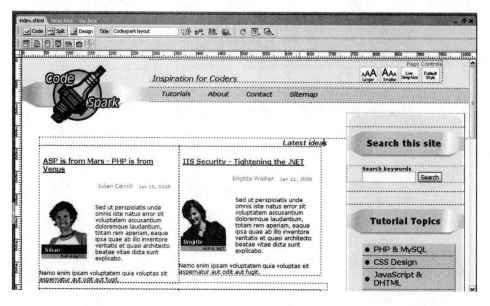

If you switch back into Design View, you should see that the parts that you have copied out of `index.shtml` are still displayed; Figure 8.3 illustrates this. This occurs because Dreamweaver understands the server-side includes in the file and automatically includes the files when displaying the document. If you view the file locally (by selecting File > Open File... in your Web browser, or by double-clicking the file in Windows Explorer), you'll see that the header of the page is missing and that most of the page is missing its CSS rules. This occurs because you're not viewing the file through the Web server, which is responsible for handling the server-side includes.

# The Final Include: `bottom.html`

The last file that we need to create and include in our document will contain the sidebar and the end of the document. Select everything from the closing `</div>` tag in the content area right down to the final `</html>` tag in the document. Copy this content into a new file, and save it as `bottom.html`. The file should contain the following code.

File: **inc/bottom.html**

```
</div>
<div id="nav">
  <div class="section">
    <h3>Search this Site</h3>
    <form id="form1" method="post" action="">
      <p><label>Search keywords
        <br />
        <input name="keywords" type="text" class="searchtxt"
          id="keywords" />
        <input type="submit" name="Submit" value="Search" />
      </label></p>
    </form>
  </div>
  <div class="section">
    <h3>Tutorial Topics</h3>
    <ul class="topics">
      <li><a href="">PHP &amp; MySQL</a></li>
      <li><a href="">CSS Design</a></li>
      <li><a href="">JavaScript &amp; DHTML</a></li>
      <li><a href="">ASP &amp; .NET</a></li>
      <li><a href="">JSP &amp; Servlets</a></li>
    </ul>
  </div>
  <div class="section">
    <h3>Reader Favorites</h3>
    <ul class="list">
      <li><a href="">Longus Imitaris</a></li>
      <li><a href="">Tu Urbanus Vero Scurra</a></li>
      <li><a href="">Lingua Factiosi, inertes opera</a></li>
      <li><a href="">Mufrius, Non Magister</a></li>
      <li><a href="">Omnis Oratio Moribus Consonet</a></li>
      <li><a href="">Quales Illic Homunculi</a></li>
      <li><a href="">Omnium Mensarum Assecula</a></li>
    </ul>
  </div>
  <img src="img/nav-bottom.gif" alt="" width="266"
      height="63" class="displayblock" />
</div>
</body>
</html>
```

Delete this code from index.shtml and insert a server-side include in its place. Save your document and check that it still displays as a complete page in Dreamweaver. Now, try viewing the page from your Web server by entering the address **http://localhost/codespark/index.shtml** into your Web browser.

You should see the complete page as you do in Dreamweaver; its display through Firefox is illustrated in Figure 8.4. If you right-click on the page and select View Source, all of the code will display, as the server includes all the files before it sends the page to the browser.

**Figure 8.4. The `index.shtml` page view in Firefox.**

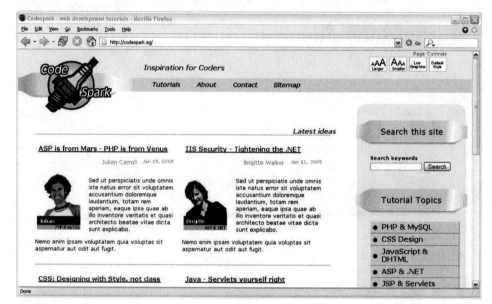

# Creating The Base Page

The `index.shtml` page that we have created will become the homepage of the site. Our next step is to create a document that will serve as a starting point for the rest of the site's pages. These pages will be less complex than the homepage, but, as we discussed when we created the layout, they will all display the header and sidebar sections that are contained in our include files; the difference will be the content that's kept within the content `div`.

The basic page layout is shown in Figure 8.5; we can use this as a starting point for all the pages of the site.

This page constitutes a base framework: every time you want to create a new page, you'll be able to do so simply by saving this framework under a new filename. All of the include files will be in the right spots, ready for you to add your content.

## Figure 8.5. The base page layout for an article.

Save `index.shtml` as `base.shtml`. Switch into Code View and delete all the code between the includes `top.shtml` and `bottom.shtml`. Insert a placeholder paragraph between the two includes:

File: **base.shtml (excerpt)**

```
<p>Content here</p>
```

You should now have a document that contains the following:

File: **base.shtml**

```
<!--#include file="inc/head.html" -->
<title>Code Spark layout</title>
<meta http-equiv="Content-Type" content="text/html;
    charset=iso-8859-1" />
<link href="inc/main.css" rel="stylesheet" type="text/css" />
</head>
```

```
<body>
<!--#include file="inc/top.html" -->
<p>Content here</p>
<!--#include file="inc/bottom.html" -->
```

### The Importance of Placeholder Text

*Tip*

This placeholder text gives you something to select and replace with your content in Dreamweaver's Design View. If you haven't inserted any content between the two includes, it becomes very difficult to start adding content.

Save the page and view it in Design View. You should see the framework of the page, as shown in Figure 8.6.

## Figure 8.6. The base page file.

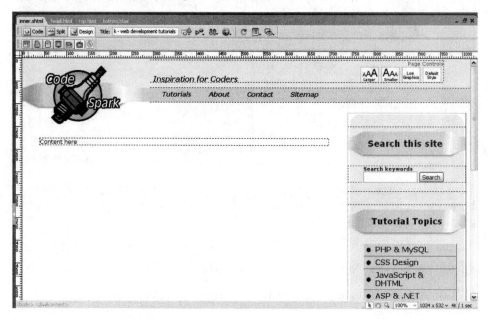

From this point forward, when we create a new page, we will simply save this `base.shtml` page with a new filename, then add to it.

# The Tutorial List Page

Save `base.shtml` as `tutorials.shtml` using File > Save As.... This page will display a list of all of the tutorials on the site, under appropriate category headings. To start with, we'll set the title of the page to reflect its contents. Page titles are important when it comes to having your site indexed by search engines—as well as for accessibility purposes—as they explain what the page is about. A good title for this page would be "Code Spark tutorials – the very best ASP, PHP, JSP and CSS tutorials." Place this text between the existing `<title>` and `</title>` tags.

Next, start the content of the page with a level one heading that reads, "Tutorials," followed by a paragraph that introduces the tutorial section of the Website.

We want to display all of the tutorials under tutorial topic headings. The Sidebar contains a list of these headings:

❑ PHP & MySQL

❑ CSS Design

❑ JavaScript & DHTML

❑ ASP & .NET

❑ JSP & Servlets

Add these to the page as level two headings, as shown in Figure 8.7.

## Figure 8.7. The tutorial headings.

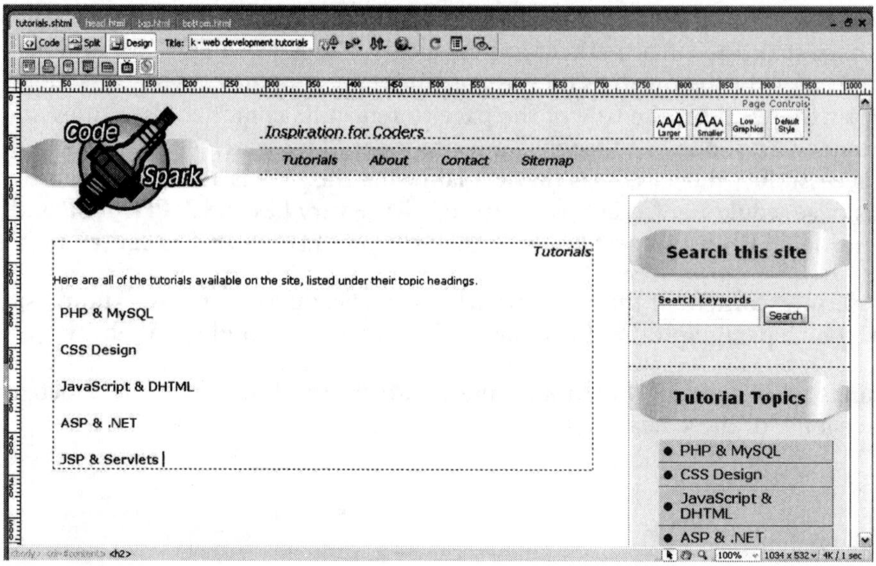

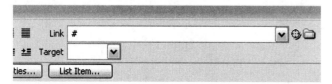

The headings have taken on the rules created for them in the style sheet, as the style sheet is attached to the page in the `top.html` include.

# Creating the Lists

Under each heading, add a list of the tutorials that are presented within that category, using the Property Inspector to mark the titles up as an unordered list. Each tutorial title will form a link to the actual tutorial page; you can make these null links (i.e., links that don't go anywhere) for now by entering a **#** in the Link field of the Property Inspector, as shown in Figure 8.8.

## Figure 8.8. Creating a null link.

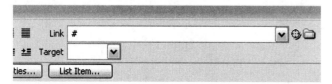

Continue until you have two or three tutorials listed under each heading.

### Make a Mockup

Even if you are going to store your tutorials in a database and list them on the page using PHP, ASP, or another server-side language, creating the page initially as a static page containing dummy data can simplify the process of sorting out the design. By the time you come to writing the server-side code, you don't have to worry about how the page will look, because you already will have created all the CSS rules, and worked out how the page will display.

Often, when I'm creating an application for a client, I'll mock up the look and feel of the site's main pages as static HTML pages. This way, I can quickly show the pages to the client, and they can understand how the site will look—and what will appear on each main page—before I begin any time-consuming development work.

# Adding to the CSS

We have now marked up our basic tutorial listing page. As we have already created some basic styles, it doesn't look too plain; however, it might be nice to style the tutorials lists.

In Dreamweaver, create a new CSS rule using the CSS Panel. Create class selector, **.tutorial-list**, as shown in Figure 8.9. Define it in our existing style sheet, `main.css`.

### Figure 8.9. Creating a new class named `tutorial-list`.

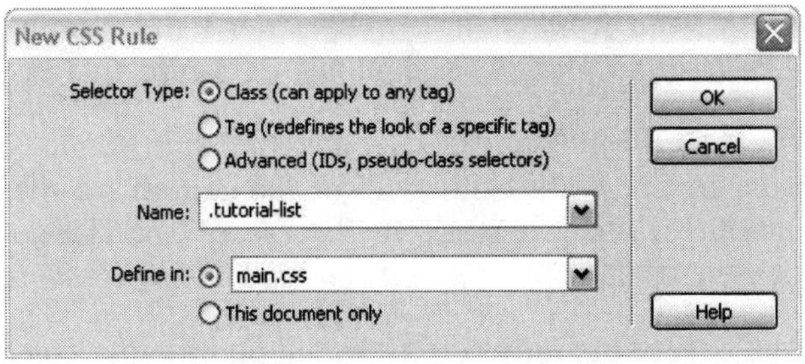

In the CSS Rule Definition dialog, go to List category and browse for the bullet image `tutorial-list-bullet.gif`. Click OK to create the class.

You will need to apply the class to the lists in order for the new bullet image to display. Select the <ul> tag of the first list using the Tag Selector at the bottom of the document window. In the Property Inspector, select from the Style drop-down the tutorial-list class that you just created. The selected list should display with images instead of the plain bullets, as shown in Figure 8.10. Select each list in turn and apply the same class to it: because we have used a class for this purpose, rather than an ID, we can apply it multiple times throughout the one document.

## Figure 8.10. The tutorial lists.

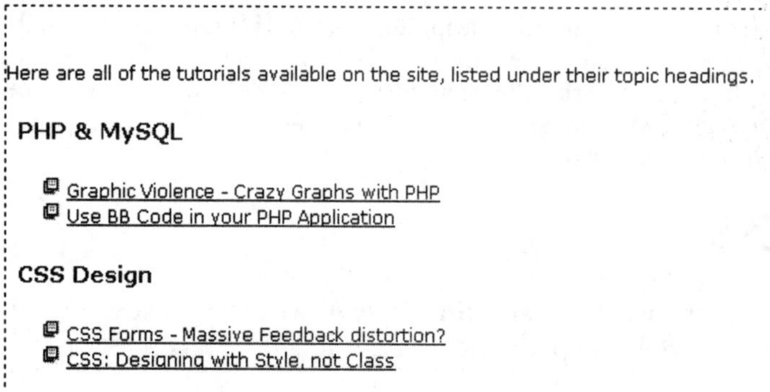

Here are all of the tutorials available on the site, listed under their topic headings.

**PHP & MySQL**

- Graphic Violence - Crazy Graphs with PHP
- Use BB Code in your PHP Application

**CSS Design**

- CSS Forms - Massive Feedback distortion?
- CSS: Designing with Style, not Class

# An Example Tutorial Page

The next page we will create is an example tutorial page. The one I'm going to create is a CSS tutorial that's linked from the front page. If you're creating all your tutorials as static pages, you could use this example page as a starting point and create as many pages as you need from it. If, on the other hand, you're working with server-side code, you could place your dynamic data into this example page.

We will start, as we did with the last page, by adding all of the content to the page, so that we can see what we have. We'll then add the necessary CSS classes to create the look and feel that we want.

Open `base.shtml` and save it as `tutorial1.shtml`. Delete the placeholder content. The first thing on our tutorials page is the breadcrumb trail that shows users where they're located within the structure of the site:

```
Home > Tutorials > CSS Design > CSS: Designing with Style, not
Class
```

Add this as the first item within the content area of the page. The first three elements will need to link back to the homepage, the tutorials list page, and the

CSS tutorials list page (if you're creating one), respectively. The final item identifies the page that the user is currently on: it doesn't need to be linked. The finished trail is shown in Figure 8.11.

**Figure 8.11. The breadcrumb trail.**

Now add the title of the article as a level one heading. We've already created a style rule for level one headings, so the text will be aligned to the right.

Below the heading, insert the author image; use the same image that we used for this author on the homepage: `georgina.jpg`. Don't forget to add the `alt` attribute that describes the image. Next to the image, add the author's name, Georgina Laidlaw, and a publication date for the article. Finally, add a few paragraphs of dummy article text. You now have the basic elements of an article page.

# Adding CSS for the Tutorial Page

Let's use CSS to style the tutorial page, starting with the first item that we added to the page. Create a new CSS rule for the class selector **.breadcrumbs** in `main.css`.

Let's add a 1 pixel border to the bottom of the breadcrumbs in order to visually separate them from the rest of the content. In the Border category, uncheck the Same for all checkboxes and create a bottom border that's solid, with a 1 pixel width, and a color of **#3C582F**.

In the Type category, set Size to 90% to make the breadcrumb text slightly smaller than that of the main content. Set Line height to 2 ems to provide some space between the bottom border and the breadcrumb text. In the Block category, set Text align to right, then click OK. In order for these rules to display, you need to apply the `breadcrumbs` class to the paragraph that wraps the breadcrumb trail. So, select the `<p>` and, in the Property Inspector, apply the class using the Style selection box.

## Level One Heading

The heading on the page has aligned right, and has taken on the styles we set for level one headings (`h1`) when we created the initial layout. But, for these tutorial pages, I'd like the heading to be left-aligned and a little larger.

We can create differently styled headings by creating a class to be applied to specific headings. That way, any heading to which no class is applied will take on the default `h1` style, but headings to which a different class is applied will also use the style properties specified for that class.

Create a new CSS rule. This time, create an Advanced selector **#content h1.tutorial**. This class will only be applied to level one headings that have a class of `tutorial` inside an element with the `content` ID. Under Block, set Text Align to left. Under Type, set Style to normal, and Size to 160%. Now, apply the `tutorial` class to the heading.

# The Author Image

The author image should display to the left of the author credit, date of publication, and the tutorial's introduction. To achieve this, we need to float the picture left, which will allow the rest of the content to wrap it.

Create for this class a new CSS class rule, **.tutorial-author**. In Box, set the Width to 104 pixels, and set Float to left, right margin to 10 pixels, and bottom margin to 10 pixels. Click OK, select the image, and apply the `tutorial-author` class. The results of this work are shown in Figure 8.12.

**Figure 8.12. The layout after the new class `tutorial-author` is applied.**

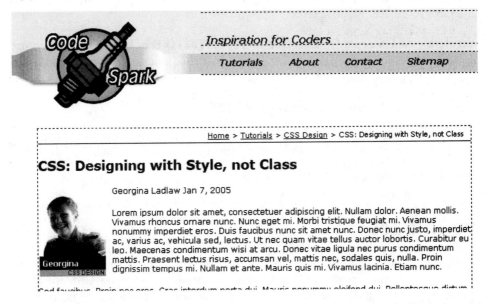

# The Author Credit and Date

The tutorial page is really starting to come together now! Preview it in the browser by typing **`http://localhost/codespark/tutorial1.shtml`** into the address bar, but make sure you select File > Save All first, so that all the changes you've made to the Web page and the style sheet are saved.

Next, let's style the author credit. Create a new CSS rule for the selector **`.tutorial-credit`**. In the Box category, set right margin to 3 ems and click OK. Apply this class to the author's name (in this case, Georgina Laidlaw) by highlighting the text and selecting tutorial-credit from the Style drop-down list. This will wrap the author name in a `span` with the class `tutorial-credit`, supplying some space between the name and the date.

# The Introduction Text

In our mockup image for this page, the first paragraph of text for the tutorial is bold. Now, we could simply select this and click the B button on the Property Inspector, which would wrap the text in `<strong>` tags. However, from the point of view of semantics, this wouldn't be the correct thing to do, as `strong` implies that the text has a special meaning: that it should be strongly emphasized. As we only want the text to *look* bold, rather than to have any special meaning, we'll use CSS to create the bold effect.

Create a new CSS rule for the selector `.tutorial-intro`. In the Type category, under Weight, select bold. Click OK, then select the paragraph that wraps the introduction text, and apply the `tutorial-intro` class to it.

### A Hidden Advantage of CSS

An additional advantage to styling this introduction with CSS is that if, in the future, you wanted the introduction to appear in a box, or to display as a different color, or in some other format, you have already added a class to it: it's easy to create a new look for that class without having to edit every page.

# Inline Images

We have now styled the basic tutorial layout. However, there are a couple of extra page elements that might appear in some tutorials; let's create CSS for these cases, so that the styles are there, ready to be applied. The first case is an inline image that displays within the text—perhaps a screenshot or figure.

As we saw when we dealt with the author image, the way to get text to flow around an image is to float that image left or right. When you insert the image, you need to insert it at the start of the text that you want to wrap around it. Normally, the text will line up with the bottom of the image, and there will be a large amount of whitespace on either side of the image. Insert the image `css-tutorial-img.gif` into the middle of a paragraph, and see for yourself.

Create for the image a CSS rule with selector `.tutorial-image`. In the Box category, set Float to left, and give the image a right margin of 10 pixels and a bottom margin of 10 pixels. If you'd rather have the image on the right and the text wrapping to the left, float the image right and apply the margin to the left and bottom. Click OK, then apply the class to your image.

### Standardize Image Sizes

In some older browsers, floated elements need to have a defined width, so it's a good idea—wherever possible—to make all of your tutorial images the same width. Then, you only need the one class to deal with them!

# Quotes

Another element we might like to have in our tutorial is a pull quote: a short quote taken from the tutorial and highlighted. Pull quotes can be used to draw the reader into the article and encourage them to read it, or to highlight important issues that the author wants the reader to remember. Just like an image, the quote will display inline within a paragraph of the article, as depicted in Figure 8.13.

## Figure 8.13. Displaying the pull quote.

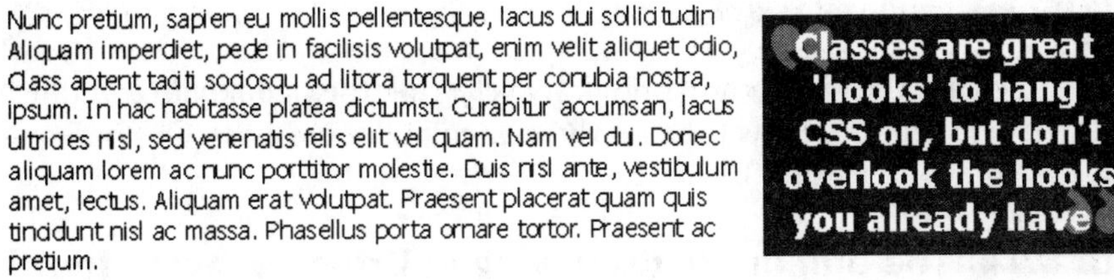

Nunc pretium, sapien eu mollis pellentesque, lacus dui sollicitudin Aliquam imperdiet, pede in facilisis volutpat, enim velit aliquet odio, class aptent taciti sociosqu ad litora torquent per conubia nostra, ipsum. In hac habitasse platea dictumst. Curabitur accumsan, lacus ultricies nisl, sed venenatis felis elit vel quam. Nam vel dui. Donec aliquam lorem ac nunc porttitor molestie. Duis nisl ante, vestibulum amet, lectus. Aliquam erat volutpat. Praesent placerat quam quis tincidunt nisl ac massa. Phasellus porta ornare tortor. Praesent ac pretium.

**Classes are great 'hooks' to hang CSS on, but don't overlook the hooks you already have**

To insert your quote, add it as an additional paragraph above the paragraph in which you would like it to float.

The correct XHTML or HTML element to use to mark up a quote is `blockquote`. You can apply this element from the Property Inspector; however, be aware that Dreamweaver confusingly calls it "Indent Text," which describes precisely what it should *not* be used for!

### Don't use Blockquote to Indent!

In the "bad old days," Web designers would often use the `blockquote` element to indent text on their pages, because browsers render the `blockquote` text as indented by default. If you want to indent text on your page, you should be using CSS to do so!

Select the quote and click the Indent Text button on the Property Inspector to add the `blockquote` element. If you switch into Code View, you'll find that it has wrapped the `<p>` and `</p>` tags `<blockquote>` and `</blockquote>` tags. In Design View, your quote will appear indented from the left margin.

To create the pull quote effect we want, we can use CSS to style the `blockquote`. We have a choice here: we can either style all `blockquotes` in the style of our pull quote, or we can apply a class to only those quotes that we want to display in this way. I think it's quite likely that I'd want to use `blockquotes` in articles for other reasons—perhaps in quoting an expert on a certain topic—so I'm going to leave the basic `blockquote` alone, and create a `pullquote` class for these special quotes.

Create a new CSS rule in Dreamweaver for the selector **`.pullquote`**. In the Type category, set Font size to 120%, Weight to bold and the Color to **#FFFFFF**. In the Background category, set the background color to **#3C582F**.

In the Box category, set Width to 160 pixels, Float to right, and assign bottom and left margins of 10 pixels. Then, set the top and right margins to 0 pixels to remove the default margin from this element. Add padding of Top 0.2 ems, Right 0.5 ems, Bottom 0.2 ems, and Left 0.2 ems.

Click OK to create the class, and apply it by selecting the `blockquote` and using the Property Inspector to select the newly created pullquote class. Our pull quote displays as shown in Figure 8.14.

**Figure 8.14. The pull quote displaying in Dreamweaver after the class is applied.**

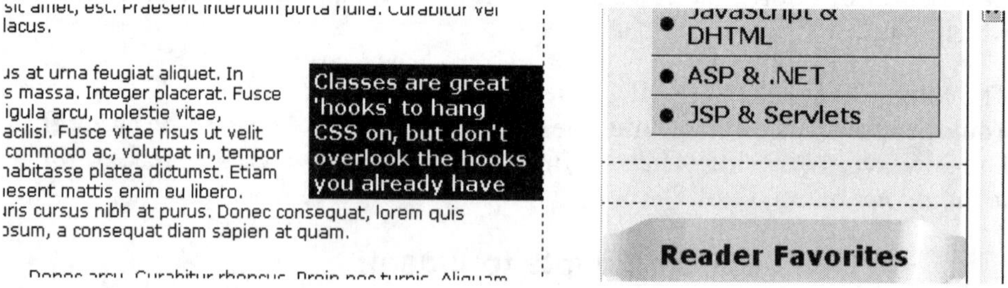

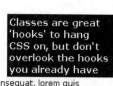

## Adding the Quote Mark Images

In our mockup layout we have quote marks within the pull quote's green background. As we don't know how tall the box will be—the quote could be any length, or the user might resize the text in the browser, causing it to expand—we can't simply have one green background image with quotes in it as the background of the box; we need to create the background in a way that will allow the box to resize. To do this, we'll use two background images: one for the top-left quotation mark, and one for the quotation mark in the bottom-right. An element can only have one background image, so we'll need to make use of both the `blockquote` element and the p that's inside it.

First, edit the `.pullquote` rule we applied to the `blockquote` element. In the Background category, browse for the `quote-bottom.gif` background image. Set Repeat to no-repeat, Horizontal Position to right, and Vertical Position to bottom. Click OK to add the bottom quote image to the bottom-right of the quote box, as shown in Figure 8.15.

**Figure 8.15. The pull quote style taking shape.**

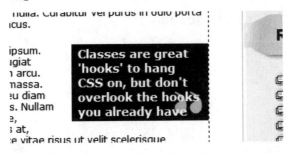

To add the top quote, create a new CSS rule for **.pullquote p** using the Advanced selector type. This will select any paragraph within any `blockquote` element to which the `pullquote` class is applied. In the Background category, browse for the background image `quote-top.gif`, and set Repeat to no-repeat. This image will be positioned from the top and left of the element. In order that we have some space before the text starts, we can tweak the padding and margins on the `p` within the `blockquote`. In the Box category, set Margin on all sides to 0 pixels, then set the Padding to Top 6 pixels, Right 4 pixels, Bottom 6 pixels, Left 8 pixels. You can tweak these values until you're happy with the amount of spacing between the edge of the box and the text. Click OK, and these rules will automatically be applied to the paragraph within the `blockquote`. You should end up with something like the display shown in Figure 8.16.

**Figure 8.16. The final pull quote displaying in Firefox.**

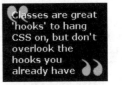

# Highlighting the Current Section in the Navigation Area

In our original layout image, the current tutorial section was highlighted, as shown in Figure 8.17, to help users identify where they were located within the site.

**Figure 8.17. Highlighting the current section.**

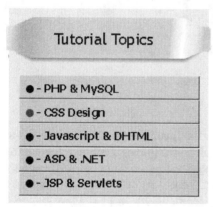

Unfortunately, as we've placed all of the sidebar in an included file, we can't change it for each individual page in order to highlight the current page or section. However, we can achieve this highlighting effect using pure CSS and some very longwinded selectors!

In your `tutorial1.shtml` file, switch into Code View and find the opening `<body>` tag. Edit this tag so that it reads as follows:

File: **tutorial1.shtml (excerpt)**

```
<body id="topic-css">
```

We are giving the body tag an ID that relates to the section of the site that it's in: if it were in the PHP section, the ID would be `topic-php`. Open `bottom.html` in Code View, and find the unordered list that displays the tutorial topics.

File: **inc/bottom.html (excerpt)**

```
<ul class="topics">
  <li><a href="">PHP &amp; MySQL</a></li>
  <li><a href="">CSS Design</a></li>
```

```
<li><a href="">JavaScript &amp; DHTML</a></li>
<li><a href="">ASP &amp; .NET</a></li>
<li><a href="">JSP &amp; Servlets</a></li>
 </ul>
```

Add the following classes to each `li` element. This class should have the same name as its corresponding ID in the body element.

File: **inc/bottom.html (excerpt)**

```
<ul class="topics">
   <li class="topic-php">
     <a href="">PHP &amp; MySQL</a></li>
   <li class="topic-css">
     <a href="">CSS Design</a></li>
   <li class="topic-javascript">
     <a href="">JavaScript &amp; DHTML</a></li>
   <li class="topic-asp">
     <a href="">ASP &amp; .NET</a></li>
   <li class="topic-jsp">
     <a href="">JSP &amp; Servlets</a></li>
   </ul>
```

## Includes Save Time!

As `bottom.html` is the navigation included on every page, we only need change one file to have our change reflected on every page that includes this file. Using includes can save a great deal of time, as you only need to change and upload one file to make a change to the site's navigation.

Save `bottom.html` and open `main.css`, your style sheet file. You could add these selectors via the CSS Panel, but as the selectors are rather longwinded, and the rule itself is quite simple, it's easier to add these rules to the style sheet directly.

Scroll through `main.css` until you find the following rule:

File: **inc/main.css (excerpt)**

```
#nav ul.topics li {
  font: 90% Verdana, Arial, Helvetica, sans-serif;
  color: #3C582F;
  background: #D9DDCF url(../img/nav-topics-bullet.gif) no-repeat
     4px center;
  padding: 0.2em 0.4em 0.3em 26px;
  border-top: 1px solid #EAEAE2;
  border-right: 1px solid #72746D;
  border-bottom: 1px solid #72746D;
```

```
    border-left: 1px solid #EAEAE2;
}
```

Among other things, this rule adds the green bullet image to the topic list. Below this, add the following:

File: **inc/main.css (excerpt)**

```
#topic-css ul.topics li.topic-css {
  background-image: url(../img/nav-topics-bullet-hilite.gif);
}
```

This rule will overwrite the "CSS Design" menu item's green bullet point with an orange one on all the CSS tutorial pages; however, it will leave the green bullet displaying on the other tutorial pages, as shown in Figure 8.17. The rule works because the selector starts with the #topic-css ID selector, so the rule will only apply when the body element has the topic-css ID.

We'll also need to add style rules for the other menu items, but, thankfully, we don't need to repeat ourselves too much: we can just add extra selectors to the same rule, separating them with commas.

File: **inc/main.css (excerpt)**

```
#topic-css ul.topics li.topic-css, #topic-php ul.topics
   li.topic-php, #topic-asp ul.topics li.topic-asp,
   #topic-javascript ul.topics li.topic-javascript,
   #topic-jsp ul.topics li.topic-jsp {
  background-image: url(../img/nav-topics-bullet-hilite.gif);
}
```

### Server-Side Language Tip

If you're using a server-side language to build your site, you could instead create a class named nav-hilite, then apply that class dynamically to the correct li element.

You have now completed your tutorial page! You can use this as a basis to create all of your static tutorial pages, or as a template to pull in dynamic content if you're working with databased content.

### Don't Forget to Validate!

Before you go on to create more pages based on this one, don't forget to validate the page! Unfortunately, because we're using server-side includes, the Dreamweaver validator will be confused by this page: it will think that you've forgotten to use the `html` and `head` elements, as they are located in the include files. One way around this would be to upload the file to a Web server, and enter the live URL into the W3C validator. However, if you aren't in a position to upload all of your files yet, a quick way to validate offline pages is to use Firefox and the Web Developer Toolbar,[1] which provide a handy method for validating your markup without having to upload the document. This solution is shown in action in Figure 8.18.

### Figure 8.18. Validating local HTML in Firefox.

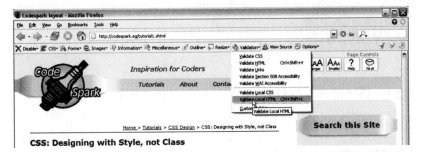

This toolbar provides all kinds of useful little tools. The one we're interested in, Validate Local HTML, basically uploads the HTML to the W3C HTML Validator Website and presents the results in a new tab in Firefox. This is also useful if you're creating pages that use server-side scripts on a local Web server, as the output of the scripts are sent to the validator.

# The Sitemap

The pages that we have created so far should provide a useful starting point for most of the other pages that you might want to create for the site. You can, of course, add to `main.css` more CSS rules to style any additional elements you need for your pages. In the next chapter, we'll look at creating forms—including building a contact form for the site—and we'll see how you can ensure that your forms are accessible and attractive. However, to complete this chapter, we will look at a very useful and helpful inclusion on any site: a sitemap.

It's easy for Website users to become confused, or to be unsure of where to find the particular content they're after, especially on large sites with complex navigational structures. A sitemap, linked from all of the pages of your site, gives users an easy way to inform and orient themselves; it also provides Web crawlers such as Google a good way to find (and index!) all the content on your site.

---

[1] http://chrispederick.com/work/firefox/webdeveloper/

The sitemap is generally a tree-like structure with at least two levels—often more. In our site, the top-level navigation is as follows:

❑ Tutorials

❑ About

❑ Contact

Under Tutorials, we have these main topic headings:

❑ PHP & MySQL

❑ CSS Design

❑ JavaScript & DHTML

❑ ASP & .NET

❑ JSP & Servlets

Under each of these topic headings, we have the list of tutorials. There are three levels in the structure of this part of the site, which is depicted in Figure 8.19.

## Figure 8.19. The Code Spark sitemap.

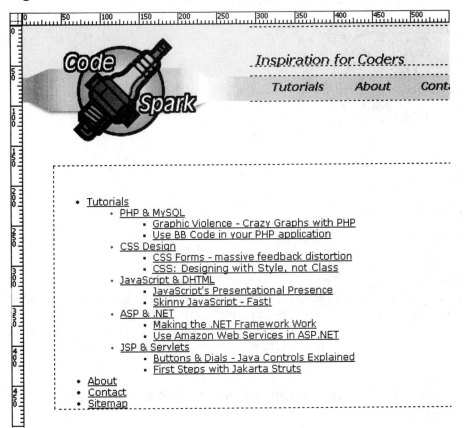

Just as we displayed our tutorials in a list on the tutorials page, we can use lists to mark up our sitemap. To describe the different levels of navigation, we can nest one list inside another: the tutorial topics will comprise a list that's nested inside the main sitemap list, and the tutorials for each topic will be nested inside the list for that topic.

# Marking up the Sitemap

Create a new page from base.shtml and save it as sitemap.shtml. Set the page's title to **Sitemap**, and add **Sitemap** as a level one heading. Enter the top level navigation as an unordered list, making each item a link, as shown in Figure 8.20.

## Figure 8.20. Marking up the top level of the sitemap as a list.

Position the cursor at the end of the text that reads, "Tutorials," and hit **Enter** to create a new list item below it. We want this item to be the first item of a list that's nested inside the Tutorials li element. To do this in Dreamweaver, hit the **Tab** key. The list item will move in, and will appear with a style of bullet that's different from the main list item, as shown in Figure 8.21. Add the tutorial topics to this list.

## Figure 8.21. Marking up the second level of the sitemap as a nested list.

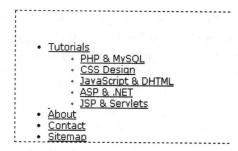

Repeat the process to add the third level to the sitemap, placing the cursor after "PHP & MySQL," hitting **Enter** to create a new list item, and then hitting **Tab** to move to a new, nested list in which you can add the tutorials for the PHP &

MySQL topic category. You should end up with the structure shown in Figure 8.22.

## Figure 8.22. Marking up the sitemap as nested lists.

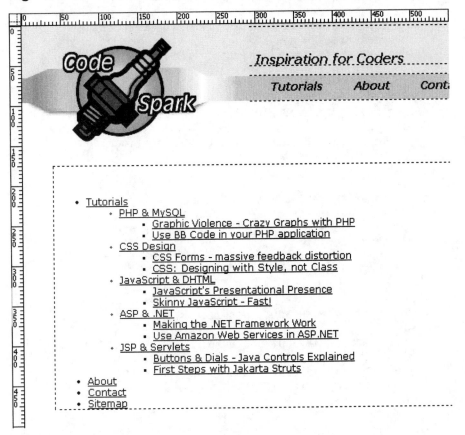

The code should look like this:

File: **sitemap.shtml** (excerpt)

```
<ul>
  <li><a href="tutorials.shtml">Tutorials</a>
    <ul>
      <li><a href="#">PHP &amp; MySQL </a>
        <ul>
          <li><a href="#">Graphic Violence - Crazy Graphs with
            PHP</a></li>
```

```
        <li><a href="#">ASP is from Mars, PHP is from
          Venus</a></li>
      </ul>
    </li>
    <li><a href="#">CSS Design</a>
      <ul>
        <li><a href="#">CSS Forms - Massive feedback
          distortion?</a></li>
        <li><a href="tutorial1.shtml">CSS: Designing with
          Style, not Class</a></li>
      </ul>
    </li>
    <li><a href="#">JavaScript &amp; DHTML</a>
      <ul>
        <li><a href="#">JavaScript's Presentational
          Presence</a></li>
      </ul>
    </li>
    <li><a href="#">ASP &amp; .NET </a>
      <ul>
        <li><a href="#">Making the .NET Framework
          Work</a></li>
        <li><a href="#">IIS Security - Tightening the
          .NET</a></li>
      </ul>
    </li>
    <li><a href="#">JSP &amp; Servlets </a>
      <ul>
        <li><a href="#">Buttons &amp; Dials - Java Controls
          Explained</a></li>
        <li><a href="#">Java - Servlets yourself
          right</a></li>
      </ul>
    </li>
  </ul>
 </li>
 <li><a href="#">About</a></li>
 <li><a href="#">Contact</a></li>
</ul>
```

If you look at the markup that Dreamweaver has generated, you'll see that the nested lists are located inside the parent li element, before the closing </li> tag.

# Styling the Sitemap with CSS

Now that we have created the structure for our sitemap, we can make it look more attractive using CSS.

First, create a new CSS rule for the selector `.sitemap`. In the Box category, set Margin and Padding to 0 pixels. In the List category, set Type to none. Click OK and apply the `sitemap` class to the outermost list's `<ul>` tag: select the first `<ul>` in the tag selector, then select the class from the Style drop-down in the Property Inspector. This will remove the outer list's default margin and padding, as well as its bullets, as shown in Figure 8.23.

**Figure 8.23. Using the Property Inspector to apply the `sitemap` class to the sitemap.**

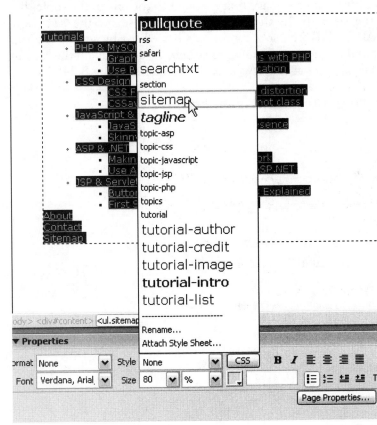

Now, create a new CSS rule using the Advanced selector `.sitemap li`. This style will only apply to `li` elements within the sitemap.

In the Border category add a solid, 1 pixel bottom border with a color of **#E4FDCC**. To space out the main list items, add a bottom padding of 0.5 ems, and a bottom margin of 0.6 ems, in the Box category. Click OK; this style rule will apply automatically to all `li` elements with the sitemap. You'll see that the rule you've just created has been applied to the nested `li` elements as well as those in the outermost list. Next, let's create rules for those nested items in order to style them differently.

Create a new CSS rule with the selector `.sitemap li ul li`. This will address the nested `li` elements, not those in the outermost list.

Set the bottom border style to none, to prevent the parent's border from displaying on these items. Let's use a bullet image that's similar to the one in the topics list for this level of the sitemap. In the List category, browse for the `sitemap-level2.gif` file. Also, adjust the spacing for this nested list by setting the top margin to 0.2 ems and the bottom padding to 0.2 ems. Click OK, and the second and third level lists will take on the new style illustrated in Figure 8.24.

## Figure 8.24. Styling the second level lists.

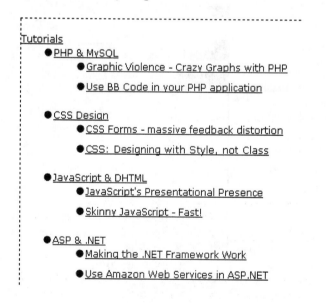

Finally, let's style the last level of the sitemap. We'll use for the third level the image that we used on the `tutorial.shtml` page. So, create a new CSS rule with the selector `.sitemap li ul ul li`; this will address the third level lists. All that's needed here is to browse for the small icon we used for the tutorial list (`tutorial-list-bullet.gif`). Select it, and click OK; the sitemap is complete, as shown in Figure 8.25.

**Figure 8.25. Displaying the completed sitemap in the browser.**

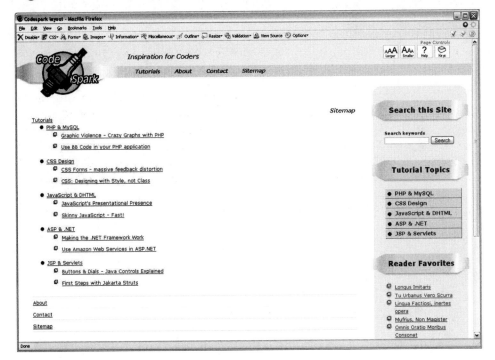

# Summary

In this chapter, we explored how to take a basic page layout and, using XHTML and CSS, turn it into the basis of a Website. The techniques used in this chapter can just as easily be used with a dynamic, database-driven site as they can with a static Website.

Once we have created our layout and the includes for the common parts of the document, we can use this to rapidly develop our site, only creating new CSS rules for new elements that we need to add to specific pages. As we know that we have a valid, accessible framework for our document, we can add new pages quickly. We need only check that the page elements we add to the content area validate, and that we bear accessibility in mind as we continue to build the site.

# Forms and Third-party Services

Now that we've created the main pages of our site, we can start to look at some additional elements, most of which are common to many sites online today.

As Web professionals move away from creating "brochureware," towards dynamic, interactive sites, they tend to require forms in order to gather user input. In this chapter, we'll use Dreamweaver to create an accessible form, which will become the contact page of our site. We'll also discuss how we can utilize a third-party service—the site search service from Atomz—on the site.

## The Contact Form

Create a new page from `base.shtml` in Dreamweaver. Save this page as `contact.shtml`—this page will contain our site's contact form. A contact form gives users an easy way to ask questions, or provide feedback about the site, and, if well-designed, ensures that the site owner can get in touch with the user as required. If we plan it well, we can use our form to ensure that, when making contact, users send in all the information we require in order to respond to their messages.

Our form will contain the following fields:

❏ A drop-down list through which the user can identify the reason they're contacting us. This will also help ensure that the message is delivered to the right person.

❏ Name

❏ Email address

❏ Phone number

❏ Comment or query

### Avoid too many Mandatory Fields

It might be tempting to include a lot of fields in the form, and to force the user to complete them all before the form can be submitted. However, this might just put people off contacting you—users may not fill in the form at all.

So, for example, if you don't require users' addresses, don't make this a required field; even better, leave it off the form entirely. If you do need specific information—for instance, you need users' addresses because they're requesting that a brochure be mailed to them—be sure to let users know why you're collecting this information. If you have a formal privacy policy, include a link to it here.

# Marking up the Form

We'll start by marking up the form; we'll use CSS to style later. You might previously have used a table to lay out a form like this, so that all the fields and their labels lined up nicely. We can achieve this effect in a far more accessible way if we use CSS for layout, and keep the markup simple and semantically meaningful.

### Make sure Dreamweaver's Form Accessibility Features are Enabled

Before you start to work on your form, open the Preferences dialog (Edit > Preferences) and, under the Accessibility category, ensure that Form objects is checked. With this preference selected, Dreamweaver will present dialogs into which you can enter form attributes to make your forms more accessible to all users. The dialogs act as a helpful reminder, and provide an easy way to add these attributes in Dreamweaver.

Insert a form into `contact.shtml` using the Forms pane of the Insert toolbar, then on the Text pane click the Paragraph button to create a paragraph inside the form. Now let's add a text field for the user's name: back in the Forms pane of the Insert toolbar, click the Text Field button, as shown in Figure 9.1.

## Figure 9.1. Inserting a Text Field using the Insert toolbar.

As we have form accessibility turned on, before the field is added to the document, the Input Tag Accessibility Attributes dialog displays. In the Label field, type **Name**; under Style, select the Attach label tag using 'for' attribute radio button; and for Position, select the Before form item radio button, as illustrated in Figure 9.2.

## Figure 9.2. Adding accessibility attributes.

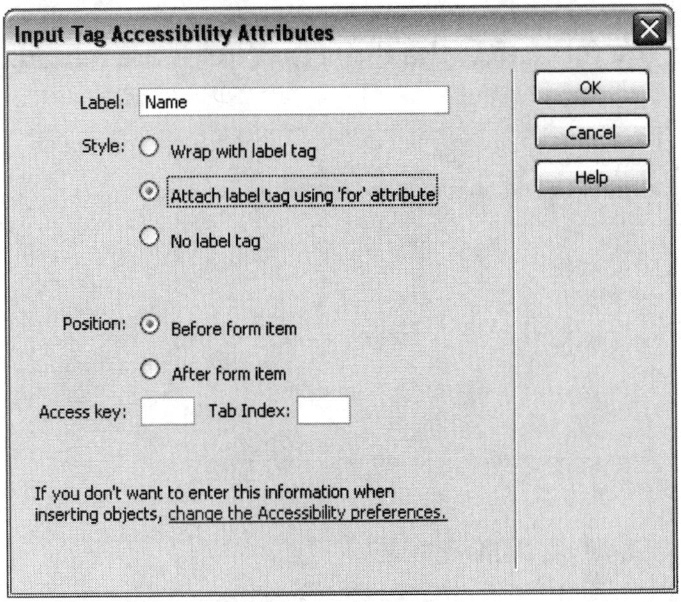

Click OK: the text field and its label will be added to your document. Select the text field and, in the Property Inspector, change the name of the field to **fullname**. If you change the name of a form element in Dreamweaver, it will change both the `name` and the `id` of the field. Switch into Code View and find the form element that you've just added; it'll look something like this:

File: **contact.shtml (excerpt)**

```
<p>
    <label for="textfield">Name</label>
    <input type="text" name="fullname" id="fullname" />
</p>
```

The `label` element is tied to a form field by its `for` attribute, which is supposed to match the `input` element's `id` attribute. As you can see from the code above, Dreamweaver has changed the `id` of the `input` element, but not the `label` element's `for` attribute, so we need to change it to `<label for="fullname">` ourselves. Unfortunately, you'll have to go through this process for every form element that you add.

Create a new paragraph by hitting **Enter** in Design View, and repeat the above process to add fields to accept the users' email addresses and telephone numbers. Also, add a paragraph of text just above the form, like that shown in Figure 9.3.

## Figure 9.3. Viewing the form after the three text fields are added.

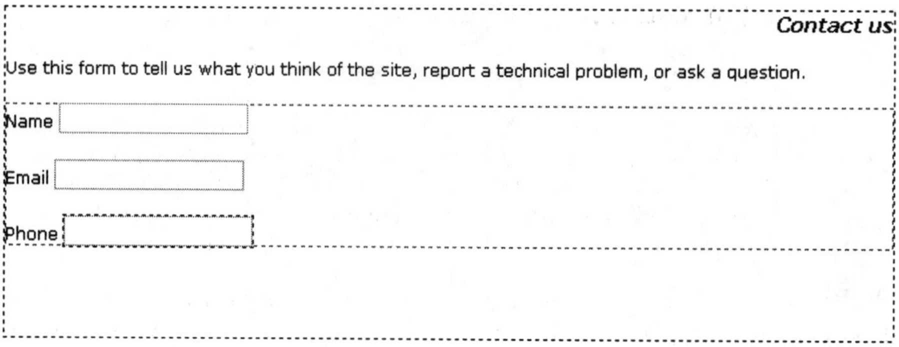

```
Contact us
Use this form to tell us what you think of the site, report a technical problem, or ask a question.
Name [            ]
Email [            ]
Phone [            ]
```

In Code View, your page should look like this:

File: **contact.shtml (excerpt)**

```
<p>Use this form to tell us what you think of the site, report
   a technical problem, or ask a question.<p>
<form id="form1" name="form1" method="post" action="">
   <p>
```

```
    <label for="fullname">Name</label>
    <input type="text" name="fullname" id="fullname" />
</p>
<p>
    <label for="email">Email</label>
    <input type="text" name="email" id="email" />
</p>
<p>
    <label for="phone">Phone</label>
    <input type="text" name="phone" id="phone" />
</p>
</form>
```

# Adding a Menu

Now, let's add a menu (or drop down list) to the form, so that users can identify the reasons for their enquiries. You could also use this tool to direct users' queries to the appropriate team members.

Click the List/Menu button on the Insert toolbar to insert a list. Once again, the Accessibility Attributes dialog displays, allowing you to add a label for the element: call it **Select subject**. This label should be positioned before the form field.

### What about Access Keys?

If you're using access keys , you could create an access key for this particular form element; however, there's limited value in adding an access key for every form element, as most keyboard users prefer to use the **Tab** key to move around a form. In addition, access keys can be confusing if they're not carefully thought through: your access keys may clash with some other browser or operating system combination, and assigning access keys to every form field increases the likelihood of such a clash occurring.

Select the menu in Design View and, in the Property Inspector, set its name to **subject**. Don't forget to switch to Code View and update the `label` element's `for` attribute, too. Switch back to the Property Inspector and click the List Values button to launch the List Values dialog, shown in Figure 9.4. In this dialog, Item Label refers to the text users will see for each item, and Value identifies the value that corresponds to that label, which will be posted to the server when the form is submitted. The server-side script could read this value and use it to determine which staff member should receive the message.

Add a list of possible subject lines, starting with **Select subject**, the Value field for which should be left empty. Use the + button to add entries to the list; Table 9.1 provides a number of example item labels and values.

## Table 9.1. Assigning Values to Item Labels

| Item Label | Value |
|---|---|
| Select subject | |
| General enquiry | general |
| Website problem | website |
| Editorial | editorial |
| Press and publicity | press |
| Advertising | advertising |

## Figure 9.4. Adding possible message subject lines through the List Values dialog.

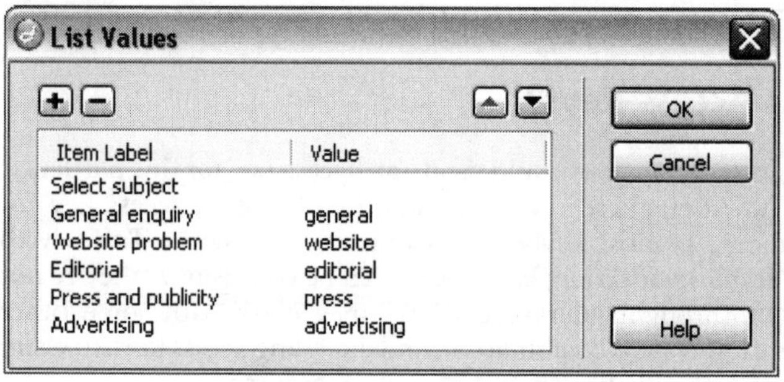

Click OK to insert these items into your menu. In Design View, you'll notice that the menu displays the Press and publicity option by default. To change this default, go to the Property Inspector and select Select subject from the Initial Selection list.

Next, we need to provide a large text box into which users can add their queries or comments. To add this field, first press **Enter** to create another paragraph, and then click the Textarea button on the Insert toolbar. Add a label that reads **Message** through the Accessibility Attributes dialog, and set the `textarea`'s name to **message** in the Property Inspector. In order to constitute valid XHTML, a `textarea` element must have values for its `cols` and `rows` attributes. In Dreamweaver, these values can be inserted via the Property Inspector, as shown in Figure 9.5. The values are Char width, which I've set to 50, and Num Lines, which I've set to 10. You can alter the size of the field using CSS, but setting these values will ensure that the textarea doesn't collapse if users' browsers fail to provide CSS support.

## Figure 9.5. Setting values for the textarea.

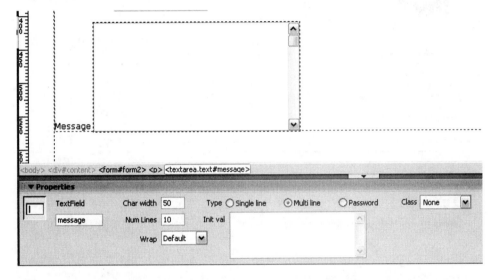

Finally, add a submit button to the form by typing **Enter** to create yet another new paragraph, then clicking the Button button on the Insert toolbar. It's not necessary to label your submit button, so select the No label tag option in the Accessibility Options dialog. However, make sure that the button's value—the text that displays on the button—makes it obvious that the button will submit the form. Leaving the value to read Submit makes this clear.

Figure 9.6 shows how the edited form displays in a browser.

## Figure 9.6. Viewing the form after the form elements are added.

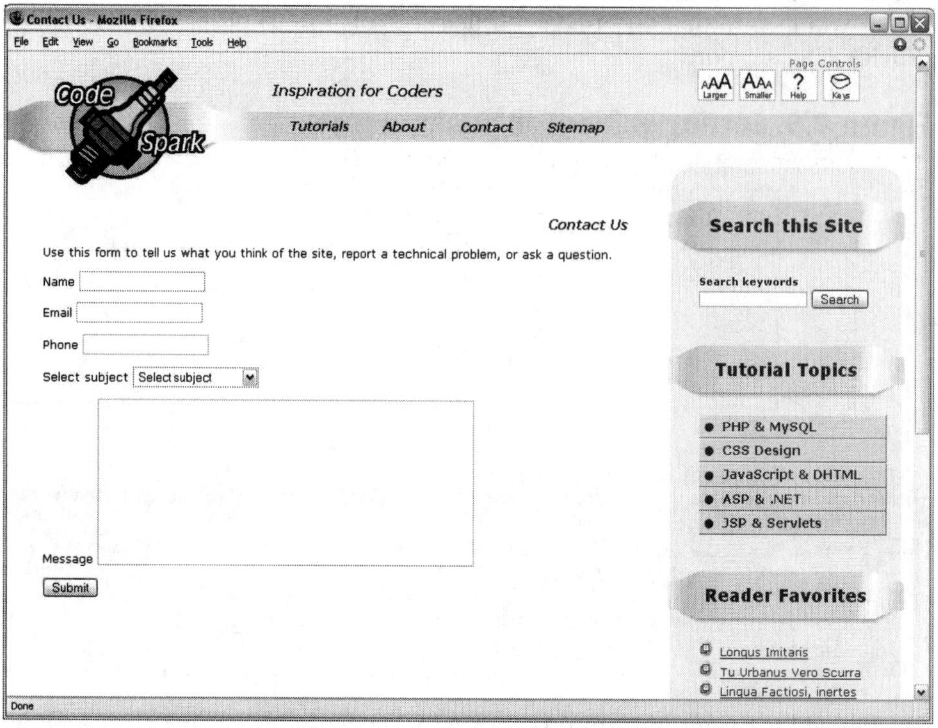

We've added all the form elements we require, but, at this point, the form looks quite plain: we haven't styled it at all. The various form controls are placed on the page immediately following each label, making the form look untidy. Let's use some CSS to tidy things up a bit!

*Tip*

### Don't Forget to Validate!

Before you start work on the form's CSS, it's a good idea to validate your form to confirm the validity of the markup you added using Dreamweaver. The validator will also tell you if you've included any labels that have a `for` attribute that doesn't match a field—this will help you spot if any such cases have slipped past.

# Laying out the Form with CSS

Switch into Code View and have a look at the markup that Dreamweaver inserted as you created your form.

File: **contact.shtml (excerpt)**

```
<form id="form2" method="post" action="">
  <p>
    <label for="fullname">Name</label>
    <input type="text" name="fullname" id="fullname" />
  </p>
  <p>
    <label for="email">Email</label>
    <input type="text" name="email" id="email" />
  </p>
  <p>
    <label for="phone">Phone</label>
    <input type="text" name="phone" id="phone" />
  </p>
  <p>
    <label for="subject">Select subject</label>
    <select name="subject" id="subject">
      <option selected="selected">Select subject</option>
      <option value="general">General enquiry</option>
      <option value="website">Website problem</option>
      <option value="editorial">Editorial</option>
      <option value="press">Press and publicity</option>
      <option value="advertising">Advertising</option>
    </select>
  </p>
  <p>
    <label for="message">Message</label>
    <textarea name="message" cols="50" rows="10" id="message">
    </textarea>
  </p>
  <p>
    <input name="submit" type="submit" id="submit"
        value="Submit" />
  </p>
</form>
```

Each field is wrapped in `<p>` and `</p>` tags and, other than the submit button, each has a `label`, followed by the form field itself. Let's make all of the form fields line up neatly by floating the `label`s left, and giving them a specified width.

Switch back into Design View and create a New CSS Rule. Select Advanced, and type the selector `.contactform p`, which will address paragraph elements within elements that have a class of `contactform`. The dialog for this rule is shown in Figure 9.7.

## Figure 9.7. Creating a New CSS Rule for `.contactform p`

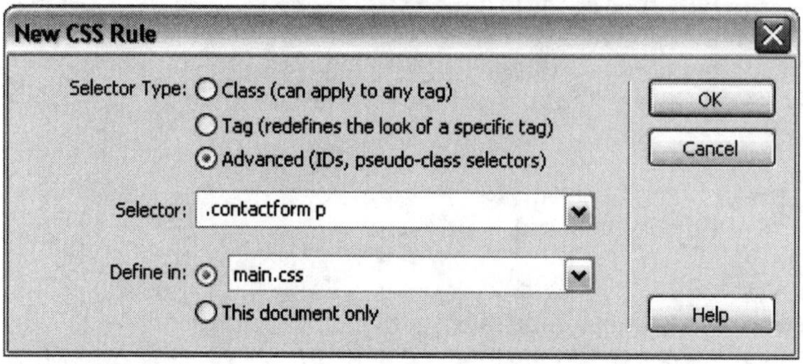

In the Box category, set the value of Clear to left. This will ensure that when we start a new line, it won't move up alongside the floated input element on the previous line—it's a technique that we used when we created the initial homepage layout. Set Margin to 0 pixels and, under Padding, set Top to 5 pixels, and Right, Bottom, and Left to 0 pixels. Now, select the form, and apply to it the class `contactform`; this should have the effect of reducing the space between the lines.

To line up the form fields, create a New CSS Rule and select Advanced. Give this rule the selector `.contactform p label`. We're now addressing the `label` elements within this form. In the Box category, set Width to 20% and the value of Float to left. I have also, in the Type category, set Weight to bold to make the labels display in bold type. Click OK: the form fields should line up neatly, and Dreamweaver should have created the following CSS:

File: **inc/main.css** (excerpt)

```
.contactform p {
  margin: 0px;
  padding: 5px 0px 0px;
  clear: left;
}
.contactform p label {
  float: left;
  width: 20%;
  font-weight: bold;
}
```

# Styling Form Fields

We can also use CSS to style the form fields, and make them more attractive. Create a New CSS Rule, select Advanced and enter the selector **.contactform .text**. Set background color to **#F5F6F2**. In the Box category set Padding to 2 pixels and Width to 280 pixels. Finally, in the Border category, give these fields a solid, 1 pixel border using color **#3C582F**. Apply the `text` class to the `textboxes` and text area.

Our form is beginning to take shape! However, the Submit button is looking a little bit lost at the far bottom-left of the form. It might be a better idea to line it up with the form fields. To do this, we will add a left margin to the <p> that contains the button.

Create a New CSS Rule, select Advanced, and enter the selector **.contactform p.submit**. In the Box category under Margin, set Left to 20%. Click OK to close the dialog. Select the p element that wraps the Submit button and, using the Property Inspector, apply the class `submit`. The Submit button will now line up to the left-hand edge of the form fields. We can also style the button itself, as it's now within a p element with a class of `submit`; we can create a selector named **.contactform p.submit input** to style the button. In the form shown in Figure 9.8, I've set the Type color to **#FFFFFF** and the background color in Background to **#3C582F**.

### Keeping Your Buttons Looking Like Buttons

As you're styling the Submit button, be aware that if you make it look too little like a button, your users may not realize that they should click it! If you decide to style your buttons, make sure they still look button-like when you've finished!

### Styling Buttons On Safari

In its current version, the Safari browser on Mac OS X doesn't allow too much modification of a button's appearance, as OS X gives them its own unique look and feel. There are plans to add button-styling support to Safari, but such changes appear to be a little ways off at the time of writing.

## Figure 9.8. Viewing the completed form styled with CSS.

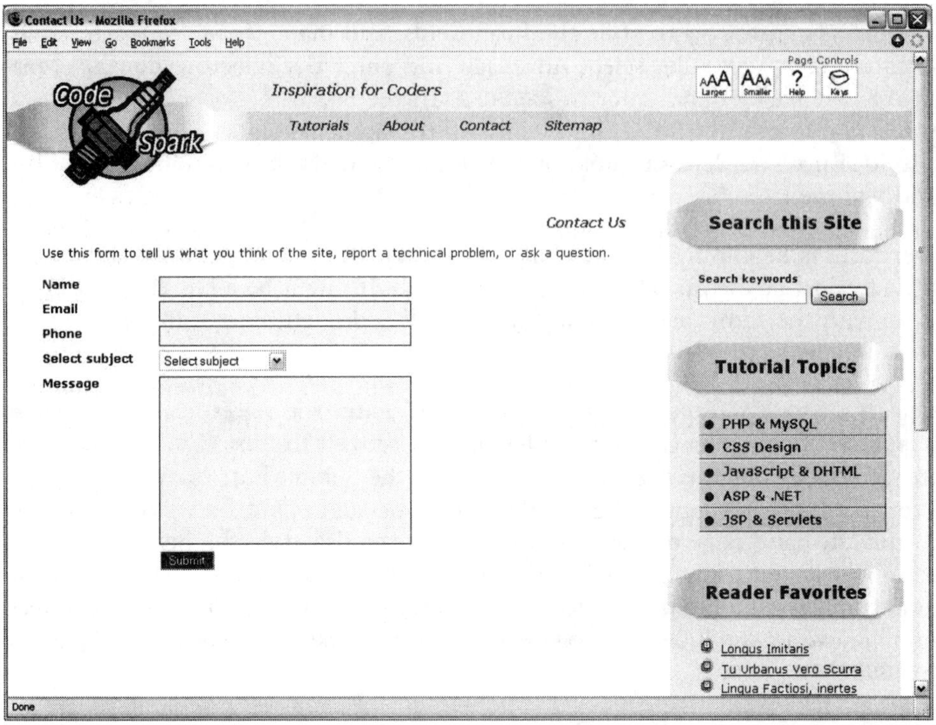

Our styled form is now complete, and looks much nicer and neater than it did before, as Figure 9.8 illustrates.

# Client-side Validation Using Dreamweaver

When creating a form, you often want to ensure that your site visitors complete certain fields. After all, if they request that you contact them, but don't leave a valid email address or telephone number, you aren't going to be able to help them. So, it's a good idea to check that the form has been filled out properly before allowing its submission to the server. One of the Dreamweaver's built-in Behaviors can add simple JavaScript validation to your forms.

## The Validate Form Behavior

First, open the Behaviors panel by selecting Window > Behaviors. In Design View, select your form, then click on the + button in the Behaviors panel to show the list of available behaviors. Select Validate Form.

The Validate Form dialog will display. The Named fields box should display a list of all of the form elements in the page, including the keywords text field that's in the search form. Select the fullname field from this list, and check the Required checkbox to indicate that this field must be completed for the form to submit successfully. Also, ensure that the radio button next to Accept is set to Anything—this means that users can enter anything they like into this field.

Next, select the email field from the Named fields list, make this field required, and select the Email address radio button. When the form is submitted, the script will do a basic check to see if the value looks like an email address. Let's also make sure that people enter something into the message box; at the end of the list, select message, and make this a required field.

Click OK to apply the behavior. Now, if you view your form in a Web browser, and click the Submit button without completing the fields, a JavaScript alert, like that shown in Figure 9.9, will appear, identifying the fields that need to be completed.

### Figure 9.9. The JavaScript alert.

Back in Dreamweaver, switch into Code View to take a look at the markup that Dreamweaver added to your document in order to create this behavior.

File: **contact.shtml**

```
<!--#include file="inc/head.html" -->
<title>Contact Us</title>
```

```
<meta http-equiv="Content-Type" content="text/html;
    charset=iso-8859-1" />
<link href="inc/main.css" rel="stylesheet" type="text/css" />
<script type="text/JavaScript">
<!--
function MM_findObj(n, d) { //v4.01
  var p,i,x;  if(!d) d=document; if((p=n.indexOf("?"))>0&&parent.
      frames.length) {
    d=parent.frames[n.substring(p+1)].document; n=n.substring(0,
        p);}
  if(!(x=d[n])&&d.all) x=d.all[n]; for (i=0;!x&&i<d.forms.length;
      i++) x=d.forms[i][n];
  for(i=0;!x&&d.layers&&i<d.layers.length;i++) x=MM_findObj(n,d.
      layers[i].document);
  if(!x && d.getElementById) x=d.getElementById(n); return x;
}

function MM_validateForm() { //v4.0
  var i,p,q,nm,test,num,min,max,errors='',args=MM_validateForm.
      arguments;
  for (i=0; i<(args.length-2); i+=3) { test=args[i+2]; val=
      MM_findObj(args[i]);
    if (val) { nm=val.name; if ((val=val.value)!="") {
      if (test.indexOf('isEmail')!=-1) { p=val.indexOf('@');
        if (p<1 || p==(val.length-1)) errors+='- '+nm+' must
            contain an e-mail address.\n';
      } else if (test!='R') { num = parseFloat(val);
        if (isNaN(val)) errors+='- '+nm+' must contain a number.
            \n';
        if (test.indexOf('inRange') != -1) { p=test.indexOf(':');
          min=test.substring(8,p); max=test.substring(p+1);
          if (num<min || max<num) errors+='- '+nm+' must contain
              a number between '+min+' and '+max+'.\n';
    } } } else if (test.charAt(0) == 'R') errors += '- '+nm+' is
        required.\n'; }
  } if (errors) alert('The following error(s) occurred:\n'+
      errors);
  document.MM_returnValue = (errors == '');
}
//-->
</script>
</head>

<body>
<!--#include file="inc/top.html" -->
  <h1>Contact Us</h1>
```

```
<p>Use this form to tell us what you think of the site, report
   a technical problem, or ask a question.</p>
<form action="" method="post" name="form2" class="contactform"
    id="form2" onsubmit="MM_validateForm('fullname','','R',
    'email','','RisEmail','message','','R');return document.
    MM_returnValue">
  <p>
    <label for="fullname">Name</label>
    <input name="fullname" type="text" class="text"
        id="fullname" />
  </p>
  <p>
    <label for="email">Email</label>
    <input name="email" type="text" class="text" id="email" />
  </p>
  <p>
    <label for="phone">Phone</label>
    <input name="phone" type="text" class="text" id="phone" />
  </p>
  <p>
    <label for="subject">Select subject</label>
    <select name="subject" id="subject">
      <option>Select subject</option>
      <option value="general">General enquiry</option>
      <option value="website">Website problem</option>
      <option value="editorial">Editorial</option>
      <option value="press">Press and publicity</option>
      <option value="advertising">Advertising</option>
    </select>
  </p>
  <p>
    <label for="message">Message</label>
    <textarea name="message" cols="50" rows="10" class="text"
        id="message"></textarea>
  </p>
  <p class="submit">
    <input name="btnSubmit" type="submit" id="btnSubmit"
        value="Submit" />
  </p>
</form>
<!--#include file="inc/bottom.html" -->
```

As you can see, Dreamweaver added a lot of code! This code comprises Dreamweaver's standard form validation functions—they'll appear on any page to which we add this behavior. As we might want to use this behavior elsewhere in the site, let's move the JavaScript from the head of the document to an external file.

This will trim the file size of the page, and also allows us to start thinking of our scripts as reusable components.

To move the JavaScript to an external file, select everything between the opening `<script type="text/JavaScript">` and the closing `</script>` tags; you can ignore the HTML comment tags that surround it. Copy this code to the clipboard. It should contain the code shown here:

File: **inc/functions.js**

```
function MM_findObj(n, d) { //v4.01
  var p,i,x;  if(!d) d=document;  if((p=n.indexOf("?"))>0&&parent.
      frames.length) {
    d=parent.frames[n.substring(p+1)].document; n=n.substring(0,
        p);}
  if(!(x=d[n])&&d.all) x=d.all[n]; for (i=0;!x&&i<d.forms.length;
      i++) x=d.forms[i][n];
  for(i=0;!x&&d.layers&&i<d.layers.length;i++) x=MM_findObj(n,d.
      layers[i].document);
  if(!x && d.getElementById) x=d.getElementById(n); return x;
}

function MM_validateForm() { //v4.0
  var i,p,q,nm,test,num,min,max,errors='',args=MM_validateForm.
      arguments;
  for (i=0; i<(args.length-2); i+=3) { test=args[i+2]; val=
      MM_findObj(args[i]);
    if (val) { nm=val.name; if ((val=val.value)!="") {
      if (test.indexOf('isEmail')!=-1) { p=val.indexOf('@');
        if (p<1 || p==(val.length-1)) errors+='- '+nm+' must
            contain an e-mail address.\n';
      } else if (test!='R') { num = parseFloat(val);
        if (isNaN(val)) errors+='- '+nm+' must contain a number.
            \n';
        if (test.indexOf('inRange') != -1) { p=test.indexOf(':');
          min=test.substring(8,p); max=test.substring(p+1);
          if (num<min || max<num) errors+='- '+nm+' must contain
              a number between '+min+' and '+max+'.\n';
    } } } else if (test.charAt(0) == 'R') errors += '- '+nm+' is
        required.\n'; }
  } if (errors) alert('The following error(s) occurred:\n'+
      errors);
  document.MM_returnValue = (errors == '');
}
```

In Dreamweaver's New Document dialog, select Basic Page, then choose JavaScript and click Create. Paste the copied functions into this document, and save it in the `inc` directory as `function.js`. Back in `contact.shtml`, delete all of the JavaScript that you pasted into `functions.js`, along with the HTML comments, leaving yourself with this:

File: **contact.shtml (excerpt)**

```
<script type="text/JavaScript"></script>
```

Edit this line to reference the external JavaScript file, like so:

File: **contact.shtml (excerpt)**

```
<script type="text/JavaScript" src="inc/functions.js"></script>
```

Save the document, and go back to your Web browser: you should find that the validation works as it did before, though the page doesn't contain all that script. If you want to use this behavior on another page, make sure that you include the JavaScript functions file before you apply the Dreamweaver behavior. Dreamweaver should notice that you already have this code in your page, and will add to the form the code that causes the behavior to run when the form is submitted.

You can also add other JavaScript functions to this same file—either before or after the validation functions—which means that you can include on your pages just one file that contains all the required JavaScript.

### Validation Using JavaScript

Validating forms using JavaScript can be a helpful way to remind users which fields they should complete. However, if it's important to your business that the data is complete, you should also check it using a server-side script before you process the form. If the user doesn't have JavaScript, or has turned off JavaScript, this simple validation technique won't work, and the incomplete form may be posted. The simple client-side check does save the user having to wait for the server to perform its own check, though, so it's always a useful step to take, even if you use server-side form validation.

# Submitting the Form

We now have a form that's ready to be submitted to a processing script. This will require some server-side scripting, which is outside the scope of this book. However, a number of excellent form-to-email scripts are available, so, rather than leave you to hunt on your own, I'll mention some of the most popular: one of these should be suitable for your server platform.

**Perl/CGI**   If your hosting account gives you the ability to run CGI scripts, they may already have a form-to-email script installed for you: check with your hosting provider. One of the most popular is FormMail, which is available from http://www.scriptarchive.com/formmail.html.

**ASP**   If your Website is hosted on a Windows Server that offers ASP, a script based on FormMail, but written in ASP,[1] might be just what you need. It comes with instructions that are very easy to follow, too.

**PHP**   A large number of email scripts are available for PHP, but there is one that acts in a similar way to those mentioned above.[2]

To implement any of the above scripts, you will need to download the files, upload them to your own server, and follow the implementation instructions provided. The scripts tend to require hidden fields to be placed in the form, which you can do using Dreamweaver and the Forms pane of the Insert toolbar. You will then need to make the action of your form refer to the URL of the processing script you're using.

These scripts also have basic server-side validation built-in, which checks that the form fields have been completed even if the user has turned JavaScript off.

# Adding a Search Facility

We've already added a search form to our basic template; in this section, we'll use a third-party search application in order to provide a search facility on our site. The third-party application we'll use is the Atomz Express Search, which is free for sites that are under 750 pages in size. To make use of Atomz, the search form on our site needs to send its queries to the Atomz Website, where all of the work is done. The real advantage of Atomz is that you can customize the search result pages so they look like they're part of your Website, even though they're hosted on Atomz.com.

You will need to upload the site we've developed to your server—even though it isn't complete—in order to make the search function: Atomz will need to index your site in order to display search results.

---

[1] http://www.brainjar.com/asp/formmail/
[2] http://www.dtheatre.com/scripts/formmail.php

# Creating an Atomz Account

To begin, go to http://www.atomz.com/applications/search/trial.htm, and sign up. The sign-up process requires you to enter your email address. Atomz will then send you a password and link, to confirm your email address. Once you return to the site and log in, you'll need to provide your complete contact details. You'll then be able to enter the main control area, where you can start to create a search facility for your site.

Once you've entered all of your contact details, click the link to create a new account, and proceed through the pages to create an Atomz Express Search account. With your Atomz login, you can create free or paid accounts for multiple sites. You'll need to enter the details of each Website, including its URL (which should be the URL to which you intend to upload your site's files), your time zone, the "category" into which the site is best grouped, and an estimate of how many pages the site contains. After verifying your details, Atomz will begin to index or catalog your site. Don't worry that there isn't much to index for the time being; you can request that it re-index the site at any time. In fact, you can set the application to index your site daily, to pick up any changes.

# Adding the Search Form to Your Site

Now that you've created an account for your site, you can change the search form so that it sends searches to Atomz.

Click on the HTML link in the menu that displays when you're logged into the Atomz Website. This will take you to a page that contains the HTML for the Standard Search Form. The page also contains an Advanced Search Form, but we're only interested in the Standard Search Form for now. The Atomz standard search form code is:

```
<!-- Atomz Search HTML for Code Spark -->
<form method="get" action="http://search.atomz.com/search/">
<input size="15" name="sp-q"><br>
<input type="submit" value="Search">
<input type="hidden" name="sp-a" value="sp12345678">
<input type="hidden" name="sp-p" value="all">
<input type="hidden" name="sp-f" value="ISO-8859-1">
</form>
```

You could simply cut and paste this code into your site, but the code is presented in HTML (rather than the XHTML we need), and we already have a search form in our site. So, instead of using the Atomz form, we shall simply edit our existing XHTML search form to include the fields from the Atomz form.

In Dreamweaver, open the include file `bottom.html`, which contains our search form. Select the `form` element and, using the Property Inspector, set the form's Method to GET and set Action to match the Atomz search form's action by entering `http://search.atomz.com/search/`. These steps are shown in Figure 9.10.

## Figure 9.10. Setting the action for the search form.

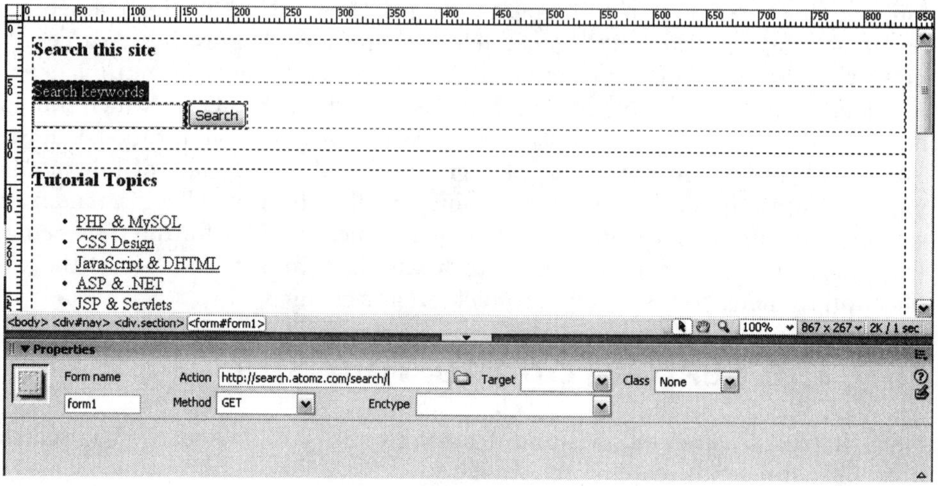

Now, select the Search keywords text field. In the Atomz search form, the text field has the name `sp-q`, so rename your `keywords` field `sp-q`. Don't worry about the `size` attribute in the Atomz search form HTML. This is a presentational attribute that defines the size at which the text field appears; we've already sized the text field with CSS.

Three hidden fields appear in the Atomz search form HTML: `sp-a`, `sp-p`, and `sp-f`.

❑ `sp-a` is the unique code that identifies your site. Use the value from your example HTML, not the one in this book.

❑ `sp-p` can have a value of `all` or `any`. If it's set to `all`, the results must contain all of the keywords; if it's set to `any`, the results can contain any of the entered keywords.

❑ sp-f is the character encoding of the page on which the search form appears. This should match the character encoding set in the meta element that controls the page's Content-Type. For example, if you have the following Content-Type, this attribute should have the value iso-8859–1.

```
<meta http-equiv="Content-Type" content="text/html;
    charset=iso-8859-1" />
```

Add these hidden fields to the search form using the Hidden Field button in the Insert toolbar. Hidden fields will appear in Dreamweaver's Design View as small yellow H icons. If you select a hidden field in Design View, you can edit its name and value in the Property Inspector. Once you've added the three hidden fields, you should have a form that, in Code View, looks like the following:

File: **inc/bottom.html (excerpt)**

```
<form id="form1" action="http://search.atomz.com/search/"
    method="get">
  <p><label>Search keywords
      <br />
      <input name="sp-q" type="text" class="searchtxt"
          id="sp-q" />
      <input type="submit" name="Submit" value="Search" />
    </label>
    <input name="sp-a" type="hidden" id="sp-a"
        value="sp12345678" />
    <input name="sp-p" type="hidden" id="sp-p" value="all" />
    <input name="sp-f" type="hidden" id="sp-f"
        value="iso-8859-1" />
  </p>
</form>
```

Assuming that you've uploaded your files, and that the Atomz application has been able to index them, and that you've added the hidden fields correctly, you should be able to run a basic search on your site. If you haven't added links to the content pages of your site, all that will appear in the index is your homepage. Search for a word that you know appears on the homepage, in order to see some results. Atomz's indexing works by following links that point to other pages in your site: if no links exist, Atomz won't know how to find the other pages of the site. As this search is part of a free Express Search Account, Atomz has included some "sponsored links" to other sites, as you can see in Figure 9.11. To remove these, you'll have to upgrade to Atomz's paid service.

## Figure 9.11. Viewing the default Atomz search results page.

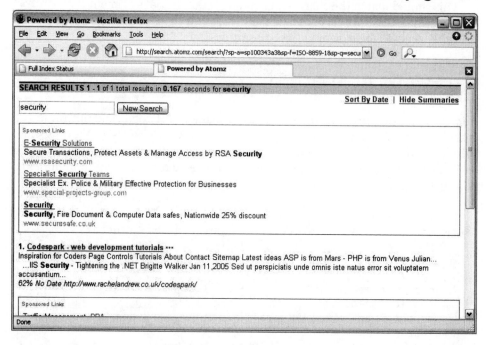

# Editing the Atomz Templates

One of the reasons I've chosen Atomz as our search provider is that the search results pages it presents are easily customizable: you can make them look like part of your own site. This gives users a seamless experience as they switch between your site and the Atomz site.

Customization is provided by Atomz templates. Log in to the Atomz Website, click the Templates link in the left menu, then click Template Editor to see the page shown in Figure 9.12.

We can change our site template into an Atomz template very easily; we just need to make a few minor alterations.

## Figure 9.12. The Atomz Search Template Editor.

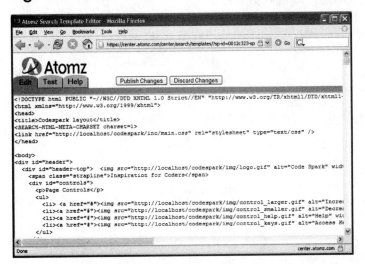

Hopefully, you still have a copy of `homepage-layout-strict.html`, the document that we used to create our layout before we cut the site up into separate includes. If not, grab it from the code archive. Open that document now, and save it as `atomz-template.html`. Change the page title to **Code Spark search results – powered by Atomz**.

Switch into Code View and replace the `meta` element that sets the `Content-Type` with the special Atomz tag, `<SEARCH-HTML-META-CHARSET charset=1>`. Take care to *not* add an XML-style / in an attempt to indicate that this is an empty element. Atomz will not recognize the element if you do.

The head of this page will also contain a link to your CSS style sheet. As this page will be hosted on the Atomz server, you need to make sure that the link to the style sheet is a link back to your own server. Change the `link` element's `href` attribute to reference the CSS file as a full URL, such as `http://www.yourdo-main.com/codespark/inc/main.css`. You also need to change all of the images' `src` attributes in the same way. When you're done, the start of your page should look something like the following:

File: **atomz-template.html** (excerpt)

```
<!DOCTYPE html PUBLIC "-//W3C//DTD XHTML 1.0 Strict//EN"
    "http://www.w3.org/TR/xhtml1/DTD/xhtml1-strict.dtd">
<html xmlns="http://www.w3.org/1999/xhtml">
<head>
```

```
<title>Code Spark search results - powered by Atomz</title>
<SEARCH-HTML-META-CHARSET charset=1>
<link href="http://www.yourdomain.com/codespark/inc/main.css"
    rel="stylesheet" type="text/css" />
</head>
<body>
<div id="header">
  <div id="header-top">
    <img src="http://www.yourdomain.com/codespark/img/logo.gif"
        alt="Code Spark" width="290" height="160" id="logo" />
    <span class="tagline">Inspiration for Coders</span>
    <div id="controls">
      <p>Page Controls</p>
      <ul>
        <li><a href="#"><img src="http://www.yourdomain.com/
codespark/img/control_larger.gif" alt="Increase Text Size"
            width="43" height="35" />
        </a></li>
        <li><a href="#"><img src="http://www.yourdomain.com/
codespark/img/control_smaller.gif" alt="Decrease Text Size"
            width="43" height="35" />
        </a></li>
        <li><a href="#"><img src="http://www.yourdomain.com/
codespark/img/control_low_graphics.gif" alt="Low Graphics"
            width="43" height="35" /></a></li>
        <li><a href="#"><img src="http://www.yourdomain.com/
codespark/img/control_default_style.gif" alt="Default Style"
            width="43" height="35" /></a></li>
      </ul>
    </div>
  </div>
```

In your template file, clear the content `div` by deleting everything from just after `<div id="content">` to the point just before the corresponding `</div>` (which occurs immediately before `<div id="nav">`); this will give us the search results area. We'll add the code that inserts the results here shortly.

Next, copy the updated search form from `bottom.html`, and paste it into this new page, so that any searches that are started from this page will work as well. You can also choose to remove the reader favorites from this page if you wish: we won't have an easy way to keep the list on this page up-to-date, other than manually updating the template, which won't be an acceptable solution if this Website is to be updated from a database. To delete this section, simply select everything including the `<div class="section">` tag, and its corresponding `</div>` closing tag, and delete it.

The markup for your Atomz template should now look something like that shown below.

File: **atomz-template.html**

```html
<!DOCTYPE html PUBLIC "-//W3C//DTD XHTML 1.0 Strict//EN"
    "http://www.w3.org/TR/xhtml1/DTD/xhtml1-strict.dtd">
<html xmlns="http://www.w3.org/1999/xhtml">
<head>
<title>Code Spark search results - powered by Atomz</title>
<SEARCH-HTML-META-CHARSET charset="1">
<link href="http://www.yourdomain.com/codespark/inc/main.css"
    rel="stylesheet" type="text/css" />
</head>
<body>
<div id="header">
  <div id="header-top">
    <img src="http://www.yourdomain.com/codespark/img/logo.gif"
        alt="Code Spark" width="290" height="160" id="logo" />
    <span class="tagline">Inspiration for Coders</span>
    <div id="controls">
      <p>Page Controls</p>
      <ul>
        <li><a href="#"><img src="http://www.yourdomain.com/
codespark/img/control_larger.gif" alt="Increase Text Size"
            width="43" height="35" />
        </a></li>
        <li><a href="#"><img src="http://www.yourdomain.com/
codespark/img/control_smaller.gif" alt="Decrease Text Size"
            width="43" height="35" />
        </a></li>
        <li><a href="#"><img src="http://www.yourdomain.com/
codespark/img/control_low_graphics.gif" alt="Low Graphics"
            width="43" height="35" /></a></li>
        <li><a href="#"><img src="http://www.yourdomain.com/
codespark/img/control_default_style.gif" alt="Default Style"
            width="43" height="35" /></a></li>
      </ul>
    </div>
  </div>
  <div id="header-bottom">
    <ul>
    <li><a href="http://www.yourdomain.com/codespark/">Tutorials
        </a></li>
    <li><a href="http://www.yourdomain.com/codespark/">About</a>
        </li>
    <li><a href="http://www.yourdomain.com/codespark/">Contact
```

```
      </a></li>
    <li><a href="http://www.yourdomain.com/codespark/">Sitemap
      </a></li>
    </ul>
  </div>
</div>
<div id="content">
</div>
<div id="nav">
  <div class="section">
    <h3>Search this Site</h3>
    <form action="http://search.atomz.com/search/" method="get"
        name="form1" id="form1">
      <p><label>Search keywords
          <br />
          <input name="sp-q" type="text" class="searchtxt"
              id="sp-q" />
          <input type="submit" name="Submit" value="Search" />
        </label>
        <input name="sp-a" type="hidden" id="sp-a"
            value="sp12345678" />
        <input name="sp-p" type="hidden" id="sp-p" value="all" />
        <input name="sp-f" type="hidden" id="sp-f"
            value="iso-8859-1" />
      </p>
    </form>
  </div>
  <div class="section">
   <h3>Tutorial Topics</h3>
   <ul class="topics">
   <li><a href="http://www.yourdomain.com/codespark/">PHP &amp;
     MySQL</a></li>
   <li><a href="http://www.yourdomain.com/codespark/">CSS Design
     </a></li>
   <li><a href="http://www.yourdomain.com/codespark/">JavaScript
     &amp; DHTML</a></li>
   <li><a href="http://www.yourdomain.com/codespark/">ASP &amp;
     .NET</a></li>
   <li><a href="http://www.yourdomain.com/codespark/">JSP &amp;
     Servlets</a></li>
    </ul>
  </div>
  <img src="http://www.yourdomain.com/codespark/img/nav-bottom.gif"
      alt="" width="266" height="63" class="displayblock" />
  </div>
```

```
</body>
</html>
```

# Adding the Atomz Search Code

We've built the shell of our search results pages. Now, it's time to fill it in.

Back on the Atomz page, return to the Templates screen and click Template Recipe. Here, you'll see the search results display code, as shown in Figure 9.13, ready to be copied and pasted into your template.

## Figure 9.13. Viewing the Template Recipe page.

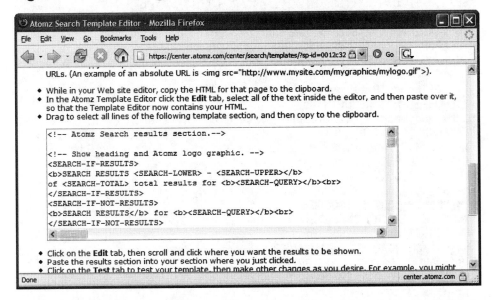

We don't actually need all of this code: the bottom section creates a search form, which we already have in our template. So, copy the markup from the beginning down to a point just before the `<!-- Put up the next form. -->` comment.

Paste this code inside the `content` div in your page. That `div` should now contain the following code:

File: **atomz-template.html** (excerpt)

```
<!-- Atomz Search results section.-->

<!-- Show heading and Atomz logo graphic. -->
```

```
<SEARCH-IF-RESULTS>
<b>SEARCH RESULTS <SEARCH-LOWER> - <SEARCH-UPPER></b>
of <SEARCH-TOTAL> total results for <b><SEARCH-QUERY></b><br>
</SEARCH-IF-RESULTS>
<SEARCH-IF-NOT-RESULTS>
<b>SEARCH RESULTS</b> for <b><SEARCH-QUERY></b><br>
</SEARCH-IF-NOT-RESULTS>
<SEARCH-LOGO><br>

<!-- Display Results. -->
<SEARCH-RESULTS LENGTH=160>
<p><b><SEARCH-LINK><SEARCH-TITLE LENGTH=160></SEARCH-LINK></b><br>
<SEARCH-IF-SHOW-SUMMARIES>
<SEARCH-IF-CONTEXT LENGTH=240><SEARCH-CONTEXT><br>
   </SEARCH-IF-CONTEXT>
<font size="-1"><SEARCH-URL></font><br>
</SEARCH-IF-SHOW-SUMMARIES>
</SEARCH-RESULTS>

<!-- If no results, show a message. -->
<SEARCH-IF-NOT-RESULTS><p>
Sorry, no matches were found containing <b><SEARCH-QUERY>.</b>
</SEARCH-IF-NOT-RESULTS>
<!-- Show By Score, By Date links, Show/Hide Summaries links. -->
<SEARCH-IF-RESULTS><p>
<SEARCH-IF-SORT-BY-DATE>
<b><SEARCH-SORT-BY-SCORE COUNT=10>Sort By Score
   </SEARCH-SORT-BY-SCORE></b>
</SEARCH-IF-SORT-BY-DATE>
<SEARCH-IF-SORT-BY-SCORE>
<b><SEARCH-SORT-BY-DATE COUNT=10>Sort By Date
   </SEARCH-SORT-BY-DATE></b>
</SEARCH-IF-SORT-BY-SCORE>
 | <b>
<SEARCH-IF-SHOW-SUMMARIES>
<SEARCH-HIDE-SUMMARIES COUNT=20>Hide Summaries
   </SEARCH-HIDE-SUMMARIES>
</SEARCH-IF-SHOW-SUMMARIES>
<SEARCH-IF-HIDE-SUMMARIES>
<SEARCH-SHOW-SUMMARIES COUNT=10>Show Summaries
   </SEARCH-SHOW-SUMMARIES>
</SEARCH-IF-HIDE-SUMMARIES>
</b><br>
</SEARCH-IF-RESULTS>

<!-- Display Prev & Next links. -->
```

```
<SEARCH-IF-RESULTS>
<SEARCH-IF-PREV-COUNT>
<b><SEARCH-PREV>Prev <SEARCH-PREV-COUNT></SEARCH-PREV></b>
<SEARCH-IF-NEXT-COUNT> | </SEARCH-IF-NEXT-COUNT>
</SEARCH-IF-PREV-COUNT>
<SEARCH-IF-NEXT-COUNT>
<b><SEARCH-NEXT>Next <SEARCH-NEXT-COUNT></SEARCH-NEXT></b><br>
</SEARCH-IF-NEXT-COUNT><p>
</SEARCH-IF-RESULTS>
```

Save your page. You may have noticed that the Atomz code contains some HTML—in its use of `<br>`, rather than `<br />`, for example. Quickly tidy up this markup by changing HTML tags to XHTML in Code View.

## Adding the Template to Atomz

We can now add our template to Atomz. Go back to the Template page, and click on Template Editor. Delete all the markup in the editor: this markup comprises the default template that we'll replace with our new template. Now, copy all of the markup from `atomz-template.html` and paste it into the Template Editor.

At the top of the editor, click the Test tab. On this screen, enter a keyword that will return some results, and click Search. A new page will open and, in it, the search results should display in your own template, as shown in Figure 9.14.

### Figure 9.14. Displaying search results in the Code Spark template.

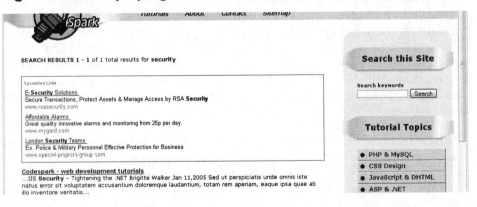

### The Problem with Third-party Services

If you look at the source of the search result page in your browser, you will see that, while your template and the results over which you have control are valid XHTML, the sponsored links that Atomz has inserted are not valid, nor are they semantically correct. Unfortunately, as with any third-party service, there isn't anything that we can do to change this. If you find yourself in this situation, all you can do is ensure that the parts of the site or template that you do have control over are valid and accessible. And don't be afraid to drop the third-party services a line to ask if they are going to update their markup any time soon!

Once you're happy with your template, click Publish Changes to publish the template, making it the template in which the results of any searches from your site will display.

Don't forget to update your template if your site template changes. As we haven't linked up the entire site yet, we'll need to go back and update the links to other parts of the site as they are created. As you upload content, you'll also need to manually re-index the site, or set it to be indexed regularly. You can do this by selecting Index from the Atomz menu that's presented when you're logged into your account.

# Summary

This chapter has discussed two ways in which you can apply additional functionality to your site. Forms can collect information from users for a variety of reasons, from simple contact purposes to complex ordering facilities and, as part of more advanced solutions, can be driven by server-side script. If you want to add server-side functionality to your site, you can write it yourself; use Dreamweaver Server Behaviors for ASP, PHP, ASP.NET, JSP or ColdFusion; install third-party scripts such as FormMail; or you can make use of remotely hosted third-party solutions such as Atomz.

Third-party solutions can improve the functionality of your site without requiring you to spend a lot of money, or learn a server-side language. However, they can force you to make some compromises in terms of validation and accessibility. Use these services with care and, in cases in which you must accept that a page won't validate because of a third-party tool you've had to use, don't use that limitation as an excuse to allow the rest of your template to be invalid or inaccessible!

# 10 Alternate Style Sheets

Over the last few chapters, we've put together the skeleton of our site and, in the process, you've learned the techniques required to build a standards compliant Website using Dreamweaver 8. In this final chapter, we'll explore the additional power that lies at your fingertips now that you've created a site using semantic markup and CSS: the power to create different style sheets that can be used to help particular users view the site.

By creating different style sheets, we can accommodate site visitors with many different needs. A visually stunning, graphically heavy site can be very difficult to view on a PDA or when printed. But, using alternate style sheets, we can provide low-graphics versions, or special versions of pages that can be used when the document is printed.

Throughout this chapter, we'll be working on the file `tutorial1.shtml` (the sample tutorial page we created in Chapter 8), adding style sheets and JavaScript to this document. At the end of the chapter, we'll move this additional markup to `head.html`, so that the functionality is available on every page of the site.

# Accessibility Controls

The header of our layout contains accessibility controls designed to enable users to resize the displayed text and view a text-only version of the site. Our next step is to implement these controls for our users.

# Text Resizing

Although we've sized our fonts in such a way that users can resize the text using the settings in their browsers, providing some means of resizing the text right there on the Web page can be particularly helpful for some users.

As users increase the size of the text in their browsers, however, parts of our carefully constructed layout can start to break, despite our best efforts to create a robust design. For example, open the Code Spark homepage in Internet Explorer and select View > Text Size > Largest. While every element of the page still works, parts of the layout have gone awry: the headings in the navigation bar on the right, for example.

## Creating a Style Sheet for Text Sizing

Currently, all of the site's style information is stored in one large style sheet. This isn't a problem: Dreamweaver enables us to manage long lists of style rules with ease. However, because we're going to change the font sizes, we'll remove all the information that relates to text sizing from our main style sheet, and place it in a separate style sheet. Then, to change the text size, we simply need to create a style sheet with larger font sizes, and use it to replace the existing text styles.

### Text Sizing Alternatives

We could just create a new style sheet that contained only font sizing information, and insert it after the existing style sheet, so that the new styles could override the existing ones. However, putting the styles that relate to font sizes in a separate file at this point makes it easy for us to see what needs to be changed; otherwise, we'd have to dig through the entire document to find the appropriate markup. This approach will also potentially be useful if we decide to offer a low graphics, large-text option: in this case, we can simply combine our low graphics and large-text style sheets.

In Dreamweaver, open the New Document dialog (File > New) and choose Basic Page, then select CSS. Save the newly created, empty style sheet in the `inc` folder as `text-regular.css`.

Open the `tutorial1.shtml` file and, using the CSS panel, click Attach Style Sheet. Browse for the file `text-regular.css` and click OK to add it to `tutorial1.shtml` along with your existing style sheet, `main.css`.

## Removing the Font Sizing from the Main Style Sheet

We now need to shift all the text styles out of the main style sheet and into our new `text-regular.css` style sheet. Open `main.css` in Dreamweaver's Code View.

The first rule we see is that for `body`, which contains the property `font-size: 1em`:

File: **inc/main.css (excerpt)**

```
body {
  font-size: 1em;
  color: #000000;
  background: #FFFFFF;
  margin: 0px;
  padding: 0px;
}
```

We'll want to remove this property from `main.css` and add it to the new style sheet, so, in `text-regular.css`, add the following rule:

File: **inc/text-regular.css (excerpt)**

```
body {
  font-size: 1em;
}
```

Now that we've put this property into our new style sheet, we can delete it from `main.css`, leaving the following rule:

File: **inc/main.css (excerpt)**

```
body {
  color: #000000;
  background: #FFFFFF;
  margin: 0px;
  padding: 0px;
}
```

The next rule that deals with font sizing has the selector #content:

File: **inc/main.css** (excerpt)
```
#content {
  margin-top: 80px;
  margin-right: 320px;
  margin-left: 40px;
  font: 80% Verdana, Arial, Helvetica, sans-serif;
}
```

In this rule, Dreamweaver has added the shorthand font property, which sizes the font and sets the font face. We'll have to split this shorthand property into its longhand equivalent. In text-regular.css, add:

File: **inc/text-regular.css** (excerpt)
```
#content {
  font-size: 80%;
}
```

Go back to main.css and change the font property to a font-family property, leaving the following rule:

File: **inc/main.css** (excerpt)
```
#content {
  margin-top: 80px;
  margin-right: 320px;
  margin-left: 40px;
  font-family: Verdana, Arial, Helvetica, sans-serif;
}
```

We'll need to do the same to the .tagline rule:

File: **inc/main.css** (excerpt)
```
.tagline {
  margin: 0px 0px 0px 300px;
  float: left;
  padding-top: 2em;
  font: italic bold 100% Verdana, Arial, Helvetica, sans-serif;
  color: #3C582F;
}
```

Create a .tagline rule in text-regular.css and add the font-size: 100% property to it. Now, we need to modify the rule in main.css: we'll need to replace the font property with the properties font-style, font-weight, and font-family, like so:

File: **inc/main.css (excerpt)**

```css
.tagline {
  margin: 0px 0px 0px 300px;
  float: left;
  padding-top: 2em;
  font-style: italic;
  font-weight: bold;
  font-family: Verdana, Arial, Helvetica, sans-serif;
  color: #3C582F;
}
```

Continue this process through the style sheet, adding each font sizing rule to text-regular.css, and removing it from main.css. This might seem like a daunting task if you don't feel comfortable editing CSS by hand, but don't worry: it's surprisingly simple once you get the hang of the way the font property works. You should soon end up with the following rules in text-regular.css:

File: **inc/text-regular.css**

```css
body {
  font-size: 1em;
}
#content {
  font-size: 80%;
}
.tagline {
  font-size: 100%;
}
#controls {
  font-size: 70%;
}
#header-bottom li {
  font-size: 90%;
}
#content h1 {
  font-size: 120%;
}
#content h2 {
  font-size: 120%;
}
#content h3 {
  font-size: 100%;
}
.credit .date {
  font-size: 80%;
}
```

```
#content .homepage-box th {
  font-size: 70%;
}
#content .homepage-box td {
  font-size: 90%;
}
#nav h3 {
  font-size: 120%;
}
#nav label {
  font-size: 70%;
}
#nav ul.topics li {
  font-size: 90%;
}
#nav ul.list a:link {
  font-size: 80%
}
#nav ul.list a:visited {
  font-size: 80%
}
p.breadcrumbs {
  font-size: 90%;
}
#content h1.tutorial {
  font-size: 160%;
}
.pullquote {
  font-size: 120%;
}
```

View your pages now: they should still look exactly the same as they did before. We haven't changed any of the CSS properties that are applied to the document; we've just moved some of these properties around a little.

## Creating the Large-text Style Sheet

We can now create the large-text style sheet. Open `text-regular.css` and save it as `text-large.css`. As you know, we've set a font size for the `body`. And all the other page elements calculate their size, as percentages, from this rule. So the first thing we'll do is to bump up the `body` font size from `1em` to `1.5em`.

File: **inc/text-large.css (excerpt)**

```
body {
  font-size: 1.5em;
}
```

This will have the effect of increasing the size of all of the text on the page. We can use some handy Dreamweaver functionality to see exactly how this will affect our page.

## Design Time Style Sheets

While we're working on an alternate style sheet, it's nice to be able to see the effect that our work has on the look of the page. We could do this by replacing the link to `text-regular.css` with a link to `text-large.css`, and switching it back later. However, Dreamweaver offers a useful tool to help us here: Design Time Style Sheets.

Design Time Style Sheets enable you to get Dreamweaver to apply one or more style sheets to your document while you're working in Dreamweaver (that is, at "design time"), but not in the browser or when the site is uploaded. To see what our site looks like when the large-text style sheet is applied, we can make that style sheet a Design Time Style Sheet.

Open `tutorial1.shtml` in Design View, right click in the CSS panel and select Design-time..., as shown in Figure 10.1.

**Figure 10.1. Launching the Design Time Style Sheets dialog.**

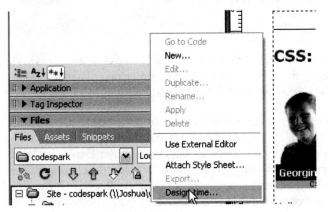

In the Design Time Style Sheets dialog, click the + button above the Show only at Design Time box, and browse for `text-large.css`. Add `text-regular.css` to the Hide at Design Time box in the same way, to hide this style sheet at design time. Click OK: your page should take on the large-text styles.

## Processing One Page at a Time

If you want this to take effect on multiple pages, you'll need to perform this process on each page.

Click OK to save the Design Time Style Sheet settings. In Design View, you should see the page take on the larger text size, as shown in Figure 10.2.

## Figure 10.2. Displaying the large font size.

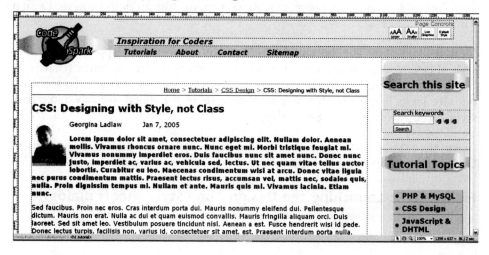

If you view this page in the browser, the text size will not have changed: this style sheet is only applied when you view the page in Dreamweaver. It will now be easy for us to work on this style sheet, as we can see our changes in Design View.

As you can see in the above screenshot, increasing all of the page text by a large amount has caused some of the layout elements to become misplaced, much like the display we'd see if we set the text size to Largest in Internet Explorer. With some layouts, we might only need to change the base font size to create a large-text effect, but with a more complex layout such as ours, we'll need to do a bit more tweaking. Now that we've got `text-large.css`, however, the tweaking will be a simple matter of altering the percentages in that file.

If you look in the CSS panel, as shown in Figure 10.3 you'll see that our `text-large.css` style sheet's listing is followed by the word "design", which shows that it's a Design Time Style Sheet. You can edit any of this document's rules by selecting them in the CSS panel, and clicking Edit Style....

## Figure 10.3. The CSS panel, showing the linked and Design Time Style Sheets.

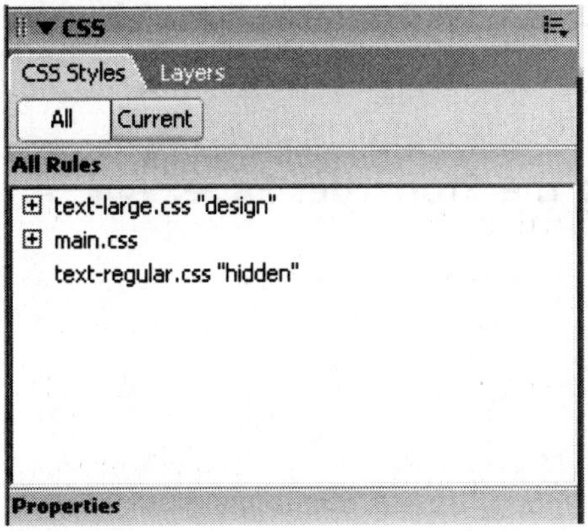

Let's reduce the font size of the menu items in the sidebar. From the CSS panel, select the `#nav ul.topics li` rule in the Design Time Style Sheet `text-large.css`, and click the Edit Style... button. In the CSS Rule Definition dialog, change the font size from 90% to 80%, as shown in Figure 10.4.

## Figure 10.4. Editing the font size to 80%.

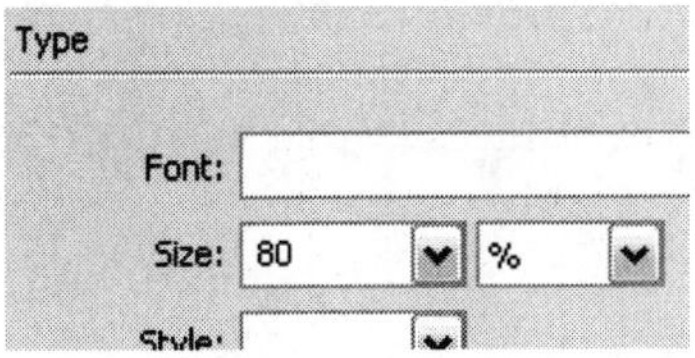

Click OK: the size of these list items should decrease slightly.

# Editing CSS Rules Using the Properties Pane

Instead of using the CSS Rule Definition dialog, we can edit properties through the Properties pane, which comprises the bottom part of Dreamweaver 8's new unified CSS panel. We will use this pane to edit the size of headings in the side navigation.

In the CSS panel, find the selector **#nav h3** and click on it, as shown in Figure 10.5. The properties that have been set for this rule will appear in the bottom portion of the panel. In this case, only the `font-size` property has been set. Click on the value, and you'll find that it becomes two editable drop down lists: one for a number and another for the unit. In this case, the lists display 120 and %. We can either type in the new size—**100**—and leave the percentage sign as-is, or we can select and entirely different method of sizing. Let's go ahead and reduce it from 120% to 100%.

### Figure 10.5. Editing #nav h3 using the Properties Pane.

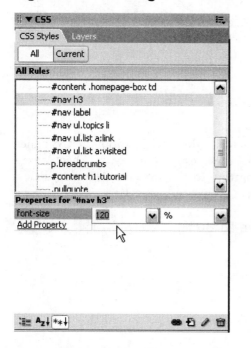

Click away from the panel to confirm the change, and the size of the heading text should decrease. Next, let's reduce the size of the "Inspiration for Coders" tagline by editing the `font-size` of the `.tagline` rule to 80%.

**Tip** 💡 **Quickly Tweaking Values**

Using the Properties pane is an excellent way to quickly edit values in your style sheet. It can be very useful when you're creating a new style sheet from an existing one: all of the rules have already been created, and you simply need to tweak the different properties and their values.

Finally, let's reduce the size of the top navigation links. Create a new CSS rule in `text-large.css` for the selector `#header-bottom li`, and set the font size to 70%.

# Switching Style Sheets

Once we're happy with the new, large-text style sheet, we need to add a tool that allows users to switch between style sheets. In some browsers, such as Firefox, the functionality to switch between alternate style sheets is built-in. All we have to do in such cases is to make sure that we've added the correct attributes to the `link` element that refers to these style sheets.

## Selecting Alternate Style Sheets in the Browser

To enable our large-text style sheet to be selected using the browser, we need to add it to the head of our document. First, we'll need to remove the page's design time style sheets settings: right-click in the CSS panel, select Design-time... and remove `text-large.css` from the list of style sheets shown at design time and remove `text-large.css` from the list of style sheets to be hidden at design time. Now, click Attach Style Sheet... in the CSS panel, and add `text-large.css` to the page as a link. Switch to Code View and find the three style sheet `link` elements. Edit the link to `text-large.css`, so that the `rel` attribute has a value of `altern-ate stylesheet`, and add a `title` attribute with a value of `Large Text`. You will also need to give the regular text style sheet a `title`: add `title="Medium Text"` to the `link` element.

The medium-text style sheet is now applied by default when the page loads. However, because we've made the large text style sheet an alternate style sheet, those browsers that support style sheet switching will see it and allow the user to switch to it. In Firefox, users can switch style sheets by selecting View > Page Style, then making a selection from the listed style sheets, as illustrated in Figure 10.6. The style sheets are listed with the names we gave to their `title` attributes.

## Figure 10.6. Switching styles in Firefox.

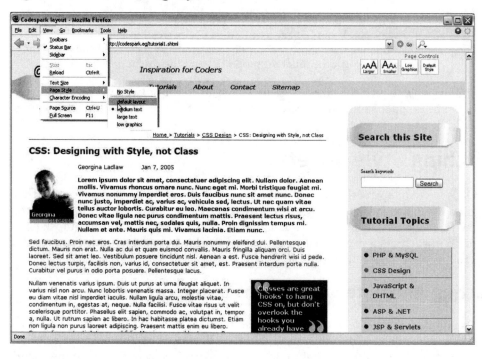

# Switching Styles with JavaScript

Not all browsers enable style sheet switching as Firefox does, and even in cases where site visitors use a browser that does allow style sheet switching, those users may not be aware of the functionality. For these reasons, we'll offer the switching functionality through the accessibility controls on our site. To do so, we'll make use of a technique described in an article written by Paul Sowden for A List Apart.[1] The method uses JavaScript to switch between style sheets, and works in tandem with the browser switching technique so that visitors can use either method to switch style sheets.

The article explains in detail how the various functions work, so if you use plan to use this method in one of your own projects, it's worth reading the entire article. For our purposes, however, you'll simply need to add the functions that are created in the article to an external JavaScript file, link that file to your document, and call in the appropriate functions when the user clicks your switching buttons. To

---

[1] http://www.alistapart.com/articles/alternate

function correctly, the style sheets that are linked to the document need to have been added using the alternate style sheet method explained above.

We already have an external JavaScript file—functions.js—which we created when we added client-side form validation in Chapter 9. Open this file, and paste in the JavaScript that's available for download as part of the ALA article.[2]

## Tip: Giving Credit where it's Due

Even if the third-party code that you use doesn't require you to credit the author, it's a good idea to leave a comment in the file that identifies where the code came from. If another developer was to maintain the site in the future, they could then easily find the article from which you took the code if they had a problem with that code, or wanted to edit it.

Your functions.js file should now contain the following JavaScript functions:

File: **inc/functions.js**

```
// JavaScript Document
function MM_findObj(n, d) { //v4.01
  var p,i,x;  if(!d) d=document; if((p=n.indexOf("?"))>0&&parent.
    frames.length) {
    d=parent.frames[n.substring(p+1)].document; n=n.substring(0,
      p);}
  if(!(x=d[n])&&d.all) x=d.all[n]; for (i=0;!x&&i<d.forms.length;
    i++) x=d.forms[i][n];
  for(i=0;!x&&d.layers&&i<d.layers.length;i++) x=MM_findObj(n,d.
    layers[i].document);
  if(!x && d.getElementById) x=d.getElementById(n); return x;
}
function MM_validateForm() { //v4.0
  var i,p,q,nm,test,num,min,max,errors='',args=MM_validateForm.
    arguments;
  for (i=0; i<(args.length-2); i+=3) { test=args[i+2]; val=
    MM_findObj(args[i]);
    if (val) { nm=val.name; if ((val=val.value)!="") {
      if (test.indexOf('isEmail')!=-1) { p=val.indexOf('@');
        if (p<1 || p==(val.length-1)) errors+='- '+nm+' must
          contain an e-mail address.\n';
      } else if (test!='R') { num = parseFloat(val);
        if (isNaN(val)) errors+='- '+nm+' must contain a number.
          \n';
        if (test.indexOf('inRange') != -1) { p=test.indexOf(':');
```

---

[2] http://www.alistapart.com/d/alternate/styleswitcher.js

```
            min=test.substring(8,p); max=test.substring(p+1);
            if (num<min || max<num) errors+='- '+nm+' must contain
              a number between '+min+' and '+max+'.\n';
      } } } else if (test.charAt(0) == 'R') errors += '- '+nm+' is
          required.\n'; }
   } if (errors) alert('The following error(s) occurred:\n'+
      errors);
   document.MM_returnValue = (errors == '');
}
// Style Sheet Switcher functions written by Paul Sowden for an
// article on A List Apart -
// http://www.alistapart.com/articles/alternate
function setActiveStyleSheet(title) {
  var i, a, main;
  for(i=0; (a = document.getElementsByTagName("link")[i]); i++) {
    if(a.getAttribute("rel").indexOf("style") != -1 &&
        a.getAttribute("title")) {
      a.disabled = true;
      if(a.getAttribute("title") == title) a.disabled = false;
    }
  }
}
function getActiveStyleSheet() {
  var i, a;
  for(i=0; (a = document.getElementsByTagName("link")[i]); i++) {
    if(a.getAttribute("rel").indexOf("style") != -1 &&
        a.getAttribute("title") && !a.disabled) return
        a.getAttribute("title");
  }
  return null;
}

function getPreferredStyleSheet() {
  var i, a;
  for(i=0; (a = document.getElementsByTagName("link")[i]); i++) {
    if(a.getAttribute("rel").indexOf("style") != -1
        && a.getAttribute("rel").indexOf("alt") == -1
        && a.getAttribute("title")
        ) return a.getAttribute("title");
  }
  return null;
}
function createCookie(name,value,days) {
  if (days) {
    var date = new Date();
    date.setTime(date.getTime()+(days*24*60*60*1000));
```

```
    var expires = "; expires="+date.toGMTString();
  }
  else expires = "";
  document.cookie = name+"="+value+expires+"; path=/";
}
function readCookie(name) {
  var nameEQ = name + "=";
  var ca = document.cookie.split(';');
  for(var i=0;i < ca.length;i++) {
    var c = ca[i];
    while (c.charAt(0)==' ') c = c.substring(1,c.length);
    if (c.indexOf(nameEQ) == 0) return c.substring(nameEQ.length,
        c.length);
  }
  return null;
}

window.onload = function(e) {
  var cookie = readCookie("style");
  var title = cookie ? cookie : getPreferredStyleSheet();
  setActiveStyleSheet(title);
}

window.onunload = function(e) {
  var title = getActiveStyleSheet();
  createCookie("style", title, 365);
}

var cookie = readCookie("style");
var title = cookie ? cookie : getPreferredStyleSheet();
setActiveStyleSheet(title);
```

Next, include functions.js in tutorial1.shtml by inserting the following
markup just below the style sheet links:

File: **tutorial1.shtml (excerpt)**

```
<script type="text/JavaScript" src="inc/functions.js"></script>
```

All we need to do now is update the control buttons so that they call the style
sheet switching functions using the onclick attribute. Open top.html in Code
View and locate the page controls. Add an onclick attribute to the first two a
elements, and set them as shown in the code below:

File: **inc/top.html** (excerpt)

```
<p>Page Controls</p>
<ul>
  <li><a href="#"
      onclick="setActiveStyleSheet('Large Text'); return false;">
    <img src="img/control_larger.gif" alt="Increase Text Size"
        width="43" height="35" /></a></li>
  <li><a href="#"
      onclick="setActiveStyleSheet('Medium Text'); return false;">
    <img src="img/control_smaller.gif" alt="Decrease Text Size"
        width="43" height="35" /></a></li>
  <li><a href="#"><img src="img/control_low_graphics.gif"
        alt="Low Graphics" width="43" height="35" /></a></li>
  <li><a href="#"><img src="img/control_default_style.gif"
        alt="Default Style" width="43" height="35" /></a></li>
</ul>
```

Save the file and load `tutorial1.shtml` in your browser. You should now be able to increase and decrease the text size using the buttons shown in Figure 10.7.

## Figure 10.7. Switching style sheets using JavaScript.

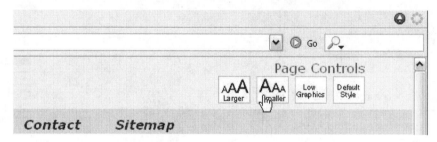

# A "Low Graphics" Layout

For some users, a low graphics, frills-free version of your documents might be useful. These users may include people who find text difficult to read when it's presented on a background color, and need high contrast, and those who access your site using a handheld device: big navigation bars and large images can make a site very hard to read on a tiny screen.

When we think of a text-only style sheet, we might think of simply removing CSS completely; after all, this will display the page's text content without any styling. However, in the case of users who can see CSS, but need—or prefer—a plainer environment for reading articles, an approach that avoids CSS entirely won't make the site very usable. A better alternative is to create for the site what is essentially an alternate layout that cuts down on images and background colors.

As a starting point, open `main.css` and save it as `textonly.css`. We can use this style sheet as a basis for our text-only style sheet by editing the properties, just as we did when we created the large-text style sheet. Add `textonly.css` as a Design Time Style Sheet for `tutorial1.shtml`, and use the same dialog to hide `main.css`.

## The Header Area

Let's start by removing some of the colors and images from the header area. In the CSS panel, find the `#logo` rule in `textonly.css`. In the Properties pane, you should see the properties that have been set for the `#logo` rule, as shown in Figure 10.8.

### Figure 10.8. Viewing the properties set for `#logo`.

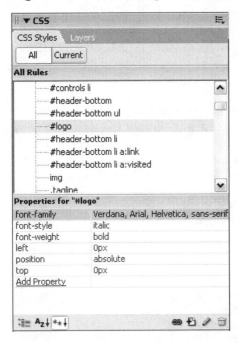

Click the Add Property link beneath the existing properties. In the drop-down list that appears, select display. Once you've made your selection, another drop-down list appears, which contains all the valid values for this property; select none from this list, as shown in Figure 10.9.

## Figure 10.9. Setting `display` to none in the Properties Pane.

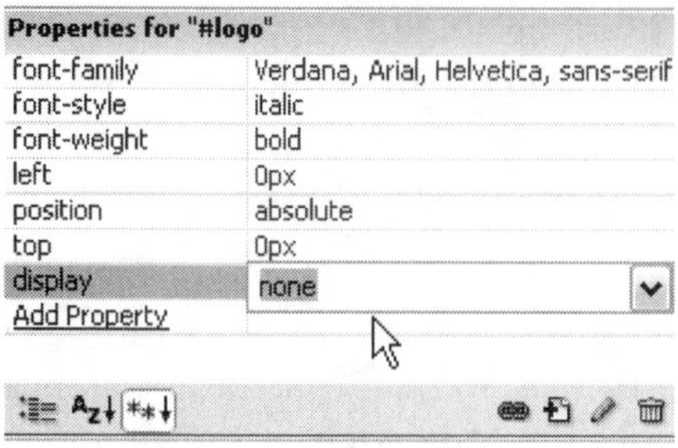

| Properties for "#logo" | |
|---|---|
| font-family | Verdana, Arial, Helvetica, sans-serif |
| font-style | italic |
| font-weight | bold |
| left | 0px |
| position | absolute |
| top | 0px |
| display | none |
| Add Property | |

This should have the effect of making the logo disappear when we view the page in Design View.

Now, select the #header-top rule in the CSS panel, and enter the background color **#FFFFFF** (white). Once you click on the existing color in the Properties pane, it will become an editable text field. Repeat this process for #header-bottom.

# Replacing the Logo with Text

As we've hidden the logo, we now find that the page no longer displays the name of our Website. In this situation, it's a good idea to replace the logo with some text whenever the text-only style sheet is in use. To do this, we need to add to the page the text that will display in place of the logo, and, in our main style sheet, hide this text, as the logo will display when that style sheet is used.

Open top.html in Code View, and after the logo, add the text **Code Spark** wrapped in <span> and </span> tags, with a class of logotext:

File: **inc/top.html (excerpt)**

```
<div id="header">
  <div id="header-top">
    <img src="img/logo.gif" alt="Code Spark"
        width="290" height="160" id="logo" />
    <span class="logotext">Code Spark</span>
    <span class="tagline">Inspiration for Coders</span>
```

Save your changes to top.html, and return to tutorial1.shtml to see the new text displaying at the top of the document window, as it does in Figure 10.10.

The text will have pushed some other page elements around; let's change that now.

### Figure 10.10. Viewing the page `tutorial1.shtml` after the Code Spark text is added.

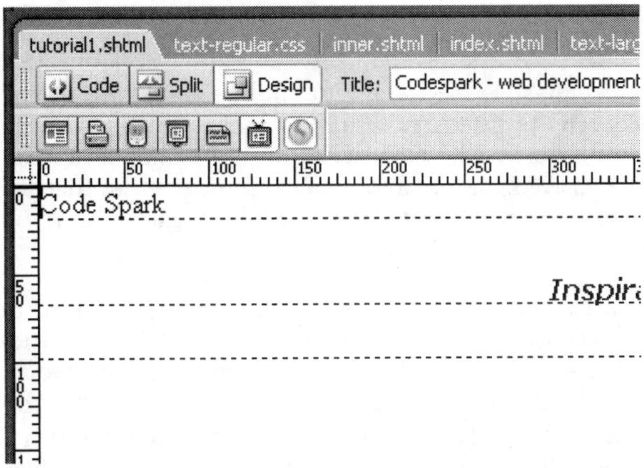

In the CSS panel, add a new CSS rule for **#header-top .logotext** to tex-tonly.css. Click OK and, in the CSS Rule Definition dialog, use the Type category to set the font to **Verdana, Arial, Helvetica, sans-serif** with a color of **#3C582F** and weight of **bold**. Then, in the Positioning category, set Type to absolute, Top to 10 pixels and Left to 10 pixels. Click OK; the Code Spark text should now display in approximately the same place where the logo appeared previously.

If we view this layout in the browser, we find that the header is pushed out of shape by the addition of the span element. Remember that this page still uses main.css; text-only.css is applied to the page only in Dreamweaver's design time style sheet. The logo remains visible in main.css, so we can simply hide the span element in that style sheet.

To edit main.css through the CSS panel, we need to open a page to which the textonly.css Design Time Style Sheet is not applied. Take your pick, then in main.css, create a new CSS Rule. Choose the Advanced Selector Type and set the selector to **#header-top .textonly**. This time, all we need to do is set the Display property—which can be found in the Block category—to none. Once this is done, the logo image will display when the main.css style sheet is in use, while the text heading appears when textonly.css is in use.

## Alternative Style Sheets: Exclusive or Cumulative?

Though it would be easy to miss, we have just made an important design decision: for `textonly.css` to work correctly (i.e. to display the alternate logo text), the default style sheet (`main.css`) must be disabled. Otherwise, `main.css` will hide the logo text, rendering the positioning properties in `textonly.css` useless.

Sadly, browsers that offer style sheet switching features don't work this way. Rather, they keep the default style sheet(s) like `main.css` perpetually active, and simply switch between the different alternate style sheets that have been provided. Although we'll shortly adjust our style sheet switching JavaScript code to provide the exclusive behavior we require, this does mean that the style sheet switching features provided by some browsers will not work on our site.

The alternative, which you may wish to consider in your own work, is to write all of your alternative style sheets such that they override the properties in your default style sheet as required. In the current example, this would mean adding the property `display: inline;` to our `#header-top .logotext` rule in `textoly.css`, which would make visible the logo replacement text that was hidden in `main.css`. You might think that sounds pretty simple, but if we were to extend this approach to the entirety of even this simple site, the style sheets would become quite convoluted in their interactions.

Instead, we'll elect to keep our style sheets simple, and add complexity to the JavaScript code that enables and disables them. As we'll see, this approach has other benefits that we'd forfeit if we limited ourselves to what the built-in style sheet switching features of some browsers can provide.

# The Sidebar

The sidebar uses several images in its display. Our challenge is to remove the images while keeping the sidebar looking like a navigation element.

In the CSS panel, scroll down and find the `#nav .section` rule in `textonly.css`. This rule displays the background image behind the headings. Right-click on the background property, and select Delete to remove it, as shown in Figure 10.11.

**Figure 10.11. Deleting the background image from #nav .section.**

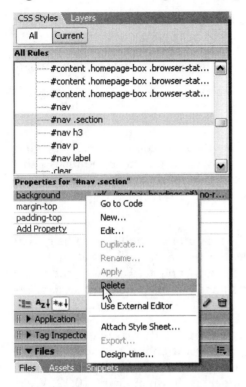

Then, find the rule for **#nav** and repeat this procedure to delete the background image. While editing **#nav**, add a 1-pixel, dotted, left-hand border to provide a sense of separation between the sidebar and the main content once the images have been removed. You can do this via the CSS Rule Definition dialog, or using the longhand `border-left-style`, `border-left-size` and `border-left-color` properties in the Properties panel. This should leave us with the bottom part of the curved box, which is actually an image that has been inserted into the page. To hide this image, we can add a new CSS rule with the selector **#nav img** and, in the Block category, set Display to none.

Other changes you can make to the sidebar include:

☐ Set the `text-align` property of #nav h3 to **left**, and add a 0.5 em left margin (you can do this by adding **0.5em** to the end of the existing `margin` property value; the four numbers will define the top, right, bottom, and left margins, respectively).

- For #nav ul.topics, reduce margin-left to 10 pixels.

- For #nav ul.topics li, change the background color to white and delete the borders.

- For #nav ul.list, delete the list-style image and reduce margin-left to 30 pixels.

# The Main Content

Next, let's tackle the removal of images from the main content area. Depending on your site and your requirements, you may wish to remove the images that appear in the content area, if they're included for decorative purposes only; alternatively, you may make the decision to include some of the smaller images from the site.

As images that appear within the body of our tutorials are likely to help users understand the articles, I've decided to leave these in this style sheet, and to remove only the unnecessary images such as the author photo. To remove the author photograph, find the .tutorial-author rule in the CSS panel, and set display to none.

Within the articles' content, we styled blockquotes with images and dark background colors. Let's use simpler styling in the text-only style sheet. Find the .pullquote rule in the CSS panel, delete the background property, set color to #000000 (black) and add a 1-pixel gray border, as shown in Figure 10.12. We're left with the top quotation mark image; select the .pullquote p rule and delete the background property there.

## Figure 10.12. Restyling the pullquotes.

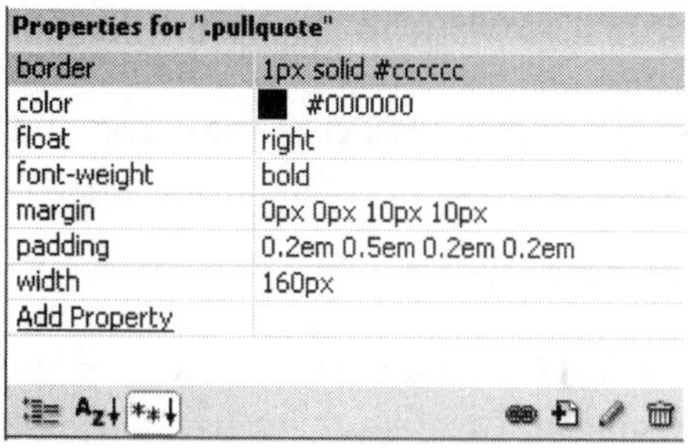

| Properties for ".pullquote" | |
| --- | --- |
| border | 1px solid #cccccc |
| color | ■ #000000 |
| float | right |
| font-weight | bold |
| margin | 0px 0px 10px 10px |
| padding | 0.2em 0.5em 0.2em 0.2em |
| width | 160px |
| Add Property | |

## Other Pages

We now need to check the other pages of the site to identify any other changes that may be required when this style sheet is in use. You'll need to apply `tex-tonly.css` as a Design Time Style Sheet to each of the pages that you work on.

The homepage, with its two column layout in the content area, would be difficult to use on a small screen. So, in our basic, low-graphics style sheet, we'll display these blocks as a single column to make the page easier to use.

Find the `#content .homepage-box` rule, delete the `float` property, then set `width` to 100%. To hide the author photo, find the `#content .homepage-box .author-pic` rule and set `display` to `none`. The homepage boxes should now take up the full width of the screen, as is the case in Figure 10.13.

### Figure 10.13. The homepage boxes using the text-only style sheet.

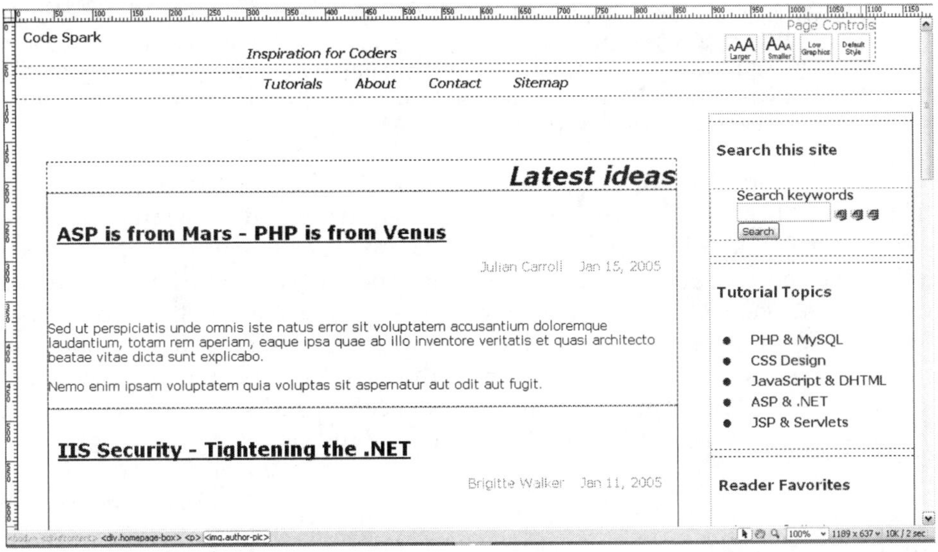

You can continue to work on your low-graphics style sheet until you're happy with the results, moving as far from the original layout as you like! If you set the `display` property for any rules to `none`, in order to hide elements in the page, you can also remove any other properties that are set for those rules: they can't take effect because the elements effectively have been deleted. I won't list the full `textonly.css` code here, as it's far too long, but you can find this file in the book's code archive.

# Modifying the JavaScript to Enable Multiple Style Sheets to be Enabled/Disabled

Now we have normal- and large-text style sheets, and regular- and low-graphics style sheets. We could decide to allow them to be used in combination: users could elect to see large or small text with either the graphics-intensive layout or the basic, low-graphics layout. Importantly, we want to be able to offer these options and still have a good looking, usable Website. To step away from the usual "default style sheets plus one selectable alternative style sheet" system supported by many browsers as well as our current script, instead adopting a system of choosing from two sets of mutually exclusive style sheets, we'll need to make some changes to the JavaScript.

### Using a Server-side Language

If you have access to a server-side language such as ASP or PHP, this process becomes much simpler: all you need to do is write out links to the selected style sheets using your server-side language. Employing a server-side language also means that your style sheet switching functionality won't rely on the users' having JavaScript enabled. The CSS-Discuss Wiki offers some links to various server-side methods.[3].

To start, open each of the pages on your site and make sure to clear any Design Time Style Sheets settings that you have applied to them. It's time to make these style sheets work as intended *outside* of Dreamweaver's design view. Next, open `top.html` and locate the Page Controls section. Currently, the function that's called by the `onclick` event handler accepts one parameter: the style sheet's title. We need to add a parameter that indicates whether it is a text or a layout style sheet that is being selected, so that the script can disable any other style sheet of that type that is currently active. We also need to add similar `onclick` event handlers to our low graphics and default layout buttons.

File: **inc/top.html (excerpt)**

```
<ul>
  <li><a href="#"
      onclick="setActiveStyleSheet('Large Text','text');
      return false;"><img src="img/control_larger.gif"
      alt="Increase Text Size" width="43" height="35" /></a></li>
  <li><a href="#"
      onclick="setActiveStyleSheet('Medium Text','text');
      return false;"><img src="img/control_smaller.gif"
```

---

[3] http://css-discuss.incutio.com/?page=StyleSwitching

```
      alt="Decrease Text Size" width="43" height="35" /></a></li>
  <li><a href="#"
      onclick="setActiveStyleSheet('Low Graphics','layout');
      return false;"><img src="img/control_low_graphics.gif"
      alt="Low Graphics" width="43" height="35" /></a></li>
  <li><a href="#"
      onclick="setActiveStyleSheet('Default Style','layout');
      return false;"><img src="img/control_default_style.gif"
      alt="Default Style" width="43" height="35" /></a></li>
</ul>
```

Now, open `tutorial1.shtml` and add `textonly.css` as another alternate style
sheet. Don't forget to give `main.css` a `title` of `Default Style`, to match the
text used in the code above. We also need to identify the style sheets by group:
we can do so by adding a `class` attribute to each `link` element that has a value
of `text` or `layout`, depending on whether the style sheet affects text or layout.
The following style sheets should now be linked from the top of your document,
with classes applied:

File: **tutorial1.shtml (excerpt)**

```
<!--#include file="inc/head.html" -->
<title>Code Spark layout</title>
<meta http-equiv="Content-Type" content="text/html;
    charset=iso-8859-1" />
<script type="text/JavaScript" src="inc/functions.js"></script>
<link href="inc/main.css" rel="stylesheet" type="text/css"
    title="Default Style" class="layout" />
<link href="inc/text-regular.css" rel="stylesheet" type="text/css"
    title="Medium Text" class="text" />
<link href="inc/text-large.css" rel="alternate stylesheet"
    type="text/css" title="Large Text" class="text" />
<link href="inc/textonly.css" rel="alternate stylesheet"
    type="text/css" title="Low Graphics" class="layout" />
</head>
```

The changes we'll made to the JavaScript code enable it to check to see which
class of style sheet the user is selecting. The changes are highlighted below:

File: **inc/functions.js (excerpt)**

```
// Style Sheet Switcher functions written by Paul Sowden for an
// article on A List Apart -
// http://www.alistapart.com/articles/alternate
function setActiveStyleSheet(title,theClass) {
  var i, a, main;
  for(i=0; (a = document.getElementsByTagName("link")[i]); i++) {
```

```
        if(a.getAttribute("rel").indexOf("style") != -1 &&
            a.getAttribute("title")
            && a.className==theClass) {
          a.disabled = true;
          if(a.getAttribute("title") == title) a.disabled = false;
        }
      }
    }
    function getActiveStyleSheet(theClass) {
      var i, a;
      for(i=0; (a = document.getElementsByTagName("link")[i]); i++) {
        if(a.getAttribute("rel").indexOf("style") != -1 &&
            a.getAttribute("title") &&
            a.className == theClass &&
            !a.disabled) return
            a.getAttribute("title");
      }
      return null;
    }

    function getPreferredStyleSheet(theClass) {
      var i, a;
      for(i=0; (a = document.getElementsByTagName("link")[i]); i++) {
        if(a.getAttribute("rel").indexOf("style") != -1
            && a.getAttribute("rel").indexOf("alt") == -1
            && a.getAttribute("title")
            && a.className == theClass
            ) return a.getAttribute("title");
      }
      return null;
    }
    function createCookie(name,value,days) {
      if (days) {
        var date = new Date();
        date.setTime(date.getTime()+(days*24*60*60*1000));
        var expires = "; expires="+date.toGMTString();
      }
      else expires = "";
      document.cookie = name+"="+value+expires+"; path=/";
    }
    function readCookie(name) {
      var nameEQ = name + "=";
      var ca = document.cookie.split(';');
      for(var i=0;i < ca.length;i++) {
        var c = ca[i];
        while (c.charAt(0)==' ') c = c.substring(1,c.length);
```

```
    if (c.indexOf(nameEQ) == 0) return c.substring(nameEQ.length,
      c.length);
  }
  return null;
}

window.onload = function(e) {
  // get text style cookie
  var cookie = readCookie("text");
  var title = cookie ? cookie : getPreferredStyleSheet("text");
  setActiveStyleSheet(title, "text");
  // get layout style cookie
  var cookie = readCookie("layout");
  var title = cookie ? cookie : getPreferredStyleSheet("layout");
  setActiveStyleSheet(title, "layout");
}

window.onunload = function(e) {
  var title = getActiveStyleSheet("text");
  createCookie("text", title, 365);
  var title = getActiveStyleSheet("layout");
  createCookie("layout", title, 365);
}

window.onload();
```

You should now be able to swap style sheets with any combination of layout and text size. You could use these techniques to create any number of style sheets, giving site users real choices about how they view your content. Figure 10.14 shows the low-graphics style sheet in action.

### Figure 10.14. Viewing the low-graphics layout in Firefox.

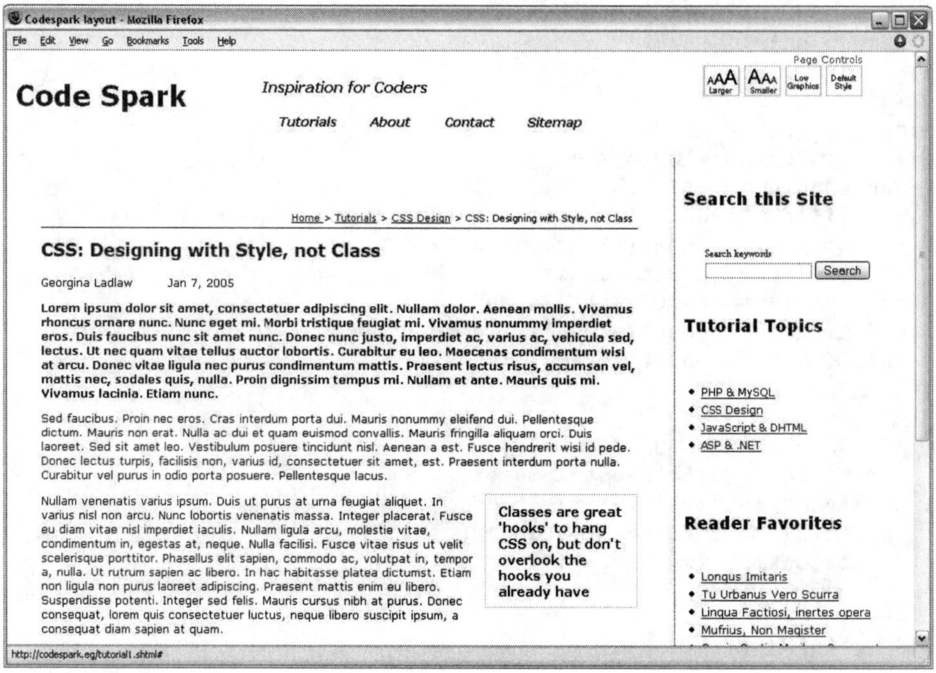

# Media Types

Another use of alternate style sheets is to provide different displays suited to the various types of devices that may access our site. When you attach a style sheet in Dreamweaver, you may notice the Media drop-down list in the Attach External Style Sheet dialog. Shown in Figure 10.15, the menu enables you to set your style sheet for:

**all**       All devices

**aural**     Screen readers

**braille**   Braille readers, which convert the text on screen to Braille

**handheld**  Handheld devices

**print**     To be used when the document is printed

| | |
|---|---|
| **projection** | For projection purposes |
| **screen** | Regular computer screens |
| **tty** | Fixed-width devices |
| **tv** | Web TV |

**Figure 10.15. Viewing the Media drop-down in the Attach External Stylesheet dialog.**

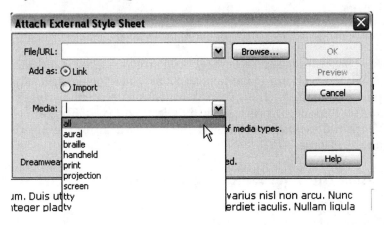

Support for these media types is still limited in most devices, so they are not as useful now as they may become in the future. However, there is one media type that is well supported in browsers, and can be very useful in your day-to-day development of Websites: the `print` media type.

# Print Style Sheet

If users want to print any of our articles, it will be helpful if they can do so without printing all of the navigation elements and images that appear on the page. We can create a separate print style sheet to be used when the document is printed.

Open `main.css` and save the style sheet as `print.css`. Attach the style sheet by clicking on the Attach Style Sheet button in the CSS panel, browse for `print.css`, and select the print media type from the Media drop-down list, as shown in Figure 10.16.

## Figure 10.16. Selecting the print media type.

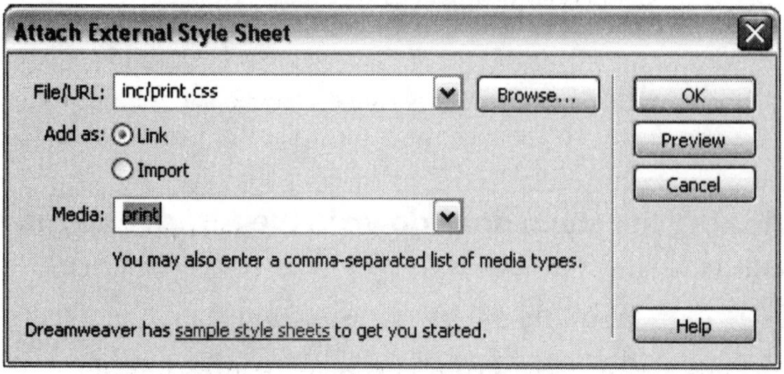

**Attach External Style Sheet**

File/URL: inc/print.css | Browse... | OK

Add as: ⦿ Link | Preview

○ Import | Cancel

Media: print

You may also enter a comma-separated list of media types.

Dreamweaver has sample style sheets to get you started. | Help

Save the document. To view the print style sheet as we work on it, we could add it as a Design Time Style Sheet, but Dreamweaver 8 has a new toolbar specially developed to help us work with different style sheets for different media types: the Style Rendering toolbar. Open this toolbar by selecting View > Toolbars > Style Rendering. When the toolbar opens, select the printer icon for the **print** media type, as shown in Figure 10.17.

## Figure 10.17. Using the Style Rendering toolbar.

# Editing the print.css Style Sheet

Expand **print.css** in the CSS panel and find the **#header** selector. In the Properties pane, add a display property, and set its value to none. This will hide the header area when the document is printed. You can now delete from **print.css** any rules that reference elements inside the header.

Now, select **#nav**, and again set display to none to hide the sidebar. Once again, you can remove from this style sheet any rules that apply to elements within the sidebar.

The breadcrumb navigation is another page element that isn't useful in a printed document, so locate the `p.breadcrumbs` rule and set display to none.

`#content` has a very wide right margin to allow space for the sidebar that won't appear in the print document; we can edit this rule to reduce the margin to 80 pixels. You should be able to see all these changes take place in Dreamweaver as you make them using the Style Rendering toolbar.

As with the text-only style sheet, a simpler treatment of the pull quote would be suitable for the print style sheet. In Figure 10.18, I've deleted the background image and made the text color black.

## Figure 10.18. Viewing the print style sheet in Dreamweaver.

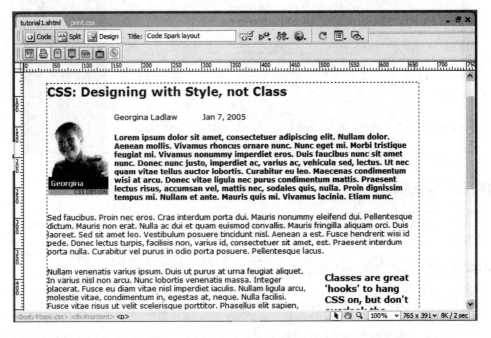

Once you're happy with the print style sheet, save it and reload the tutorial page in your browser. If you print the page, or access your browser's print preview feature, you should see the `print.css`-styled document shown in Figure 10.19. The `print.css` file is available in the code archive.

## Figure 10.19. Viewing the page in print preview.

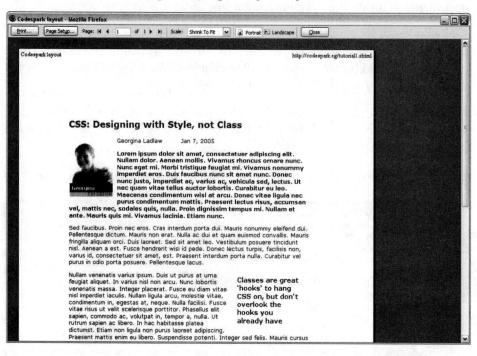

# Final Tasks

Throughout this chapter, we've been working to add functionality to one of our documents: `tutorial1.shtml`. The style sheets we've created will need to be added to every page of the site if the style switching is to work properly. The easiest way to do this is to move the style sheets from `tutorial1.shtml` and add them to `head.html`. This file is included in all of your documents, so doing this will ensure that your style sheets are available to every page.

### A Technical Hitch

We didn't include the style sheets in the head document from the outset because some of the Design Time Style Sheets functionality we used in this chapter doesn't work very well when the style sheets aren't linked within the file that's being worked on. However, once you've finished the design phase, moving these style sheets isn't a problem.

Once we've moved the style sheets, our `head.html` include contains the following:

File: **inc/head.html**

```
<!DOCTYPE html PUBLIC "-//W3C//DTD XHTML 1.0 Strict//EN"
    "http://www.w3.org/TR/xhtml1/DTD/xhtml1-strict.dtd">
<html xmlns="http://www.w3.org/1999/xhtml">
<head>
  <meta http-equiv="Content-Type" content="text/html;
      charset=iso-8859-1" />
  <script type="text/JavaScript" src="inc/functions.js"></script>
  <link href="inc/main.css" rel="stylesheet" type="text/css"
      title="Default Style" class="layout" media="all" />
  <link href="inc/text-regular.css" rel="stylesheet"
      type="text/css" title="Medium Text" class="text" />
  <link href="inc/text-large.css" rel="alternate stylesheet"
      type="text/css" title="Large Text" class="text" />
  <link href="inc/textonly.css" rel="alternate stylesheet"
      type="text/css" title="Low Graphics" class="layout" />
  <link href="inc/print.css" rel="stylesheet" type="text/css"
      media="print" />
```

Now that you've moved the link to main.css and the meta element into an include, you'll need to go through each of your pages and remove them.

# Final Validation

Once you've uploaded your files to your Web server, go to each page and validate it using the W3C online validator. You should check all your CSS files, as well. Whenever you make changes to any documents or includes, remember to revalidate after you upload those files, just to ensure that no errors have crept in.

# Summary

In this chapter we've looked at a few different ways in which alternate style sheets can be used to make your site more interesting and usable for different types of site visitor. As we've seen here, style sheet switching does not have to be a gimmick, nor a way to showcase different designs: it can be a way of adding useful functionality to the site. Of course, switching layouts for fun is perfectly justifiable on some sites, and a great way to showcase your design skills on a portfolio site.

This chapter also gave us the chance to look at some functionality—new in Dreamweaver 8—that assists you in working with alternate style sheets. There are several ways of working with CSS in Dreamweaver: use the techniques that you find most helpful to your workflow.

I hope that, by following this project, you've gained an understanding of how you can develop sites to Web standards using Dreamweaver 8. A knowledge of what you're doing in your markup, and your CSS, is important if you want to fully understand what you're doing and why. However, Dreamweaver 8 can help you to create standards-compliant, accessible documents. With a little care and the right preferences, using a visual tool shouldn't stand in the way of your developing a standards compliant Website.

# Index

# Books for Web Developers
## from SitePoint

Visit http://www.sitepoint.com/books/
for sample chapters or to order!

# Build Your Own

# Database Driven Website

## Using PHP & MySQL

By Kevin Yank

A Practical Step-by-Step Guide

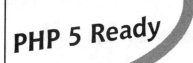

The PHP Anthology

# Object Oriented PHP Solutions
## Volume I

By Harry Fuecks

Practical Solutions to Common Problems

PHP 5 Ready

sitepoint

## The PHP Anthology

# Object Oriented PHP Solutions

## Volume II

By Harry Fuecks

Practical Solutions to Common Problems

## No Nonsense

# XML Web Development

## With PHP

*By Thomas Myer*

A Practical Step-by-Step Guide

# Build Your Own

# *ASP.NET Website*

## Using C# & VB.NET

By Zak Ruvalcaba

A Practical Step-by-Step Guide

Includes the most **Complete CSS2** property reference!

 sitepoint

# *HTML Utopia:*

# Designing Without Tables
## Using CSS

By Dan Shafer

A Practical Step-by-Step Guide

Covers
CSS 2.1

sitepoint

# The CSS Anthology

# 101 Essential Tips, Tricks & Hacks

Practical Solutions to Common Problems

By Rachel Andrew

# *DHTML Utopia:*

# Modern Web Design

## Using JavaScript & DOM

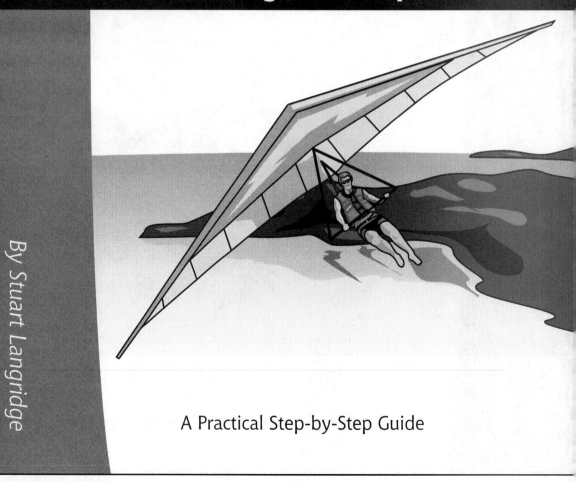

By Stuart Langridge

A Practical Step-by-Step Guide

Flash
MX 2004

sitepoint

## The Flash Anthology

# Cool Effects &
# Practical ActionScript

*By Steven Grosvenor*

Practical Solutions to Common Problems